MOVING THE GUNS
THE MECHANISATION OF THE ROYAL ARTILLERY 1854-1939

Philip Ventham and David Fletcher

© The Tank Museum 2022

All rights reserved. No part of this publication may be reproduced or stored in a retrieval system or transmitted, in any form or by any means, electronic, mechanical, photocopying, recording or otherwise, without prior permission in writing from The Tank Museum.

First published in 1990 by HMSO
This edition published in 2022 by The Tank Museum

Philip Ventham and David Fletcher have asserted their moral right to be identified as the authors of this work.

British Library Cataloguing in Publication Data.
A catalogue record for this book is available from the British Library.

Printed book ISBN 9781739902742

Designed and produced for The Tank Museum by JJN Publishing Ltd.

Printed and bound in Malta.

MIX
Paper from responsible sources
FSC® C022612
www.fsc.org

The Dragon, Field Artillery, Mark I was the first purpose designed, full-track gun tractor to enter service with the Royal Artillery. Yet something in the way the gun detachment is perched on top, in vulnerable splendour, suggests that even in 1923 the lessons of the Great War were being purposely ignored in order to create an effect. The event is a parade in Long Valley, Aldershot, for HM King George V by 28 Field Battery RA.

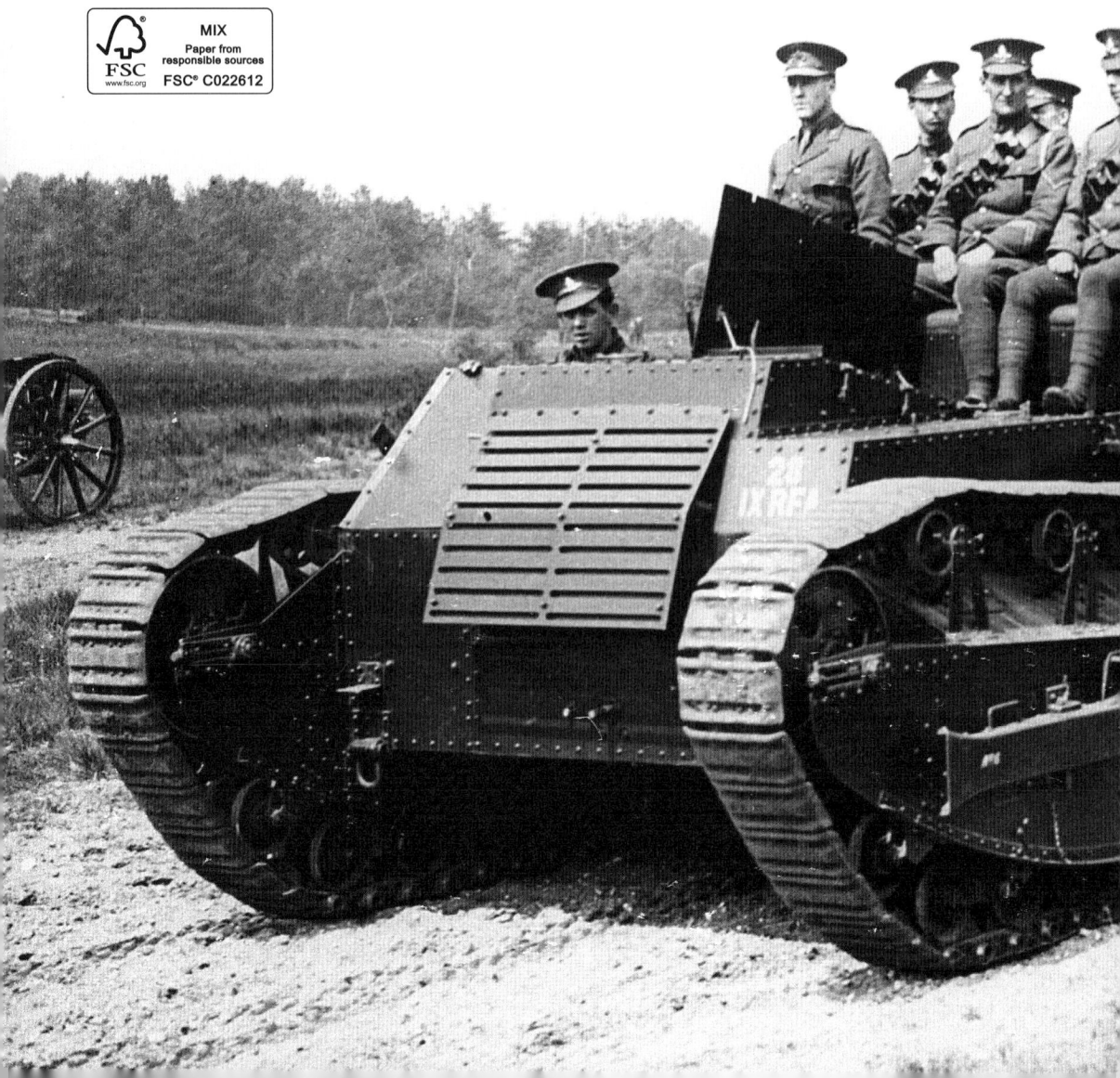

CONTENTS

INTRODUCTION 4
1 EARLY EXPERIMENTS 6
2 THE FIRST WORLD WAR 24
3 FIELD ARTILLERY - EXPERIMENTATION, 1920-30 38
4 THE ARMOURED FORCE EXPERIMENTS, 1925-29 80
5 FIELD ARTILLERY - CONSOLIDATION, 1930-39 88
6 MEDIUM AND HEAVY ARTILLERY, 1919-39 116
7 ANTI-AIRCRAFT ARTILLERY 126
8 THE MECHANISATION OF THE TERRITORIAL ARMY ARTILLERY 138

APPENDICES
A - NOTES ON THE ORGANISATION AND EQUIPMENT OF THE ROYAL ARTILLERY 144
B - THE MECHANISATION OF THE ROYAL HORSE ARTILLERY 150
C - VEHICLE DEVELOPMENTS IN INDIA 158
D - THE PROGRESS OF MECHANISATION FIELD BATTERIES 164
INDEX 166

MOVING THE GUNS

INTRODUCTION 1989/2022

In January 1976, on the last but one day of his two-year posting as Assistant Senior Instructor at the Royal Artillery Wing of the Driving and Maintenance School at Bovington, Captain Philip Ventham received on behalf of the Royal Regiment of Artillery, a 1940 Mark I Morris Commercial C8 Field Artillery Quad Tractor.

The vehicle had been bought from the previous owner, Steve Stephenson, with a sum of money raised by voluntary subscriptions around the Royal Regiment. A limber had already been donated, a 25pdr gun had been issued as a 'saluting gun' and the Quad spent several months in 18 Command Workshop REME at Bovington being stripped and restored under the guidance of a fitter who had worked on Quads during the Second World War.

It emerged in near perfect condition and since then the unique set of Quad, limber and gun appears regularly at military shows and events, manned by students and instructors from the Royal Artillery Wing and it raises a great deal of interest wherever it appears.

Incidental to the acquisition of the Quad was the production of a small booklet outlining the history and development of the various types of Quad. As Captain Ventham dug into the archives, it became obvious that a wealth of fascinating information about the development of artillery gun tractors, self-propelled guns and associated vehicles was available and that much of this information had been largely glossed over or ignored in the past in the various standard Gunner regimental histories of the period.

There the matter rested, apart from spasmodic correspondence with owners of restored gun tractors around the world, until a chance conversation with David Fletcher, the Librarian of The Tank Museum at Bovington, revealed not only David's encyclopaedic knowledge and enthusiasm for all forms of military transport, but also his particular interest in military vehicle development in the interwar period – the main period covered by this book. Thus, the partnership was formed and this book is the result of that partnership.

Much of the research for this book took place among the archive material held at the library of the Royal Artillery Institution at Woolwich and the library of The Tank Museum at Bovington. The authors would like to thank Brigadier Lewendon and his Staff at the Royal Artillery Institution, in particular Mrs Brigitte Timbers, for their help and patience in locating Battery diaries and other material. Our thanks go also to Lieutenant Colonel George Forty at The Tank Museum for permission to use the facilities there and to have access to the library's collection of photographs of military vehicles. Particular thanks must go to Roland Groom for his technical skill in copying many of the photographs used in this book, some from original photographs little bigger than a postage stamp. Lieutenant Colonel Hugh Stott RA was instrumental in obtaining access to the vast and largely untapped source of material, photographs and drawings held at the Royal Arsenal at Woolwich, and we are most grateful to him for arranging it. Major Dennis Rollo RA very kindly agreed to read the script and offered advice on artillery organisational matters and on the nomenclature of Royal Artillery units

INTRODUCTION

over the time span covered by this book, as well as general and much appreciated comments about the book as a whole.

Our thanks must go to Richard Peacock of Leeds, the owner of a beautiful restored 1937 Morris Commercial CDSW Field Artillery Tractor, for his recollections of prewar Territorial soldiering and to numerous other ex-Gunners who have loaned photographs and produced reminiscences and anecdotes, which have been incorporated in this book.

Finally, this book is dedicated to the generations of Drivers IC, Drivers RA, and Artificers RA who have looked after their vehicles, maintained them, painted and polished them and often cussed at them, probably long after the remainder of the gun detachment had cleaned, polished, put away the gun and retired to the NAAFI, knowing that, if 'his' gun tractor failed to start the next morning, the gun would not make it to the gun position and give the guaranteed fire support to the rest of the Army.

Philip Ventham and David Fletcher
August 1989

Moving the Guns was first published in 1990. It was and, we believe, still is the only definitive work dealing largely with this very interesting and important interwar period of British military vehicle development. It has been out of print for some time and surviving copies command high prices when they become available. For this reason, it was decided to republish the book to meet the increased interest in military transport and related artillery.

The content remains largely unchanged apart from the correction of a few minor textual errors. The original sources are unchanged and still available to researchers: the Archives and Library of The Tank Museum at Bovington in Dorset; the Royal Artillery Archives, now held at the Royal School of Artillery at Larkhill Camp near Salisbury, Wiltshire; and The National Archives (formerly the Public Record Office) at Kew in West London.

Moving the Guns has been completely redesigned and the 150 or so contemporary photographs and manufacturer's line drawings used in the original publication have been enhanced using modern imaging techniques. We hope you enjoy this revised edition.

Philip Ventham and David Fletcher
October 2022

MOVING THE GUNS

1 EARLY EXPERIMENTS STEAM TRACTION

In the 1850s, 'Steam Sapper' traction engines were adapted from their agricultural cousins to haul heavy artillery, but what to specify for the next generation of military steam traction tied the Army in knots. Developments in compounding and axle springs moved the technology forward, while the Boer War in 1899–1902 taught important lessons about how mechanical transport could be used.

1 EARLY EXPERIMENTS STEAM TRACTION

A Burrell-Boydell engine at Woolwich Arsenal c. 1857. In keeping with the practice at that time the steersman occupies a platform on the fore carriage, which pivots against the boiler section. Although it cannot be seen, the nautical effect of the ship's wheel is further enhanced by a sort of bowsprit, sticking out at the front, which supports the steering chains.

Among the exhibits at the Chelmsford Show of the Royal Agricultural Society of England in 1856 was a steam traction engine described as weighing nine tons. It was built by the firm of Richard Garrett and Sons of Leiston, Suffolk, but entered for the show by Messrs Boydell and Glasier of the Traction Engine and Endless Railway Company Ltd of Mark Lane, London. Novel though it was at this time, the Garrett engine was only really serving as a model to display the Boydell Endless Railway system, and it was this that attracted the attention of the military.

James Boydell took out his first patent in 1846 and subsequently registered an improved pattern in 1854. His idea was to produce a form of wheel that could be used successfully on soft or uneven ground without sinking in. He achieved this by fitting a series of large wooden feet around the circumference of the wheel, fitted in such a way that they interlocked and lay flat on the ground as the wheel passed over them. It was an ingenious system, but very much at the mercy of contemporary materials, particularly the ironwork, which was much too brittle to withstand such strain for long. Hitherto, their use had been confined to horse-drawn carts and, it is believed, the Army had fitted some to gun carriages during the Crimean War.

The Garrett engine was in London in November of the same year when it took part in the Lord Mayor's Show and it seems that the military authorities took this opportunity to give it a trial of their own. A contemporary press report describes how it managed an 18-ton load, including a heavy siege gun, over a route between Woolwich Arsenal and Plumstead Common, and then helped to emplace the gun. There may have been more to this evolution than meets the eye. The Crimean War, so recently concluded, had been a chastening experience for the British Army in more ways than one. In winter, for instance, the road between the port at Balaclava and the uplands before Sevastopol, where the Army was encamped, became a sea of mud, impassable to man or beast, let alone a fully laden wagon or heavy gun. Despite the construction of a railway, it was clear that movement away from the railhead would still be difficult, and means to overcome this problem had to be found. In any case, ordnance was getting heavier, and one piece, then under construction at Woolwich, could have proved a nightmare to move at all if it was to rely on animal haulage, never mind the mud. This was the 36in Mallett mortar

7

designed specifically to shell Sevastopol. When fully assembled it weighed 42 tons and it fired spherical bombs that weighed up to 3,000lbs each. If it had ever got as far as the Crimea in the first place, Boydell wheels and even perhaps a Boydell traction engine would have been needed to get it within the 2,500yd range necessary for it to have a chance of hitting its target.

The brief trial of the Garrett engine proved that it was hardly robust enough for this kind of work, but the potential was there for all to see. As a consequence, an Ordnance Select Committee was asked to investigate further. At the same time, the Honourable East India Company asked two colonels, Sir Frederick Abbott and Sir Probey Cautley, to attend the Committee meetings and any trials on their behalf. Then an event occurred that fired everyone's imagination. In 1856, Boydell concluded an agreement with the celebrated firm, Charles Burrell and Sons of Thetford, Norfolk, who were to become the largest builders of Boydell-type engines over the next few years. They had a prototype on the road in 1856 but an improved version appeared in 1857. On 17 May that year, this new Burrell-Boydell engine left the works in Thetford hauling a mixed train of wagons, threshing machines and a portable engine, with a total weight of more than 30 tons, bound for London on the turnpike. Three days and 85 miles later the train limped into London having survived, to say no more, the first long distance mechanical road run in history. A year later, the journey was repeated by another engine, one of two ordered by the Royal Carriage Department for trials at Woolwich Arsenal.

Trials of these two engines included some prodigious feats, hauling heavy artillery up some of the steepest hills in the area, and the largest of the two is recorded as having successfully shifted a total weight of 43 tons in one go. For all that, they had their problems. Since no differential was fitted, the drive from the two cylinders passed, via the crankshaft, to only one of the hind wheels and this had an adverse effect on its ability to turn corners when the driven wheel was on the inside. It was difficult to get a grip on a paved surface and, if the road was cambered, the engine was forever trying to work its way into the gutter. Despite this, both Abbott and Cautley were impressed with its potential and, pending certain improvements, advised the East India Company to acquire one.

In 1859, this new engine, which now had drive to both hind wheels (one wheel or the other had to be thrown out of gear when turning), gave a demonstration in Hyde Park hauling five wagons containing 160 guardsmen. In the event, none of these engines turned out to be of much use. A letter from the Royal Arsenal dated 4 February 1860 describes them as being of less use than horses, adding, 'We do not use them at all, they cut up our roads and the vibration in consequence of the nature of the ground is very great.' They were offered for sale but this did not work either, for a photograph taken of one of them some time later shows that the boiler had been replaced with an enormous manually operated treadmill. It was used in this form to move large baulks of timber around the Arsenal or the Dockyard.

Correspondence from India suggests that the engine sent out to Bombay was little better. They complained that it would rear up until the front wheels lifted clear of the ground when trying to start a heavy load on a steep hill, but this malfunctioning could probably be attributed to misuse in some circumstances.

One of Boydell's contemporaries was William Bray, Chief Engineer of the cross-Channel paddle steamer *Lord Warden* of Folkestone. Perhaps it was

1 EARLY EXPERIMENTS STEAM TRACTION

Bray's engine of 1858 with three 68pdrs in tow during trials at Woolwich. Once again, the steersman is stationed at the front, but the main object of interest should be the blades, protruding through the rim of the hind wheel.

Bray's familiarity with the action of paddle wheels that led him to design another means of improving cross-country traction for steam engines. The main feature of his design again lay in the driving wheels, which were so arranged that a series of retractable blades could be set to project through the rim of the wheel by cam action. The cam could be adjusted by a handle on the footplate to cause the blades to project at the top or bottom of the wheel as required. In the former case this meant that the part of the wheel in contact with the road was smooth, for operation on firm ground. Turned the other way, the blades projected downwards and dug into the ground to give better adhesion.

In 1858, one of these machines, described as Messrs Paul and Bray's Traction Engine, was given a series of trials at Woolwich where it was photographed hauling three 68pdr guns and attendant wagons. The results of the trials were inconclusive although Abbott and Cautley commented on the better workmanship of the Bray engine compared to the Burrell. Returning to the subject of the driving wheels, which were the main object of the trial, they noted that the Boydell system gave better results on sand or marshy ground, while the Bray principle worked better on smooth roads. Presumably this was with the spades withdrawn and, if they had thought about it, they might have realised what railway engineers had discovered thirty years before, that a smooth wheel on a smooth surface gave all the adhesion necessary in all but the most exceptional circumstances.

A few engines – most of them unconventional – by Bray and others, were purchased by the Admiralty over the next few years but the War Office seemed to lose interest. From the manufacturers' point of view, trade was beginning to boom in the agricultural sector, both at home and abroad, so they had less need to cater to the costly and eccentric needs of the military. The 'little wars' that kept the British Army busy for the second half of the 19th century did not generally call for the use of heavy artillery, and the need for mechanised haulage consequently only aroused the mildest interest. There were occasional flurries of interest and one occurred, purely by chance, at Dover in 1869. It was Easter and the occasion of the Volunteer Review which, that year, included an assault on Dover Castle. The Volunteers' artillery had arrived by

9

Steam Gunner No 1? Thomson's road steamer *Advance*, from a contemporary engraving. Perhaps that is a likeness of Mr Stranger at the controls.

rail at Dover station and the problem was how to get it up Castle Hill and into action. Standing in the station on their way to a customer in France, were two new Aveling and Porter traction engines from the factory in Rochester. They were quickly put to good use and the guns were hauled away to their battery positions followed by a crowd of excited townsfolk.

Despite Burrell's attempt to sell the idea of heavy road haulage, the real market for steam engines was in agriculture. Indeed, the rapidly expanding network of railways appeared to rule out the need for long distance haulage by road and the idea that it might be useful for colonial expansion had hardly been grasped, with one exception. This was due to the efforts of a Scots inventor, R.W. Thomson of Edinburgh. His original claim to fame was a patent for a pneumatic tyre taken out in 1845, which only enjoyed limited success.

He next devised a form of solid rubber tyre in segments, which could be fitted to the driving wheels of heavier machines for road work. Again, Thomson found himself ahead of his time since no suitable road locomotives existed on which his patent could be tested. He therefore set about designing his own model, which appeared in 1867. Thomson Road Steamers were compact three-wheelers with one small steerable wheel at the front and two big driving wheels at the rear. A vertical boiler and cylinders helped to keep the wheel base short and to concentrate most of the weight over the driven axle. In 1870, the War Office bought one of his machines, the Advance built by Robey and Sons of Lincoln. In the hands of a Mr Stranger – 'the Instructor of Engine Driving at Woolwich and Aldershot' – it was noticeable both for speed and pulling power despite a tendency, according to the Army, to 'capsize' from time to time. In 1871, another unidentified Thomson steamer with 5,000 miles 'on the clock' was purchased for service at Aldershot and Woolwich. It may well be that this and Advance were the two so-called 'Steam Gunners Nos 1 and 2', which were reported as working at Woolwich in 1873. A report on these engines, in respect of their work with the siege train, claimed they were too heavy to be a practical proposition.

Thomson's work on rubber tyres brought him into contact with a young lieutenant of the Rifle Brigade, R.E.B. Crompton, who was posted to India in 1864. As a schoolboy, Crompton had designed and built a small steam cart and he contacted Thomson when he needed rubber tyres for an improved model, which he wanted to perfect while he was in India. Impressed by the road steamers, Crompton persuaded the Indian Government to buy one for hauling the mail on the Grand Trunk Road which, in due course, led to an

1 EARLY EXPERIMENTS STEAM TRACTION

order being placed for an improved version with Messrs Ransomes, Simms and Head of Ipswich. They built four such engines in 1871, named *Chenab*, *Indus*, *Ravee* and *Sutlej*, with Crompton acting as the government's agent and inspector in England. On his direction, a new type of boiler was used, which gave a much better performance and the four engines entered service with the Indian Post Office, although the Army was allowed to use them for annual camps, to which they hauled guns and supplies. Crompton was duly appointed 'Superintendent of the Government Steam Train'.

Meanwhile, back in Britain, the War Office was poised to take traction engines seriously. In 1868, they ordered a special lightweight machine from Aveling and Porter, which was followed in 1871 by a production model called the Steam Sapper. These famous engines were an immediate success and their versatility became a byword. In addition to haulage, they could drive machinery, pumps and dynamos from the flywheel, mount a light crane or even run on rails, if necessary. Steam Sappers were single-cylinder, two-speed engines rated at six nominal horse power (6nhp) – a figure that should be taken with a pinch of salt since it derived from a theoretical formula, whereas in practice engines could develop six times this figure. Weight was an important consideration since they were required to work over Army pontoon bridges and careful design meant that the engines tipped the scales at around five tons. One of these engines accompanied Sir Garnet Wolseley's expedition to the Gold Coast in 1873 – known as the Ashanti War – but little use was found for it. Yet engines of the same type were purchased by the military authorities in France, Italy and Russia, where they served, along with other makes, during the Russo-Turkish War in 1877.

The success of the Steam Sappers appears to have inspired other manufacturers and for the next 20 years few self-respecting British companies issued a catalogue unless it contained an engraving of a locomotive, fitted with a jib, lifting the barrel of a field gun from its carriage. Even so, the Army only obtained a few new engines and most of these came from Aveling and Porter. By now, the name Steam Sapper

One of the Thomson road steamers operated by Lieutenant R.E.B. Crompton in India. Water is being fed into the tender, which also has a load of wood aboard. The boiler has a good head of steam and the safety valve is blowing off. These engines were supplied with canopies fitted over the driver's platform, but this one has been removed. The picture provides a good view of Thomson's segmented rubber tyres on the wheels.

The Aveling and Porter Steam Sapper that accompanied Sir Garnet Wolseley's expedition against the Ashanti. They were single-cylinder machines rated at 6nhp, and this example had a jib fitted at the front with a manually operated hoist.

had become almost generic for military traction engines, whereas the term 'Steam Gunner' was never heard again. This, of course, reflects the fact that all such mechanical equipment was viewed as a species of plant, which only the Sappers had the wit to deal with.

The Siege of Chatham in 1877 was not the bloody business it sounds, but an exercise, or a 'sham fight', as *The Times* put it. At least two engines were used and, at the parade at the end of the exercise, they marched past the Commander-in-Chief: an 8nhp model pulling three 32pdrs and a 6nhp model with two 12pdrs in tow. These were probably Avelings since two 6nhp and two 8nhp models had been added to the fleet that year.

For all their obvious usefulness and versatility, it was still true to say that even Steam Sappers were little more than modified civilian vehicles, conscripted sons of the soil. By 1879, the Army had a much clearer idea of what it wanted from a traction engine but, as usual, it was at odds with civilian requirements and commercial economics. If the Army wanted something special then, clearly, it must specify the design requirements and fund the development itself. This was to be a constant thread throughout the history of military vehicle development.

A Mr Hay of the Ordnance Department was the first to draw up a design specification for a particular vehicle and an order was placed with John Fowler and Company of Leeds for what was described as the Fowler-Hay Siege Traction Engine, which was delivered in 1880. It was a vertical-boiler, single-cylinder machine rated at 8nhp with a driving platform, under a canopy, in front of the boiler, rather like a four-wheeled version of a Thomson engine. It had a large winch and capstan at the rear, a substantial crane at the front, and the ability to run on standard gauge railway lines if necessary. The total weight was 12 tons. Extensive trials were carried out at Shoeburyness, since the main idea of the engine was to haul artillery. It was found to be capable of handling 34 tons on the road, and 38 tons on rails, and of winching a heavy gun ashore from a barge. The 5-ton crane could lift a gun barrel, while a belt drive from the fly wheel could be used to drive pumps and other appliances.

All in all, it was a most useful machine, if rather heavy. It was also rather expensive, which no doubt explains why no more were built.

In the late 1880s, two developments took place in traction engine design that were of considerable importance, since they marked a move away from agriculture towards heavy haulage. The most significant development was the adoption of compounding, which increased the available power output by making more efficient use of the steam. The other was a springing system for the rear axle that gave a much smoother ride. Some firms went a stage further and introduced a third speed, an intermediate gear between high and low gears, but this was considered a bit of a luxury. Since farmers, in general, were happy with simple, un-sprung, single-cylinder engines, two streams developed: the agricultural engine,

A later example of the Steam Sapper crane engine, this time equipped with a power-operated hoist. Photographs of this type, usually with the background blanked out, were often used in publicity brochures and this trick of lifting a gun barrel was a favourite feature.

The unique Fowler-Hay siege train engine of 1880. This rear view shows the vertical boiler and power-driven capstan, which is an extension of the winch drum shaft just visible beneath the frame. Flanged wheels could be fitted to allow the engine to operate over standard gauge railway lines.

13

MOVING THE GUNS

Two big Fowler compound road locomotives, each hauling three wagons and a heavy gun up a steep mountain road in South Africa during the Boer War. Notice the dapper, if somewhat incongruous civilian accompanying the troops!

Another Fowler, an A4 class compound, pauses at a roadside water tank in Cape Town while moving a large gun.

One of the special armoured engines gives a demonstration in Fowler's yard at Leeds. The winch rope leads from the engine, through the armoured wagon, to haul the gun up the ramps.

and its big brother, the compound road locomotive. Trends towards specialisation in manufacturing also presaged change. Aveling and Porter, for instance, began to concentrate on steam road rollers while Fowlers, in addition to their celebrated ploughing rigs, began to take the lead in road locomotion. The War Office started to change its allegiance accordingly.

Two more large-scale manoeuvres, in Berkshire in 1893 and in Salisbury in 1898, saw various engines in action, both service and hired civilian models, but they were not used in the front line. Although they effectively halved the cost of hauling supplies by horsepower and pumped water at a rate never seen before, they stayed very much in the background, earning scant praise, such as the following comment from Lord Wolseley's report of 1898, 'the manoeuvres show clearly that mechanical traction by means of traction engines is an efficient supplement to animal traction, especially in carrying supplies in rear of the Army.' There was no suggestion that they could, or indeed should, replace horses for moving guns.

In 1898, Crompton, now a distinguished electrical engineer in civilian life, was retained by the War Office to inspect a massive four-wheel-drive engine built by William Tasker and Sons of Andover. It was designed by an eccentric genius who rejoiced in the name of Bramah J. Diplock. It was not the first machine of its kind, but it was the best engineered so far and it might have led to a great new military future for steam. One reason why it did not, was that there was a great new power in the land, the four-cycle internal combustion engine. Three years previously, pioneering British motorists had celebrated emancipation day with a run down to Brighton, freed at last from a series of petty restrictions imposed by a reactionary, horse orientated government. Now there was a new mood in the air, a new century just around the corner, and a new war to get involved in.

The Boer War

The Boer War began in October 1899 and the British Army started to mobilise in the traditional way. The British military hierarchy, with its unbending faith in the past, showed its usual reluctance to change, even in the age of steam, but some concessions were necessary. On the 1 November, No 45 Steam Road Transport Company RE, was raised at Aldershot, officered by a small band of enthusiasts who had championed the cause of mechanisation for the previous 20 years, but it was not the most popular branch of the Army. Over the next four years some 55 engines of various makes, but predominantly Fowlers, served in South Africa.

Their initial reception was decidedly chilly and it was only patience and hard work that eventually got them accepted; together with the realisation that traction engines did not catch any of the diseases, which depleted the stocks of horses and oxen. In addition, of course, they did not eat their way through mountains of fodder when they were not working. Most of their work involved carrying supplies but now and then, when a heavy gun was needed at the top of some rocky outcrop, the engines were brought out to do the job. Their supporters within the Army in Britain insisted they could do much more and persuaded the War Office to place an order with Fowlers for a series of armoured road trains, which, it was hoped, would do for road transport what armoured trains were already doing on the railways in the war zone. These trains consisted of a large road locomotive, fully enclosed in steel plate, with three armoured wagons capable of carrying troops or supplies. They concern us here because they were also designed to take artillery pieces. Steel channels carried by each wagon acted as ramps so that the guns could be winched aboard, though there was no suggestion that they could be fired from inside the wagon. Despite the fact that two complete trains were sent to the Cape, they were never used as intended. Indeed, the first thing the Army did was to strip off the armour plate for use on the railways.

Crompton was by now retired and pursuing varied interests, but still maintained a firm commitment to the electrical industry with which his name is associated. However, his strong military associations led him to form a curious unit known as the Electrical Engineers (Volunteers), RE, which was ready to mobilise and put its expertise at the service of the country. The Volunteers took three Burrell engines with dynamos with them to South Africa, which they used to haul equipment and provide electrical lighting in the field. On arrival in Pretoria, they came across a lone Fowler of 45 Company driven by an incompetent driver. Tired of rescuing him from muddy river beds and water holes, they added the engine to their own fleet and took upon themselves the task of emplacing a number of 6in guns on the hills around Pretoria. As the war progressed, the value of the engines was appreciated more and more by the establishment and demand for their services grew. But wars have that effect – novelties rapidly become essentials when there is a job to be done. It is what happens afterwards that really counts, and that very often becomes a different matter.

The lessons of the Boer War and the postwar trials

Even before the war had ended, the commander-in-chief had established a Mechanical Transport Committee to consider, among other lessons from the war, the extent to which mechanical transport could be used by the Army and what the best types of vehicles would be for the various services. One lesson was that the self-contained steam lorry – or waggon, as it was then known – was a better proposition than the road train with its string of wagons. One of the first things the Committee therefore did was to hold the first of a series of competitive trials for tractors, which were open to the trade to produce what they thought were suitable contenders. The 1901 trial attracted seven competitors of which only one was an internal combustion-engine lorry. First and second were a Foden and a Thornycroft steam waggon and they were both sent out to South Africa for a brief trial. From the results of the trial, the Committee was able to report that a 'suitable self-propelled steam lorry had been selected for present use' and that they were looking for a suitable internal combustion-engine lorry that would increase the 'radius of action'. The interim report produced in 1902 recommended that 'in general, there was a role for mechanical transport in the Army and that, until the emergence of a suitable tractor with a satisfactory "radius of action", steam haulage offered the best solution for the Army'. As a result of the trials, the Army purchased a small number of Thornycroft steam waggons for general haulage duties. Their appearance, however, inspired some further ideas, some more bizarre than others. Major Bethell of the Royal Field Artillery (RFA), for instance, proposed that they could be adapted as gun tractors, or a 'Mobile Field Battery' as he put it in an article published in the *Proceedings of the Royal Artillery Institute*. Oddly, Bethell based his design around the special 'Colonial' pattern of the Thornycroft, which was only placed third in the trials. In an effort to get the best possible traction on poor roads and rough ground the designers had placed the boiler, engine and even the driver at the rear of the machine where the latter's view was seriously impeded. The major envisaged a six-man crew and 100 rounds of ammunition being carried on the front platform and suggested that the 15pdr high-velocity gun would be the best weapon to be towed by it. There is no evidence that he was actually asked to leave the regiment but he must have earned a lot

A Burrell of the Electrical Engineers (Volunteers) hauling a box van and heavy gun, probably in the hills above Pretoria. The extension ahead of the chimney normally supported a Lawrence and Scott dynamo, which was belt-driven from the flywheel.

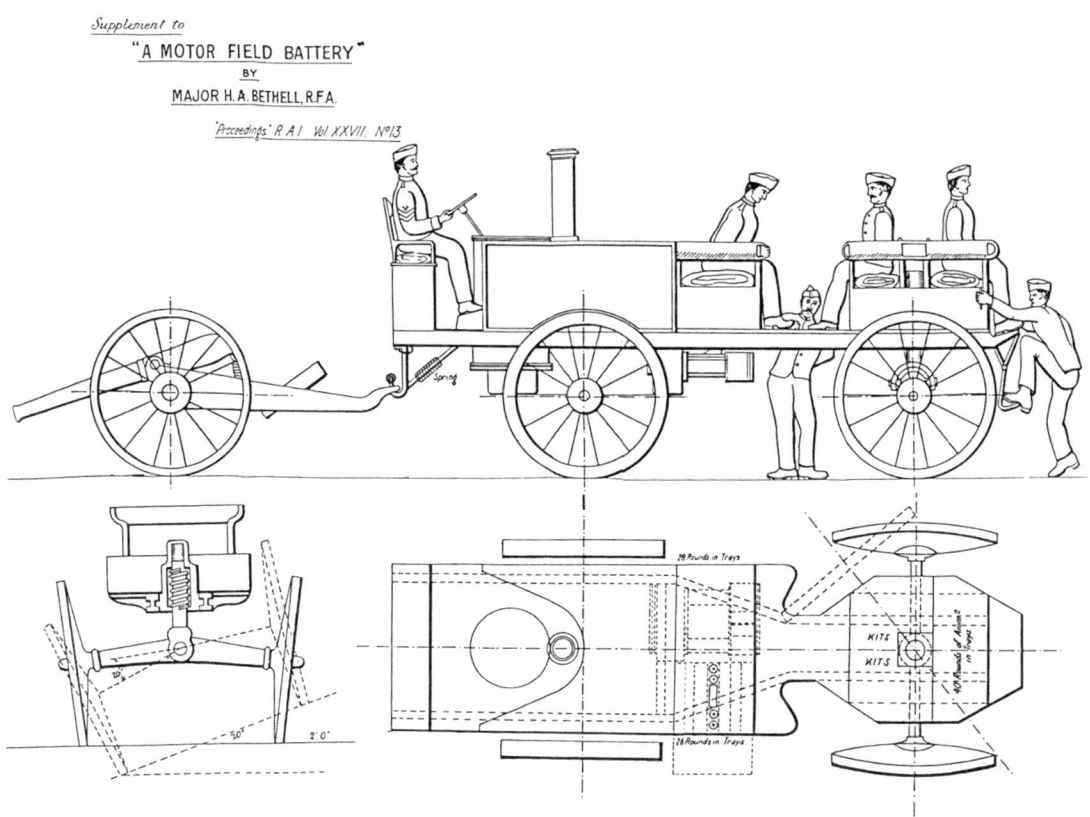

of sideways glances in the mess. The Royal Artillery Sub-Committee, meanwhile, was carrying out its own trials with gun haulage at Lydd and came to the conclusion that teams of horses could perform as well as tractors, albeit for shorter duration.

The emergence of the internal combustion engine
A further trial was held in October 1903 and this time it was an internal combustion-engined tractor that took the £1,000 first prize. This was an enormous wheeled, heavy-oil engine tractor built by Richard Hornsby and Sons of Grantham and it marked the beginning of the Army's long association with the internal combustion engine. However, in 1903, the government passed the Heavy Motor Car Order, which permitted operators to use machines of up to five tons in weight with a crew of just one man at speeds of up to 5mph. This led to a rash of light steam tractors from all the major manufacturers, but it was really steam's last fling. The Army took an interest and a number of light tractors were put through their paces hauling field guns around a course in Long Valley in Aldershot. A Tasker *Little Giant* was put to the test as was an Ackroyd Safety Oil Engine fitted with Robert's Patent Chain Track, of which more anon. Bramah J. Diplock re-emerged, having discontinued his four-wheel drive tractor, with another vehicle fitted with driving wheels, which had moveable feet attached to them, which he called Pedrails. A Foster engine fitted with Pedrails did the Long Valley course in 1904 but it did not impress the authorities.

Major Bethell's design for a steam-powered gun tractor. Although clearly based on the Thornycroft it lacks a winch, which is a strange omission, but the front end of the chassis has been cleverly shaped to give a good lock for a cart-type axle.

17

MOVING THE GUNS

By 1906, the Committee was pinning its hopes on the Hornsby tractor, which was sent back to Grantham in 1907 to be fitted with a chain track designed and patented by their managing director, David Roberts. The Committee thought that this vehicle would be particularly suitable for the haulage of heavy artillery and various trials were carried out in 1907 and 1908.

Meanwhile, in 1906, the Newcastle firm of Sir W.G. Armstrong Whitworth and Company, Britain's leading commercial armaments manufacturers, decided to take a part in military mechanisation. They had been in the automobile business since 1901 and one of their first designers, Walter Wilson, a retired naval officer, put forward an interesting proposition. His gun tractor was a lightweight compared to the big tractors then in vogue, but it was versatile and eminently suited to its task. Basically, it was a four-wheeled car chassis, powered by a four-cylinder petrol engine and probably featured its designer's highly effective pre-selector epicyclic gearbox. It differed from its contemporaries in that it was armoured to some extent. A common feature of early armoured vehicles was a strange concern on the part of the designer to over-protect the machinery at the expense of the unfortunate driver who, presumably, was thought to be bullet-proof or perhaps expendable. Thus, Wilson's vehicle was covered from stem to stern with sheets of armoured plate while the driver sat amidships in a sort of open cockpit with his head and shoulders sticking out. Like the big tractors, the car had a small capstan winch on the left side of the body with a two-legged ground anchor alongside it to act as a holdfast. Although it was a rear-wheel drive, some concessions were made to cross-country

The big Hornsby tractor was rebuilt with David Roberts's patent track-laying system and tested again by the War Department in 1907. Now known as Caterpillar No 1, its trials were witnessed by King Edward VII and The Prince of Wales. In this form the machine had air assisted steering controls, worked from a hand-operated compressor.

performance since the front axle was mounted as far forward as possible. In this way, the front wheels could tackle an obstacle without any risk of the chassis or main body getting in the way. Yet there was one design feature that any self-respecting Gunner could only see as a snag – the four wheels were identical to those fitted to a field gun. The intention was perfectly clear: if one of the wheels was damaged in action, the crew had only to look around and take one off the nearest field gun to be on their way.

In 1909, there was a further tractor trial and it was an oil-engined Thornycroft that won against competitors from Hornsby's and Broom and Wade. The Committee purchased three Thornycrofts and three Hornsby wheeled tractors, which were delivered in May and June 1910. A new chain-track tractor was ordered from

In 1905 the War Office purchased this huge, two-cylinder heavy oil-engined tractor from Richard Hornsby and Sons of Grantham. It proved capable of moving eight tons. Despite being smellier, noisier and a lot less attractive to look at than a steam engine, it was much quicker to start from cold.

The Armstrong-Whitworth gun tractor, designed by W.G. Wilson, makes a spectacle of itself during a demonstration at Newcastle. Although the body is armoured the driver, as may be seen, was rather vulnerable.

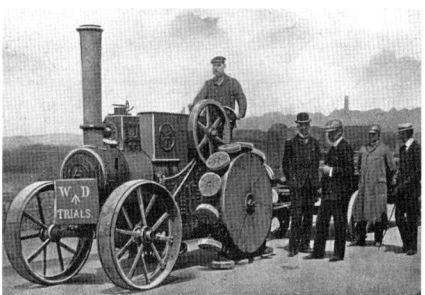

Another contestant in the 1904 Trials was this single-cylinder Foster tractor fitted with Pedrail driving wheels. J.B. Diplock, inventor of the Pedrail system, is believed to be the tall figure in the bowler hat.

MOVING THE GUNS

The Thornycroft Gun Tractor was built in 1909 specially to compete in the Mechanical Transport Committee Trials at Aldershot, which it won. A four-cylinder paraffin engine, driving through a three-speed gearbox, gave a top speed of 7mph. This machine still survives as an exhibit in the British Commercial Vehicle Museum at Leyland in Lancashire.

Hornsbys built six of these 50hp tractors to a War Office order even though they had not participated in the 1909 trials. They served with the Army Service Corps who, by this time, had taken over responsibility for mechanical transport from the Royal Engineers.

Hornsby's in 1909. This new version was much lighter at eight tons fully laden and was designed to tow the 60pdr gun. A 70hp six-cylinder vertical engine was fitted, replacing the 60hp engine of the original. The engine was started on petrol and run on paraffin vapourised by the heat of the exhaust gases. The vehicle could also be started from cold using paraffin, but this required the use of a blowlamp and took about an hour to accomplish. The vehicle steered using a crude braking system on the appropriate driving sprocket.

This vehicle was put through extensive road trials on a route which ran from Grantham to Aldershot via the Peak District. It was reported that, 'although the tractor is of an unusual shape, the delays from restive horses were not so numerous as had been expected'.

The vehicle covered the 284 miles in 8½ working days at an average speed of 6mph. When it arrived at Aldershot, the tractor was put through a series of cross-country trials at which it performed very well. The only mishap occurred after the official trials had ended when the manufacturers attempted to give an additional demonstration of its slope-climbing abilities. Unfortunately, the tractor slipped out of gear and ran back down the slope complete with the towed gun. A bit of deft handling by the driver and brakeman managed to avert a major disaster.

Following the Aldershot trial, the tractor was dispatched to join 1st Heavy Brigade at Practice Camp at Trawsfynydd in North Wales in July. It was used to haul a 60pdr gun in comparison with a horse-drawn section. At the conclusion of the trial, the Battery Commander of 35 Heavy Battery produced a damning report that condemned the tractor for practically every conceivable reason, 'to sum up, it is impossible in a column with other troops, its noise and smell are abominable and very few horses will pass it. The wooden blocks forming its feet are nearly worn away, it is unable to carry sufficient fuel for itself for any length of time and its machinery appears to be unreliable. The team of eight horses is, in my opinion, far superior in any circumstances.'

This sweeping condemnation, not untypical of many such opinions that were to be expressed about mechanisation in the years ahead, provoked the Committee into a somewhat hurt and self-defensive retort, and there the matter rested for a while. It was accepted that the engine was somewhat underpowered and Hornsby managed, with a minimum of modification, to make the engine run on petrol alone, which increased the brake horsepower to 100 at an increased output speed. The petrol lorry was by now a viable proposition and many of the original advocates of steam traction, such as Leyland and Thornycroft, joined dozens of newcomers in an effort to survive the change. The Army did not like petrol and considered it to be dangerous, inflammable stuff that did not mix with ammunition. It was tolerated for

The Hornsby Little Caterpillar was basically a tracked version of the wheeled tractor. Only one was purchased, with artillery haulage in mind, and as seen here it was quite capable of handling a 60pdr gun. It was later converted to run on petrol and in this form still survives as an exhibit at The Tank Museum.

staff cars and ambulances but smelly, inefficient paraffin was preferred where guns and ammunition were concerned. Meanwhile, trials continued with the three Thornycroft lorries and the three-wheeled Hornsby tractors, which suffered from a number of problems.

Following its rebuff at the hands of 35 Heavy Battery, the Mechanical Transport Committee then requested a comparative trial of a tractor-drawn section against a horse-drawn section coming into action after a move of approximately 30 miles. However, before this came about, the Director of Artillery intervened in a matter that he obviously thought was in danger of getting out of hand. He posed a number of fundamental questions that he felt needed addressing before any trial took place. The nature of the questions leaves the inevitable feeling that perhaps he himself was not entirely unbiased in the matter, and they are worth reproducing in full as an example of the misgivings felt about mechanisation at the highest level in the Army at this time:

> Before going further with these trials, it would be well to discuss the object of introducing this form of tractor into the Service. What is it for?
>
> 1 Is it to take the place of horses altogether for drawing the guns of the Heavy Artillery, and if so, is it because horses are getting scarce, or because it is thought that mechanical draught is better? Or
>
> 2 Is it to be used as an additional means of moving the guns either
> a when the distance is great or
> b the ground is too heavy for the Horses? Or
>
> 3 Is it in the event of the horses being done away with as in (1), to be used in conjunction with the more simple form of tractor, the latter type to be employed normally, for the purpose of drawing the heavy guns over ordinary ground and a small proportion of the chain tractors to be utilised as well so that they could be ready to help in getting the guns over ground too difficult for the simple form of tractor?
>
> When this subject was first started, I see that the Director of Artillery, when agreeing to the commencement of the trials, expressed a hope that the tractor would do with a gun of nearly six tons all that horses could.
>
> From the report of the trials recently carried out, the conclusion arrived at seems to be that, while this consummation has not been reached, yet:
>
> 1 That on moderately steep and trackless slopes the horses have the advantage, although on excessively severe gradients the tractor is best.
>
> 2 That for long distances the tractor is best. I think no trial is necessary to show that to cover a distance of 30 miles with a 60pdr gun, the tractor (if it does not break down) is the best and will be better able to surmount any difficult gradient at the end.
>
> The present seems to be the time to settle whether we are to aim at replacing the draught horses of Heavy Artillery and Siege Artillery entirely by tractors, or whether we merely wish to have additional means at our disposal for helping the guns over long distances or difficult ground.

A conference was held in December 1911 to discuss these questions at which Colonel Holden, the chairman of the Royal Artillery Sub-Committee, considered the advantages of mechanical traction to be:

> 1 Increase in distance that can be covered

2 Savings in water and forage supplies

3 Economy in men

4 Saving of space in line of march

5 Suitable for use over country unsuitable for horses.

It was agreed that a modified comparative trial should be carried out and this was conducted by an ASC officer in Long Valley, Aldershot on 5 July 1911. Once again, the nature of the trials were such that the relative advantages of the tractor over horses were not readily apparent. The conclusion of the officer conducting the trial was that the 'tractor's work seems to begin where that of the horse ends, i.e., when distances are too long or gradients are too severe to justify attempting them with the horse teams . . . it has a value for artillery purposes, not to replace horses but to carry on when the limit of horse flesh has been reached.'

This was really the end, for the moment, of the Army's brief flirtation with track-laying vehicles. The Hornsby tractor passed through the hands of the RASC who eventually passed it on to the Royal Tank Corps (RTC) Driving and Maintenance School. It now resides at The Tank Museum at Bovington and it is said to have provided some of the inspiration to the designers of the first tank a few years later. It is interesting to note in conclusion, that in 1908 Major Donohue, a member of the Royal Artillery Sub-Committee, had proposed that the tractor should be armoured and a gun mounted on it. Unfortunately, it was a suggestion that was ignored at the time.

It is worth mentioning in passing, that in 1910 the Mechanical Transport Committee had noted the existence in America of Holt gasoline caterpillar tractors and had unsuccessfully attempted to get authority to purchase one for evaluation purposes. The Military Attaché in Washington could throw very little light on it – he had probably never seen anything quite like it before – and the Committee rather condescendingly reported that, 'it did not anticipate that the design and workmanship, particularly of the engine would be beyond reproach. They are still of the opinion, however, that the general arrangement and design is a good one.'

Following the failure to pursue the Hornsby tractor to a satisfactory conclusion, the British Army was forced to buy large quantities of Holt tractors for the use of the Heavy and Medium Artillery during the First World War. One wonders whether that Battery Commander of 35 Heavy Battery had cause to regret his comments about mechanical traction as, some five years later, he perhaps struggled to move his guns through the mud of Flanders.

So, as the armies of Europe prepared for the coming conflict, the Gunners went back to their stables, to the well-matched teams of chestnuts and greys, and dreamt of galloping into action as they had done in the past. Mechanisation was coming, there was no doubt about that, but let's leave it to the Army Service Corps (ASC) and the chaps in the rear, meanwhile we'll fight the war the proper way, the way we always have done. In 1911, the last of a series of Subsidy Trials gave the British Army a range of top quality 3-ton vehicles, all designed to a common specification, which were the envy of Britain's allies. There was not, however, a single vehicle that could be called an artillery tractor.

MOVING THE GUNS

2 THE FIRST WORLD WAR

On the eve of the First World War there was no doubt that mechanisation was coming to the British Army, but there were misgivings about this new technology at the highest levels of command. And as the lamps were going out all over Europe, the Army prepared to fight the war the proper way, the way they had always done.

2 THE FIRST WORLD WAR

A British-built version of the Holt tractor by Ruston, Proctor & Company of Lincoln. For some reason they never proved capable of matching the performance of their American counterparts.

On 19 July 1914, an interesting experiment took place in Yorkshire. The Horse Artillery of the local Territorial Force formed a motorised battery for the day and, with General Plumer as the official observer, moved over a distance of 89 miles before coming into action. The cars used for the exercise were of a local make – Sheffield Simplex – and it appears the makers loaned the unit four new chassis fitted with improvised bodies. The guns were 15pdr Erhardts manufactured in Germany and used as a stopgap before the issue of the new 18pdrs to the Territorial Force.

Each gun, complete with limber, was towed behind a car and the starting point was Earl Fitzwilliam's estate at Wentworth Woodhouse near Rotherham. Since they were designed for the altogether more stately progress of a horse team, there was a very real fear that the gun carriages would shake themselves to pieces on the road. As a precaution, all the wheels were soaked for seven days in the kennel pond before the trip. A good deal of attention was also paid to lubrication. In the event, the entire operation was carried out without serious trouble and it might have had considerable influence on future practice were it not for the fact that the First World War broke out exactly three weeks later. As it was, no attempt was made to mechanise either Horse or Field Artillery during the First World War and, where it was used, mechanical traction was restricted to the heavy guns.

At first, it was the trusty old steam traction engine that was called upon to perform this service but, once the lines of trenches became stabilised, its unsuitability for the task became apparent. Close to the front line the merest wisp of smoke or steam brought a swift response from the enemy guns. As the battle zone deteriorated into a morass the big engines floundered like beached whales if they ventured off the roads. It was time to look elsewhere.

Steam still dominated British agriculture and, even where it was being ousted by the petrol-engined tractor, this was generally a small type of machine that would have been hopeless as an artillery tractor. In the United States things were quite different. The vast prairie plains and the swamps of Florida and Louisiana required massive tractors and, in the latter areas in particular, tracklayers were preferred. With the collapse of the Hornsby Roberts project in Great Britain, the type was virtually unknown at home, but a number of firms were making them in the United States and foremost among them was the Holt Company. Their 75hp model was chosen by the War Office and well over 1,000 were imported by the British agents, Balfour Williamson and Company. They were a typical American design of the period, powered by a four-cylinder engine at the front with the driver at the rear. The track units, too, were located at the rear of the machine with a single roller at the front to help with the steering and to lift the nose when it first encountered a slope. However, the centre of gravity was so arranged that almost all the weight rested on the tracks. The name 'Caterpillar', first coined for the Hornsby tractors, was adopted as a trademark by Holts.

The Holts were operated by Caterpillar Companies of the ASC attached to the Heavy or Siege Batteries of the Royal Garrison Artillery (RGA). In addition to the Western Front, they saw service in Palestine, Mesopotamia and in Salonika. The ability of the tracklayer to cross uneven ground was not so important, in this context, as its raw pulling power. The weapons most commonly hauled were the 6in gun and the 8in howitzer. Holts produced a smaller 45hp model, which was popular with the French Army, and a six-cylinder 120hp version, which was used in small numbers

Holt 75hp Caterpillar tractors towing 8in howitzers take a rest by the roadside in France. Such heavy guns would have required vast teams of horses to move them if the American Holts had not been available.

by the British. Holts also played a significant part in the evolution of the tank, and both French and German heavy tanks built during the war in fact used Holt-type components for their suspension. Such was the demand for Holts in Britain and Russia that Rustons of Lincoln were authorised to build them under licence – but results, by all accounts, were not very successful.

Another American vehicle that served in large numbers with the British Army was the FWD 3-ton lorry. Manufactured by the Four-Wheel Drive Auto Company of Clintonville, Wisconsin, it was a forward control lorry with, as its name implies, drive to all four wheels. A prototype had put up a good performance during the US Army trials in 1912. The British Government started by buying the firm's Model B in 1915 and the demand grew to such an extent that other American manufacturers, including Peerless, began building them. Indeed, by about 1917, a version built under licence known as the British Quad was being built in this country and, all told, British forces operated some 3,000 of them from all sources, in various parts of the world. Photographs taken in France show that they were sometimes used for hauling guns like the 6in howitzer in forward areas.

Oddly enough, one of the pioneers of heavy artillery haulage in the First World War was the Royal Navy and, since the equipment subsequently passed into the Army's hands, the details are worth recording. In 1915, Coventry Ordnance Works, based in Glasgow, built a 15in howitzer, a scaled-up version of their successful 9.2in howitzer. The new weapon was offered to the Admiralty and accepted for the Royal Marine Artillery on condition that a suitable heavy tractor could be provided to move it. Admiral Sir Reginald Bacon of Coventry Ordnance Works approached the Lincoln firm of agricultural engineers, William Foster and Company, who, in addition to building their range of steam traction engines, were also building internal combustion engines of 60 and 90hp using Daimler engines. The firm undertook to build an even bigger version based around the Daimler six-cylinder sleeve valve engine rated at 105hp. This Foster Daimler tractor was built along normal traction engine lines with massive 8-foot diameter rear wheels. It proved to be eminently successful, which is more than can be said for the big howitzer. Admiral Bacon later took command of the Dover Patrol but expanded his interests to the extent of installing a battery of 12in guns on the Belgian coast in an attempt to deal with the Germans' heavy Tirpitz Battery near Westende. The British guns landed at Dunkirk and Bacon chose to move

26

them by road to the firing site in order to avoid leaving tell-tale signs that would be obvious from the air if a railway were built for the purpose. Once again Foster Daimler tractors were used and plans were afoot to install an 18in gun inside the Palace Hotel in Westende. The tractors would have been used to move the gun components to the site and a complicated procedure was worked out using models to accomplish this.

By 1916, the Navy was ready to hand over most of its shoreside commitments in heavy artillery to the Army and the tractors, too, changed hands – but there is little evidence that they were used to any great extent to move the heavy guns. In passing, it should be noted that Foster Daimlers also played an important part in the development of the tank. Since they were already contractors to the Admiralty, Fosters were consulted by the Landships Committee when the initial design of the tank was being considered. This led to an order for an experimental landship called Little Willie and its successor, Mother, the prototype of the British tank. Fosters also built some production tanks of the Mark I, II and IV types, which used the engine and transmission components first designed for the tractors.

This was not all that the Army inherited from the Navy. In the summer of 1915, they took over a large fleet of armoured cars, the design and use of which had been pioneered by the Royal Naval Air Service (RNAS) for airfield defence. This equipment included some 3pdr semi-automatic guns on improvised two-wheeled carriages, towed by Rolls-Royce armoured cars, which remained in service until the spring of 1917. There were also some heavy

Another excellent American product was the FWD (Four Wheel Drive) B Type truck. This one was photographed hauling a 6in howitzer and limber over a plank road near the front.

Three of the Royal Navy's big 105hp Foster Daimler tractors hauling the barrel of a 12in gun – weighing 50 tons – to a site on the Belgian coast east of Dunkirk, where it could be used to shell the German Tirpitz Battery.

MOVING THE GUNS

armoured Seabrook lorries mounting the same weapon, which were designed to support the RNAS armoured cars in action. The Seabrooks operated for a while under Army control as Heavy Car Sections 1 to 6, but it is believed that they came under overall command of the Machine Gun Corps not the Royal Artillery.

The Gun Carriers

The advent of the tank and its first appearance in action in September 1916 seemed set to revolutionise warfare, though its potential at the time was hardly recognised. However, it was soon realised that if tanks did succeed in breaking the German line and forcing the enemy back to new positions, they would need swift and substantial support. It was equally clear that the state of the ground in the battle zone would prove a serious obstacle to the forward movement of heavy artillery, even if it was hauled by crawler tractors. An attempt was therefore made to adapt the new technology to artillery movement. In the summer of 1916, work began on the design of a new type of track-laying machine capable of transporting heavy artillery. A prototype, built by Metropolitan Carriage, Wagon and Finance Company of Birmingham, was demonstrated at Oldbury in March 1917. An order for 50 (later reduced to 48) Gun Carrier Machines Mark I was placed with Kitson and Company of Leeds and they entered service in France in 1917.

The Gun Carrier was an interesting machine based on the mechanical components of the Mark I tank. Low-profile track frames on each side were surmounted, at the rear, by a large armoured superstructure containing the engine and transmission from a Foster Daimler along with a supply of ammunition, while the front end formed an open platform. At the front, small armoured cabs sat astride the track frames with a driver on the right, and a commander/steersman on the left. These cabs were open to the rear and had a series of hinged panels on the other three faces, which could be held open or closed when under fire. They also folded forward onto the track

A Seabrook armoured lorry of the Royal Naval Air Service. It mounts a 3pdr gun for close support of armoured cars and a Maxim machine-gun for immediate protection. Taken over later by the Army, these trucks had been used on occasions as mobile artillery; moving into the front line after dark to snipe at known German positions

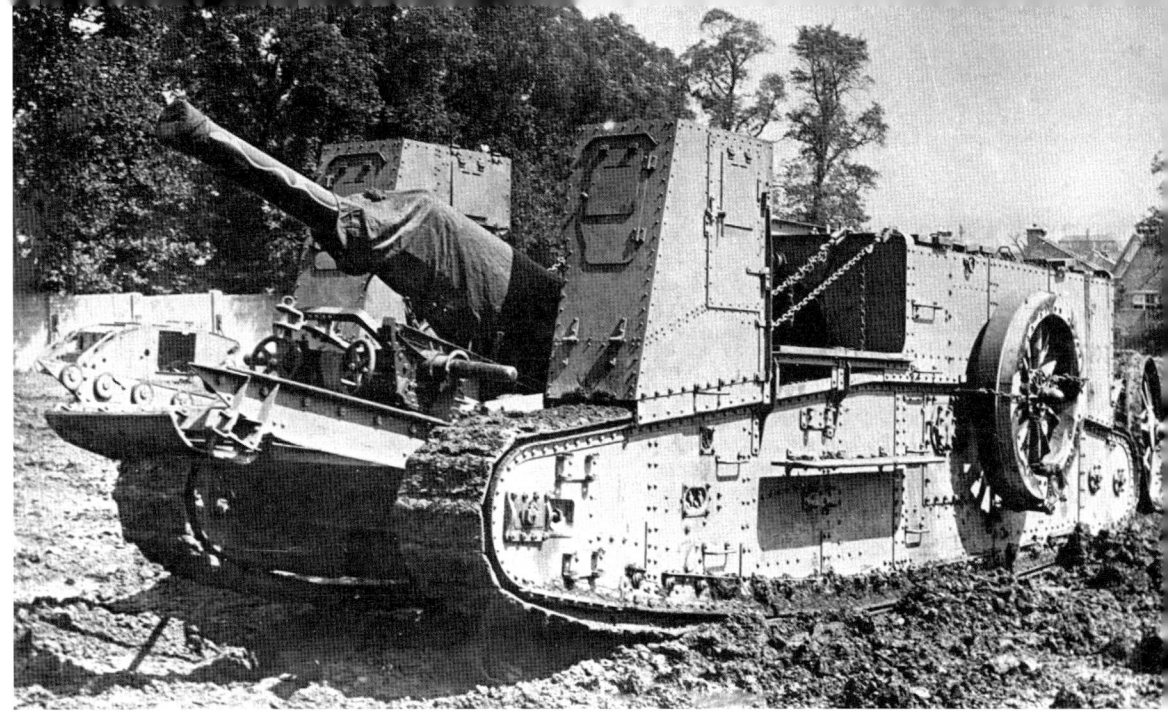

A Gun Carrier Mark I with a 60pdr emplaced. The gun's wheels hang from the sides of the body while the gun is supported by a sliding cradle mounted on the ramp seen protruding from the front. Armoured cabs for the driver and steersman fit astride the tracks, with the auxiliary steering wheels visible at the back.

frames to reduce overall height when the machine was being transported by rail. Originally, Gun Carriers were fitted with a rear steering tail, as on the early tanks, but these were later removed.

In the open platform between the track frames at the front was a long sliding frame up which moved a small cradle mounted on rollers. Gun Carriers were designed to handle either the 6in 26cwt BL howitzer or the 60pdr BL Mark I gun, and the procedure for mounting either was as follows. The sliding frame was pulled forwards until the front end rested on the ground and the cradle was moved to the front of the frame. The gun was then manhandled astride the frame until the axle rested on the cradle. The whole assembly was then winched backwards by a power take-off from the transmission until the gun was secured inboard. At this stage the end of the trail rested against a solid transverse oak beam between the track frames and the wheels were removed and hung on the sides of the superstructure. In place, the gun assumed a position similar to its normal posture on wheels.

These machines were, in effect, the first self-propelled guns, particularly since the 6in howitzer, but not the 60pdr gun, could be fired from the vehicle.

They were operated by Gun Carrier Companies of the Tank Corps who supplied a crew of four, the commander and driver already mentioned, and two gearsmen who worked inside the superstructure. The guns were served by detachments of the RGA. Ammunition was stowed in five-round drums within the vehicle and was also carried loose on the hull roof and on the gun platform itself. The carriers arrived in France in July 1917 in time for the Third Battle of Ypres, which they took part in. The 6in howitzer was used for night sniping at enemy gun positions from firing positions, which were inaccessible to other guns. They could achieve three shoots from different positions in the course of a short summer night. However, their use did not seem to catch on, and the fact that they could carry 200 6in shells weighing nearly 10 tons across broken country dictated their ultimate role as supply carriers. The two vehicles not completed as Gun Carriers were fitted with cranes and used for salvage work.

Two other gun-carrier designs existed. One, which never developed beyond the drawing board stage, had larger frames and no superstructure. It seems to have been designed to handle lighter pieces, which were loaded aboard by engaging

29

MOVING THE GUNS

the axle with a pair of horizontal prongs pivoted between the frames at the front. A winch was then used to jack-knife the prongs into a vertical position, which lifted the gun into firing position. The other type, the Gun Carrier Mark II appeared as a full-sized wooden mock-up late in 1917. The outline in this case was not unlike that of a contemporary tank with a large open area at the rear between the track frames. Here an 18pdr or a 4.5in howitzer could be mounted for transportation and firing.

One unsuccessful candidate in the race to design a tank was the venerable Colonel Crompton of steam engine fame. Indeed, he was one of the first experts to be called in by the Landships Committee in 1915. His original designs were rejected when development passed to Fosters but he continued to work on the project as a private venture. Realising that the fighting tank was only one aspect of mechanised warfare, he abandoned landships in favour of what he called 'emplacement destroyers'. These were basically box-like tracked vehicles mounting one or two guns of about 4.5in calibre inside the hull, protected by armoured doors when not in action. Throughout 1916 and 1917 he bombarded the War Office with a whole series of designs, none of which were accepted, although a model exists at The Tank Museum.

Another, more successful, tank pioneer was Walter Gordon Wilson, who, with William Tritton of Fosters, is one of the acknowledged inventors of the tank. Before he was called to this work, he

A Gun Carrier on active service in France. This one carries the 6in howitzer, the only weapon that could be fired from the vehicle. Notice how extra ammunition has been stowed everywhere. This machine, Darlington, has the usual mixed Gunner and Tank Corps crew, it is running without the useless tail wheels.

2 THE FIRST WORLD WAR

acted as supervisor for the RNAS with the Portholme Aerodrome Company of Huntingdon who were building the Seabrook armoured gun lorries already mentioned. An expert in vehicle transmissions, Wilson became a leading figure in this field between the wars. But he had his share of disasters. One of these was the Portholme Tractor, though the actual extent of his involvement in its design is debatable.

Correspondence certainly exists, which indicates that the Company kept him informed of its progress but they may simply have hoped that his influence would help them to sell it. The Portholme Tractor was a strange-looking machine by any standards and, even now, it is not quite clear which was the front and which was the back. It was a four-wheeled machine of very light construction and a minimal amount of bodywork. The wheels were of two different sizes. The smaller ones steered while the larger ones were the driving wheels. Wire spokes, tensioned by turnkeys, were used and the driving wheels had a broad serrated tread that could be fitted with detachable spuds to aid traction. The four-cylinder engine of unknown make was housed in a small armoured box at the steering end of the vehicle. An armoured screen with a hole in it, rather like the shield of a gun, was mounted crosswise between the driving wheels. Evidently, the gun was mounted here so that, if the steering wheels represented the front of the machine, the gun was trained backwards. According to the makers, any gun up to field-gun size could be mounted. They also specified a top speed of 15mph, a range of 100 miles, and a crew of three. The crew occupied a space (a cab would be too grand a title) between the driving wheels and within the shield. Makers' trials, as is often the case, were perfectly satisfactory but when it went to Shoeburyness for military trials the results were not so good. The vehicle was photographed in the yard of the

Two views showing the wooden mock-up of the Gun Carrier Mark II outside the Metropolitan Works in Birmingham. The general layout is much closer to that of a tank of the period, with a driving cab at the front. The pictures show the method devised to lift the gun aboard and carry it. The winch would be driven off the engine but the means of raising the ramps is not known.

An original scale model, now in the collection of The Tank Museum, of one of Colonel Crompton's designs for an Emplacement Destroyer. Although it lacks any tracks the model displays some ingenious features. The double doors at the front open to release the gun – the wheels for which are stowed on the back – although it was intended to be fired from the vehicle. The roof is formed from separate strips of armour which, in the event of damage, could be replaced as required without having to handle one enormous sheet of plate.

MOVING THE GUNS

Mechanical Warfare Supply Department at Cricklewood in August 1916 and it probably ended its days there.

In saying that British field artillery was not mechanised during the war, one has to allow for the inevitable exception. This was No 10 Section RFA, which was formed in Egypt in August 1916 as a mobile unit to support armoured cars on desert raids. The Section used six Talbot tenders, two of which carried 10pdr BL mountain pack guns, a weapon of some age that was still in service with the Indian Army. From November 1917 onwards, this unit served with armoured cars of the Hedjaz Battery in support of Lawrence of Arabia's force. As far as it is known, no attempt was ever made to fire the guns from the vehicles.

Back in France, a plan was hatched to effect a landing on the Belgian coast in the summer of 1917. A mixed force, including tanks, would land from gigantic pontoons, pushed by warships, at three points on the coast. They would climb off the pontoons, scramble over a steep sea wall and make for Ostend. Three pontoons carrying, among other things, three tanks and 12 guns and limbers, were to be used and the whole scheme was ready and well-rehearsed up to the point at which it was cancelled when the Ypres offensive ground to a halt. Although it was abortive, many useful lessons were learned, some of which bore fruit later. For instance, the amount of ingenuity expended in an effort to cross the sea wall was prodigious. The tanks were equipped with winches, and various ramps and see-saws were produced to enable the guns and wagons to negotiate the awkward lip of the sea wall. One aspect that remains unclear is how the guns were to be handled once ashore. No horses were included in the scheme and there were insufficient other vehicles to do the job.

The 'Hush Operation', as this secret enterprise was known, relied to a great extent on the strength of flexible steel wire to haul everything over the wall, including stores sledges, and this system

In order to bring heavy guns forward across broken ground in the wake of a tank attack this system was devised but never used. The 60pdr gun and limber each rest on a wooden skid, connected to one another and the tank by steel wire rope. In this picture – which shows the gun travelling muzzle first – the towing tank is the experimental Mark IV Tadpole Tail machine of 1917.

was adopted for use on the battlefield generally. The idea was that any tank could, if required, haul a train of stores sledges during an attack, dropping them off at selected points as required. Towards the end of the war, a similar idea was tried for moving guns. A Mark V tank towed a pair of flat sledges with cables, the leading sledge carried the limber and the following one a 60pdr gun. Presumably, the idea was that in a major assault second- or third-wave tanks could take their artillery support with them, drop it off at some pre-arranged spot and then move on to continue the attack. How the various gun detachments were to catch up with their guns is not made clear. In the event, the scheme never got beyond the experimental stage.

The First World War has, justifiably, been called a Gunners' war. Never before had artillery been used on such a massive scale. The science of gunnery made tremendous strides but the need for improved mobility hardly progressed at all, largely because of the static nature of the war. But things would have to change, heavy guns were getting heavier and becoming beyond the power of draught animals to shift them. Equally, lighter field pieces were finding it increasingly difficult to move across a landscape churned up by incessant bombardment. Only tanks could move in these conditions but, without artillery support there was a limit to how far even these vehicles could move. Unless a way could be found to bring guns forward quickly in the wake of an advance, tanks were doomed to very limited advances. The only answer, for those with the imagination to see it, was universal mechanisation for all fighting vehicles.

The lessons of the First World War
At the end of the First World War, the Royal Artillery could reflect on the many lessons learned during the war. From the point of view of mechanisation, experience had been largely restricted to medium and heavy artillery and to the specialised role of anti-aircraft artillery. There had been no role for mechanical draught for horse and field batteries engaged on the Western Front. It was only in Mesopotamia and in the latter stages of the war in Europe that there was a more mobile role for field artillery. The advent of the tank as a practical and powerful weapon of war convinced many that mechanisation of the entire Army was an inevitable and logical progression. Yet many factors at national, Army and regimental level inhibited the rapid progress of mechanisation after the war.

At the national level, there was an understandable attitude, now the 'war to end wars' had finally drawn to a close, that it would never again be necessary to conduct war on such a scale. Admittedly, Britain still had her numerous colonial commitments and therefore it would always be necessary to maintain a small professional army whose primary role would be the 'policing' of the Empire. Never again, it was argued, would Britain need to mobilise the entire nation to fight such a conflict as that which had just finished.

The formation of the League of Nations after the Armistice committed member nations to settling disputes by negotiation rather than force. They were also committed to a degree of disarmament, a policy that was pursued by Britain more actively than most other nations. Lloyd George's policies from 1919 were based on the assumption that there would be no major war for ten years, and this policy was pursued with varying degrees of naivety until about 1933 when it became obvious that the resurgence of the German nation was going to be a future source of trouble.

Such a policy inevitably meant that cuts in government expenditure in the recession that followed the war fell most heavily on the armed services. Resources for research and development and weapons production were very limited indeed and this had inevitable consequences both on government projects and on private armaments manufacturers such as Vickers Ltd. Indeed, in the period up to 1933, the size of the defence budget actually fell in real terms. In the wake of the most costly and destructive conflict known to man, it was not the most auspicious time for military leaders to be pressing for increased expenditure on more military hardware.

Within the Army itself, opinion was divided on the lessons to be drawn from the First World War. Among the more thoughtful officers, opinion was polarised into two categories: conservatives and progressives. The conservatives saw the First World War as an aberration, which was unlikely to be repeated and that any lessons drawn from the conflict would be of limited value. The tank, in their view, was a creature born of the peculiar circumstances of war in Northern France, of poorly drained land turned into a quagmire by freak weather conditions and incessant artillery bombardments. In these conditions, they argued, it was inevitable that the tank had emerged as a suitable weapon of war. However, once the Army settled back into its pre-war role of imperial policing, what role would there then be for the tank? The horse, they believed, would continue to be the main means of transport for the Army for the foreseeable future, though they did acknowledge that some degree of mechanisation was inevitable, particularly in the supply role. Less extreme conservatives accepted that improvements would be necessary to existing guns and equipment and they could see the advantages of the newly issued wireless equipment. They saw all these changes, however, as evolutionary rather than revolutionary.

In the meantime, it is probably not too cynical to suggest that the longer the Army delayed mechanisation, the longer individuals would have access to their government issued chargers, with all the attendant opportunities for sport and recreation, together with a forage allowance generous enough to feed a second, privately owned hunter.

The progressives, on the other hand, saw war as the inevitable clash between expanding industrial societies. The leading military intellectuals of the day such as Liddell Hart and Fuller saw the tank as the supreme war-winning weapon, totally impregnable and with all other arms subordinate to it. Artillery would be unnecessary as the tank would take over that function – even aircraft would become part of a greatly expanded Tank Corps. Unfortunately, some of these luminaries caught the popular imagination and exerted an influence out of all proportion to the validity of their views. Liddell Hart in particular had considerable influence as the military correspondent of the *Daily Telegraph* at the time of the Experimental Armoured Force trials (EAF) in 1928 and 1929. He was undoubtedly influenced, some would say biased, by his experiences in the First World War and expressed an open dislike for professional soldiers, particularly those not wearing a Tank Corps cap badge. We shall never know how much his views influenced the decision not to proceed with the first self-propelled gun, the Birch gun, in 1929, a decision which was to have far-reaching consequences more than a decade later.

Within the Royal Artillery, opinion was divided. There was a strong body of professional Gunners who hankered back to the days before the war when the horse was predominant and mechanical transport was a rarity. They fell into the conservative way of thinking within the Army and, like them, were happy for change to take place, if it had to, all in good time. In the meantime, there was no great interest or enthusiasm for things mechanical.

The more thoughtful body of Gunner officers saw mechanisation as inevitable. They remembered the difficulty there had been in the latter stages of the war in acquiring sufficient horses for the needs of the Army. Indeed, the combined resources of Australia, Canada and India – and in the later years, of America – had barely managed to make good the losses of horses on the Western Front. In addition, after the war ended, horsemanship skills were fast becoming a rarity in a civilian society, which was becoming more and more reliant on mechanical transport. This was likely to become a major problem if the Army ever needed to mobilise large numbers of the civilian population again.

From a technical point of view, the weight of gun that can be towed behind a six- or eight-horse team is limited. As the Gunners experimented with a longer ranged replacement for the 18pdr gun and the 4.5in howitzer in the 1930s, it was inevitable that a more powerful means of haulage would be required to tow the heavier gun. The weight of a mechanically drawn gun, in theory, is only limited by the available horsepower of the tractor. Besides, a 12hp tractor is infinitely more manageable than a 12-horse team in harness (though to be fair, the two cannot strictly be compared in terms of 'drawbar pull'). It had already been discovered by the medium and heavy batteries, that mechanisation was the only sensible solution to the problem of hauling heavier guns over rough ground.

Many Gunners had recognised the need during the First World War for artillery to remain mobile despite the increasingly static nature of its task on the Western Front. Major General Uniacke, Major General, Royal Artillery to General Gough's 5th Army and later Inspector General of Training of the Armies in France, had constantly preached the need for all types of artillery to remain mobile, so that batteries could help exploit any Allied breakthrough, while, at the same time, not run any danger of being overwhelmed in the event of an enemy advance. It was his teaching that undoubtedly saved many batteries during the German offensive in 1918 and helped them to exploit the Allied advances later in the year. Yet, for the field artillery, this mobility relied solely on horse teams.

The Duncan Prize Essay, 1921
That the effects of mechanisation were of concern amongst senior Gunner officers in the immediate postwar years is reflected in the fact that this was the subject of the annual Duncan Prize Essay in 1921. The Royal Artillery, together with the RE, were the two professional and technical arms of the Army from early days. They were the first two corps to provide technical training for their officers at the Royal Military Academy, Woolwich and the Gunners had produced a professional journal, *The Proceedings of the Royal Artillery Institute*, later the *Royal Artillery Journal*, since the mid-19th century. This journal was the organ of the Royal Artillery Institute, itself the 'learned society' of the regiment. It was the forum in which officers of the regiment could express their views on all nature of subjects, though they were mainly of a technical nature. The Duncan Prize Essay was an annual competition designed to stimulate thought and debate on a topical issue of interest to the regiment. It has to be admitted that the competition never attracted a large number of entries compared with the total number of officers serving in the regiment, but the standard of entries was generally high and provides an accurate barometer of current thinking in the regiment. This is reflected in the fact that the Gold Medal was not

automatically awarded each year if the panel of judges considered that the necessary high level of excellence had not been achieved.

What influence the views expressed in the essays had on the policymakers in the regiment is difficult, if not impossible, to judge. Conversely, it may be true that the essays reflected to some degree views and ideas already being expressed in the regiment. Nonetheless, it is interesting to note that many of the ideas expressed in the Duncan essays seemed to find their way into official thinking not long after they were first discussed in the *Journal*. It is not without significance, therefore, that the subject of the Duncan Prize Essay for 1921 was, 'In view of the improvements in mechanical transport that are likely in the near future, discuss the possibilities of its use for all natures of mobile field artillery (including horse artillery) in substitution for horse draught, both on the road and across country.' It attracted a large number of entries and, though no Gold Medal was awarded that year, some seven entries were published in the *Journal* during 1921. They reflect a wide variety of views and opinions on the necessity for and the probable effects of mechanisation in the Royal Artillery.

The winner of the Silver Medal in 1921 was Captain D.R.D. Fisher of the RFA. Having discussed the future role of the Army which included, in his view, a further 'Great War' role in Europe, he emphasised the need for the Army to maintain standardisation of organisation and equipment between the Regular Army at home and in India, and between the Indian and Dominion Armies, and with the Territorial Army. He saw the artillery performing two specific roles: in support of a 'supermobile' division and in support of a 'normal division'. In the former role, the ideal means of moving artillery would be to carry the existing carriages on a tracked vehicle.

The vehicle would be capable of 15 to 20mph and of moving across country, and would be designed to permit the gun to be fired off it in an emergency. Wheeled vehicles were dismissed as being incapable, at that time, of adequate cross-country performance. Towing guns would cause so much damage to the existing carriages as to be out of the question, while the provision of an auxiliary carriage would be too costly or complicated. A permanent 'pedestal' mounting on a tracked vehicle was discussed and rejected on the grounds of excessive height, difficulty of concealment of the vehicle in action, and the lack of flexibility in having one gun dedicated to one means of transport.

The ideal organisation would be one tracked vehicle (or 'vector' as he called it) and one tracked ammunition carrier per gun. The Battery Commander and Observation Post Officer would travel in a Whippet-like tank while the battery staff and signallers would travel in another 'vector'.

Artillery designed for the support of a 'normal' division – i.e., an infantry division – would need to travel at no more than 5 to 10mph, and therefore a vehicle capable of towing the gun was all that was necessary. However, Captain Fisher argued that rather than develop another type of vehicle to meet this requirement, energy and money should be devoted to the production of one type of gun carrier. With regard to horse artillery, he argued that as long as cavalry existed there would be a need for horse artillery support. Furthermore, he believed that the problem of mechanising the horse artillery would not arise for at least ten years – a fairly accurate forecast as it turned out.

With regard to medium artillery, he believed that a tractor was necessary with better performance than the existing Holts and FWDs. Suitable commercial 10-ton tractors existed, which could be used with minimum conversion. He emphasised the need for mechanisation of what he termed 'special weapons' – anti-tank and anti-aircraft guns. Their role would be mainly for the protection of the tank dominated 'land army' on the line of march.

In conclusion, Captain Fisher catalogued the problems of 'scarcity of horse flesh, the increased cost of buying, hiring, feeding and maintaining horses'. A revolutionary and costly change in the method of artillery transport could only be justified on the grounds of military efficiency, though this would obviously have to have regard to economic factors.

Other factors worked against the rapid mechanisation of the Army after the war. The very fact that the Army had used large quantities of vehicles, mainly in the second- and third-line transport role, contributed to a lack of progress when the war came to an end. Vast numbers of surplus vehicles suddenly became available on the civilian market. Postwar auctions of vehicles, some ordered late in 1918 and never used, flooded the market. There was therefore little incentive for civilian manufacturers to develop and produce new vehicles. Some leading manufacturers such as Thornycroft and Leyland actually purchased their vehicles back from the government and refurbished them for resale to private contractors. The early postwar years were therefore a period of virtual stagnation in the motor industry, not helped by the horsepower-rating tax provisions of the Road Traffic Act 1930, which penalised the use of larger commercial engines and inhibited research and development in this field.

Nonetheless, operating within the constraints of a very tight budget, mechanisation made progress within the Army as a whole and in the Royal Artillery in particular. The eight years following the First World War were a period devoted almost exclusively to experimental work on a large number of vehicles but not of any large-scale production. In 1926, the Minister for War was able to report, in the introduction to the catalogue that accompanied the Demonstration to the Dominion Premiers at Camberley in 1926:

The problem is now a dual one –

(a) to build machines which will enable a force of men to be moved across country under the protection of armour, and to be supplied by vehicles which can closely follow the fighting cars.

(b) to base production, so far as this is possible, on a commercial foundation so that civil supply may, in wartime, meet military demands.

This problem has been complicated by the fact that strategic commitments forbid a rapid change in our organisation.

The experiments have consequently been directed along two channels: firstly, to reinforce and strengthen the existing Arms; secondly, gradually to place them on a mechanised footing.

3 FIELD ARTILLERY – EXPERIMENTATION, 1920–30

The decade that followed the First World War was a period devoted almost exclusively to experimental work on a large number of British military vehicles. Despite an unyielding budget and the virtual stagnation in the motor industry in the early post-war years, mechanisation still made progress within the Army generally and in the Royal Artillery in particular.

The experiments with various types of artillery traction developed along many of the lines discussed in the Duncan Prize Essays. In summary, there were a number of ways of moving artillery. The simplest way was to replace the horse team with a tractor and to tow the gun behind. The tractor could be wheeled or tracked or a combination of both. Alternatively, the gun itself could be carried on a wheeled or tracked vehicle, the gun being permanently mounted on the vehicle or the gun and carriage being carried on the vehicle and then dismounted for firing. All these various combinations were tried experimentally during the early postwar period in an attempt to find the best way of moving a gun into action on roads and across country.

During the First World War, vehicle development had been carried out under stress and to meet the immediate requirements of a particular problem. As a result, solutions were very often compromises. There was little time to experiment and many vehicles were adaptations of standard commercial designs. Once the war was over, designers and engineers were able to devote more time and energy to the development of new vehicles. They were able to build upon their experiences of the First World War and take advantage of new technical improvements. There was also the commercial possibility of developing vehicles that would be suitable for use in the many colonial areas being developed at the time.

There were three main sources of experimental vehicles. First, there were those produced by the Department of Tank Design and Experiment at Charlton Park run by Lieutenant Colonel Philip Johnson of the Tank Corps. This department produced many interesting designs, some of which were then manufactured by the Royal Ordnance Factory at Woolwich. The second source of vehicles were those produced commercially by Vickers Ltd and other firms, sometimes in conjunction with Johnson's department. The third source was the various foreign vehicles bought for trial by the British Army. In the main, these vehicles were tried by the Mechanisation Experimental Establishment (MEE) at Farnborough before being handed over to a field unit for extensive user trials under service conditions.

The trials units

Three Field Artillery Brigades and two Light Batteries were involved in this initial period of experimentation. The 9th Field Brigade was originally stationed at Deepcut and formed part of the 2nd Divisional Artillery. It was commanded by Lieutenant Colonel Clement Armitage who was both a very good Commanding Officer and a very able and well-trained staff officer, who later went on to command the 7th Brigade, one of the units that continued the mechanised experiments after the demise of the EAF in 1929. The brigade consisted of 19, 20 and 29 Batteries equipped with the 18pdr QF gun and 76 Battery with the 4.5in howitzer.

The 1st Field Brigade was stationed at Bulford Camp on Salisbury Plain as part of 3rd Divisional Artillery and was commanded by Lieutenant Colonel Naper. In 1923, the brigade consisted of 11, 52 and 80 Batteries with the 18pdr QF gun and 98 Battery with the 4.5in howitzer.

It was not the custom to select particular officers and men for these trial brigades and they had the normal field-brigade establishment, with the addition of an assistant adjutant who was responsible for the Brigade Workshop. Nonetheless, there was a high proportion of soldiers on longer engagements, which contributed to a sense of continuity and experience. Each brigade also had a high proportion of RA Artificers, the technical experts

One of the two turreted Birch guns – the third pattern – at the Vickers works. The turret is in reality more a barbette, with a higher sloping shield at the front.

MOVING THE GUNS

of the regiment before the advent of the Royal Electrical and Mechanical Engineers, responsible for the maintenance of the new and innovative equipment that began to arrive in the brigades after 1923.

In 1922, 9th Brigade received its first vehicles: a Sunbeam car, a Ford van and three Triumph motorcycle combinations, together with a Thornycroft 3-ton lorry, which was 'taken on charge for the purpose of training drivers in the changing of heavy gears'. Citroën-Kégresse half-track vehicles were also issued for the use of the battery staff personnel, signallers, range-takers and command-post assistants. Between April and July 1922, the batteries were issued with 18pdr guns on the newly designed Mark IV carriage and in the following April, the issue of Mark I Dragon gun tractors began.

The 1st Brigade was mechanised one year later, being warned in November 1923 and receiving Mark I Dragons in April and May 1924 from 9th Brigade when that brigade upgraded to Mark II Dragons. In October 1925, the two brigades swapped stations and 9th Brigade moved to Bulford where it remained for many years. There it was co-located with 7th Infantry Brigade, which was involved with the initial mechanisation experiments prior to the formation of the Experimental Mechanised Force (EMF) in 1927. Presumably it was intended that these two artillery brigades would continue to be the trial units for all future experimentation, but in 1927, events in China brought 9th Brigade's involvement in the mechanisation trials to an abrupt halt.

After the First World War, the Nationalist Party of China made it clear that it was intent on the expulsion of all foreign nationals and interests from China and, in particular, from the International Treaty Port of Shanghai. In 1927, the British government sent a strong force, known as the Shanghai Defence Force, to protect British interests and the international community in Shanghai. The 1st Field Brigade was warned in late January 1927 of its involvement in this force and the first two batteries, 11 and 80, were sent out in February to be joined by the remaining batteries in May. The batteries

Colonel Johnson's Tropical Supply Tank viewed from the rear to show the towing gear. The engine was a 45hp Tylor, located beneath the superstructure, while the driver occupies a compartment on the right.

40

The Royal Ordnance Factory's artillery transporter AT2 was similar to the Vickers transporter, although the driver sat on the right side. The gun detachment seats were crude and extremely uncomfortable but AT2 was only regarded as a prototype machine.

went as mechanised field batteries, being specially equipped with Burford and Crossley half-track tractors in place of their Mark II Dragons.

It has been suggested that the decision to send one of the two experimental mechanised brigades to China was a deliberate and perverse attempt to hinder the progress of mechanisation in the Gunners. It seems much more likely that a mechanised field brigade was required at very short notice to accompany a force that was partly mechanised. Also, the problems of trooping a horse-drawn brigade to China, or of acquiring sufficient mounts locally, would have been immeasurably difficult. To meet an emergency situation, it seems to have been entirely logical to send one of the trained mechanised brigades from England. In the event, the international situation improved to such an extent that the Shanghai Defence Force was withdrawn in January 1928. Rather than return to England, 1st Field Brigade moved to India as part of the normal trooping pattern, where it reverted to a horse-drawn brigade. What happened to the various tractors that were sent to China is not recorded and there is no record of Burford or Crossley-Kégresse half-tracks being used in India. It is tempting to think that they were left behind in Shanghai and perhaps served on with one of the locally raised militia forces, and that even now they may lie derelict at the bottom of a Chinese scrapyard.

In order to replace 1st Brigade in England it was necessary to form a third mechanised brigade. The 10th Brigade, consisting of 51, 54 and 46 Batteries each equipped with the 18pdr gun and 30 Battery with the 4.5in howitzer, was moved from Newcastle upon Tyne in January 1927 to Deepcut to replace 1st Field Brigade, and in February 1928 the brigade was officially mechanised. As 9th Field Brigade was being used to support the EMF and the Experimental Armoured Force (EAF), 10th Brigade was used to trial various alternative methods of hauling and transporting guns, which are described in more detail later. Thus, 30 Battery had Burford-Kégresse half-tracks, 51 Battery had Pavesi articulated tractors, 54 Battery had the various types of portées, and 46 Battery had the Morris-Roadless half-tracks.

41

MOVING THE GUNS

Two Light Batteries were also involved in the mechanisation trials during this period. The 9 Light Battery of 2nd Light Brigade Royal Artillery, stationed at Bulford, and armed with the 3.7in pack howitzer formed part of the EMF and EAF in 1927 and 1928. It used Burford-Kégresse 30cwt half-tracks modified to take the 3.7in howitzer portée-fashion throughout the two years of trials, which are described later. After the disbandment of the EAF in 1929, the battery was organised into two experimental batteries. One was equipped with 3.7in howitzers drawn by Carden-Loyd Carriers and used in support of the 2nd Cavalry Brigade, while the other was equipped with carrier-mounted 3in mortars in support of 7th Infantry Brigade. The 15 Light Battery, part of 4th Light Brigade Royal Artillery, was identically organised and was stationed at Deepcut as part of the 2nd Division.

The Mark I Dragon

This vehicle was the first postwar attempt at mechanised haulage in the field artillery. Its origins lay in a series of four experimental tropical tanks produced by Johnson's Design Department at Charlton Park. They were based on the Medium D tank and incorporated some of Johnson's design features such as the wire cable suspension system. The fourth of the experimental tanks, Mechanical Warfare Experimental Establishment (MWEE) No 8, was sent to 9th Field Brigade in 1922 for trials in gun haulage. In August 1921, while Johnson's Design Department was being closed down, the Army negotiated with Vickers Ltd to produce three rival tropical tanks, but the third of these, B6E1, was actually completed as a transporter for an 18pdr gun. Photographs of this vehicle show an 18pdr QF gun mounted on the Mark 4 split trail carriage being carried on top of the vehicle facing forwards. The gun and carriage were manhandled onto the vehicle over ramps built into the tailgate. This vehicle was also trialled by the 9th Field Brigade where it was known as the 'Vickers transporter'. It was, in effect, a tracked portée. Based on the experience gained with the tropical tank variants, the Royal Ordnance Factory then produced two prototype tractors,

A fully equipped Mark I Dragon of 11 Battery, 1st Field Brigade. Notice how the detachments' personal kit is stowed on the back of their seats. The Dragon was boarded from the rear where one could also gain access to the ammunition lockers. The channels stowed on the sides were used to provide a path for the gun and limber across a trench.

known as AT 1 and AT2 ('Artillery Transporter'), one of which, MWEE 9, was subsequently sent to India for trials and the other was trialled by 9th Field Brigade in August 1922.

Production of the Mark I Dragon was at the Royal Ordnance Factory at Woolwich, which produced 18 vehicles for the Army and two for the RAF. The Dragon was fitted with a Leyland 60hp water-cooled engine, which produced a top speed of 12mph towing the 18pdr gun and limber. It had seating for 11 men on the vehicle and there was provision for 14cwt of ammunition.

Following issue in 1923, the batteries began training with the new equipment. On 24 May, the King and Queen Mary watched a demonstration by 76 Battery in Long Valley, Aldershot. The battery diary recorded, 'the first demonstration ever given for HM The King by a mechanicalised battery of the Royal Field Artillery' On the same occasion, 20 Battery, who had provided a Citroën-Kégresse 15cwt half-track staff car for Queen Mary, were given permission to carry her cypher on their vehicles 'to commemorate the first occasion on which she had driven in a Royal Field Artillery mechanicalized vehicle'.

In July 1923, the brigade took their Dragons and guns on a road march from Deepcut to Larkhill – a distance of 58 miles – in approximately ten hours and it was reported that the detachments arrived far less tired than if they had done 20 miles with the horses. In August 1923, the brigade took part in manoeuvres in the area of Petworth in Sussex for a fortnight, 'frequently covering 30 miles in the day and proving the efficiency of mechanicalisation for the Royal Artillery'. Only minor problems were reported, mainly fan bearings breaking up. This was reported as the first exercise in which a mechanised field battery had taken part.

A Mark I Dragon of 76 Battery, 9th Field Brigade with 18pdr QF gun on the road in Sussex during the 1925 summer exercise. The canopy has been dismounted and the driver's front door removed to help keep him cool. The armoured louvres were usually removed from in front of the radiator for the same reason.

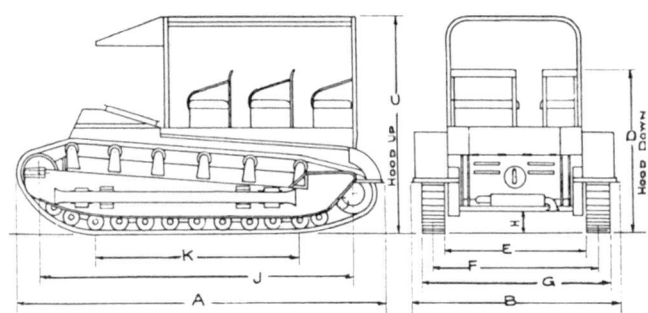

In April and May 1924, all Mark I Dragons on the charge of 9th Field Brigade were withdrawn and replaced with Mark IIs, the Mark Is being handed over to the 1st Field Brigade

Data sheet for Dragon FA Mark I.

43

at Bulford. In the summer of 1925, 1st Brigade used their Mark I Dragons on manoeuvres in the area of Andover, Whitchurch and Salisbury, and it was reported that, 'Due to their age, the Dragons caused considerable problems through minor breakdowns. The Dragons fully justified their existence and successfully completed marches which would have been impossible to a horse-drawn battery.'

In October 1925, 1st Brigade moved from Bulford to Deepcut by road on change of station and 52 Battery (the Bengal Rocket Troop) reported that, 'it must be realised by now that the Dragons are suffering from anno domini ... the most frequent cause of breakdown is through the breakages of tracks. They are now in a state of rapid decline and we anxiously await their final despatch.'

In June and July 1926, the Mark I Dragons were finally handed back to Ordnance with the exception of one per battery for training purposes, to be replaced by Mark II Dragons and Burford-Kégresse 30cwt half-tracks.

The Commanding Officer of 9th Brigade, Lieutenant Colonel Armitage, gave his verdict on the Mark I Dragon in the course of a lecture at the Royal Artillery Institute in January 1924, 'the Dragon, Field Artillery Mark I has been a success as an experimental machine, but cannot be considered suitable or sufficiently reliable for active service. Its chief defects are its weight, width, height, noise and lack of power. The track has done remarkably well; the average distance run by machines of the 9th Brigade RFA is 656 miles. One battery has done 829 per machine and one machine has completed 930 miles. An experimental machine has done 1,200 miles. The life of the track is probably between 1,000 and 1,500 miles and with further improvements a minimum of 1,500 miles should be possible.'

So ended the first three years of experimentation with mechanised transport. Although the Mark I Dragon had many mechanical problems, a lot of useful experience had been gained in handling mechanical transport. In 1928, the Tank Board recorded that all 18 of the Mark I Dragons were by then only being used for training. One was converted into an experimental bridge-layer and was used at the Experimental Bridging Establishment at Christchurch in Dorset.

The Mark II Dragon
The Mark II Dragon was developed by Armstrong Siddeley Ltd as a result of the lessons learnt with the Mark I. The Leyland water-cooled engine of the Mark I, which was under-powered and which had considerable problems caused by over-heating, was replaced by the more powerful air-cooled V8 82bhp engine. The Mark II had a lower profile achieved by seating the detachment in the well of the vehicle with the driver sitting forward alongside the engine compartment. The suspension system consisted of a number of small bogies on vertical coiled springs. The built-up tracks had a driving sprocket at the rear and an adjustable track idler at the front. The Mark II was designed as an 18pdr tractor and ammunition stowage was provided in lockers that were accessible from the outside of the vehicle.

Twenty-eight vehicles were ordered from Armstrong Siddeley in 1922 and the first vehicles were issued to 9thField Brigade in April and May 1924 as replacements for the Mark Is. From the outset, the vehicles were mechanically reliable and popular with the detachments. The 20 Battery reported that it was 'a great improvement on the Mark I. It is reliable while the Mark I is not.' In February 1925, a Mark II of 28 Battery took part in comparative cross-country and road trials at Wool and came second to a Crossley-Kégresse half-track vehicle.

In 1928, the Mechanical Warfare Board was able to report, 'the mechanical design of Dragons has proved so reliable and satisfactory that modifications to tanks have been in some cases based upon Dragon design; as examples might be cited the brakes of the latest Medium Mark IIA Tank and the bogie frames of the suspension, upon which system, certain experimental bogie frames for Medium Tanks Mark II have been made and tried.' An officer who served in 9th Brigade at the time recalls, 'the Dragon was very efficient, a bit overpowered for the job but it was armoured, almost an APC, and would have been useful in war.' In fact the Dragon was not armoured in modern terms, being clad in 1/8th mild steel plate.

The Mark II Dragon remained in service with 9th Field Brigade throughout the period of the EAF trials of 1928 and 1929 before being replaced by Crossley-Kégresse and Burford-Kégresse half-tracks. From 1927, all existing Mark IIs were converted into Medium Dragons Mark II* and used for medium artillery haulage with modified final drives and reduction gears and converted ammunition stowage.

The self-propelled gun
The second main line of experimentation was the production of a self-propelled gun along the lines proposed by several of the Duncan essayists. The idea was to carry a gun fixed permanently to a 'pedestal mounting' on a self-propelled chassis. The limitations of the system have already been mentioned and the main concern was that of tying one gun exclusively to one means of transportation with the danger of losing the use of that gun should the chassis become immobilised for any reason. Against this was the fact that a self-propelled gun would be able to come into action very much quicker than either towed or portéed equipment.

The concept was not entirely new. The 60pdr and 6in howitzer gun-carriers of the First World War, although they were primarily tracked portées, did have the capability of firing the gun from the

A Mark II Dragon on test during the Wool Trials of 1925. Note that although it was still technically a field artillery tractor, a 6in howitzer and limber were employed for this event; clear evidence of its power.

carrier and were thus an early form of self-propelled gun. It was only because scarce resources had to be channelled towards tank production in the later stages of the war that the gun-carrier concept was not pursued. Had it been, it is possible that a true self-propelled gun might have been produced during the First World War.

Armstrong Whitworth produced what was known as a 'Light Artillery Transporter', which was displayed at the demonstration of tanks and cross-country vehicles organised for the Dominion Premiers in November 1926. Little is known of this vehicle, which appears to have been a one-off experimental machine. Photographs show a 13pdr QF gun mounted on a tracked chassis. The 1926 demonstration catalogue described the engine as the 48hp four-cylinder water-cooled AEC type with two standard AEC radiators mounted side by side at the back. It could carry five fully equipped men and 15cwt of ammunition. The vehicle was capable of 13mph on the road and 8mph across country with a range of 90 miles. The modified 13pdr QF gun was mounted at the front with a driver's seat, which could be folded down and swung out of the way to enable the gun to be traversed. How much traverse and elevation was possible is not known. It is interesting to note that while the catalogue describes the vehicle as being 'designed to be inconspicuous, in order that it might be used for close support', and indeed the gun is mounted low in the hull of the vehicle, by far the most conspicuous and vulnerable parts are the radiators and what appear to be the ammunition lockers. It would appear from the photographs that the area behind the breech of the gun was very restricted and must have made loading a difficult task. There is no record of this vehicle ever being trialled by a service unit and it appears never to have gone into series production.

The Birch Gun
The first self-propelled gun to go into limited production was the 'Mounting SP QF 18pdr Mark I', more popularly known as the 'Birch Gun' after the then Master General of the Ordnance, General Sir Noel Birch. The whole of this vehicle was specially designed but incorporated many of the design features of the Dragons and the Vickers Medium Tank. The 12-ton vehicle was fitted with the 8-cylinder Armstrong Siddeley air-cooled engine that developed 82bhp and which was fitted to the contemporary Mark I Light Tanks and the Mark II Dragons. It could achieve 15mph by road and 10mph across country with a range of 80 miles. It carried an 18pdr QF gun and the gun was capable of all-round traverse and of elevation up to 90° for use in an anti-aircraft role.

The first pattern of Birch Gun to appear was a single prototype, distinguishable by the fitting of the hydro-pneumatic recuperator along the top of the barrel and a complex system of sighting gear

3 FIELD ARTILLERY EXPERIMENTATION, 1920-30

above the recuperator. This vehicle first made its appearance in January 1925 when it was attached to 28 Battery of 9th Field Brigade for experimental purposes. The remainder of 28 Battery was at this time equipped with Mark II Dragons. It is recorded that it was sent by rail to Shoeburyness on 5 January 1925 for experiments at the Air Defence Wing RA with the detachment travelling by road. The Mark I Birch Gun remained with the battery during 1925, carrying out satisfactory trials at Larkhill in May and rejoining the battery for Practice Camp in July. In September, it was recorded that the 'Birch Gun had also taken part in the Cavalry manoeuvres under Second Lieutenant R.A.G. Nicholson for the first week and had rejoined us for the Inter-Divisional operations'. At the end of September, at the conclusion of the Army manoeuvres, the Birch Gun was inspected by 'foreign officers, the Secretary of State for War and distinguished Generals'. In November 1925, the Birch Gun was handed over to Field Stores at Aldershot to be sent to 1st Field Brigade to equip 98 Battery with 'guns on self-propelled mountings'. In July 1926, it was recorded that another battery in 9th Field Brigade was to be equipped with Birch Guns in place of 98 Battery. The 1st Field Brigade was, as we have seen, posted to China in early 1927 as part of the Shanghai Defence Force. It seems that there was a change of policy when the likelihood of foreign service became evident and that it was decided to equip a battery of 9th Field Brigade instead because, in July 1926, this gun is reported as being received by 20 Battery.

The Mark II Birch Guns with which 20th Battery was equipped were improvements on the Mark I. Four of these vehicles were produced and they mounted a modified form of 18pdr QF gun with the recuperator below the barrel and a small shield for crew protection. Three SP guns were received by the battery on 31 July 1926 direct from the manufacturers, Vickers Ltd.

The unique Light Artillery Transporter C1E1. The 13pdr sits in a well at the front and the driver would be seated alongside it. Directly behind are the ammunition lockers, then the exposed AEC engine and, at the very back the two large AEC radiators, which form the highest part of the whole vehicle. As a guide the height is given as 5ft 5in; the length 16ft 3in, including the gun.

47

MOVING THE GUNS

One of the very few shots showing the prototype Birch Gun actually doing something. This rear view shows the complex sighting arrangements and the gun close to full elevation.

On 3 September, the fourth gun arrived from the Experimental Establishment at Farnborough and all four were fired at Larkhill ranges to prove the mountings. The recoil was short in all cases and two were sent back to Vickers for modification.

In September 1926, one section under Lieutenant Fernyhough went to the Air Defence School at Watchet to practice the anti-aircraft role of the gun using the Vickers predictor, a device which automatically predicted the future position of the target and passed the information electrically to dials on the gun mounting. The anti-aircraft role of the Birch Gun was one that was experimented with more fully later on and will be described in due course. On 13 November 1926, all five guns took part in the demonstration for the Dominion Premiers at Camberley, but hints of future mechanical problems were already becoming apparent with two guns having to be left behind with a seized steering clutch and a broken drive clutch.

Throughout August and September 1927, 20 Battery took part with the remainder of 9th Brigade in the manoeuvres of the EMF, then in 1928 with the EAF, until the Force was dispersed in February 1929. The objects and lessons of the EAF are dealt with in a separate section, so all that is necessary here is to chronicle the fortunes of the Birch Guns during this critical period of experimentation

During the 1927 exercise season, the battery had the primary role of the close support of tanks. This was a development of the traditional horse-artillery function of the close support of the cavalry, involving the rapid deployment of the battery when the supported cavalry required additional firepower onto an objective or to a vulnerable flank. There was often little time or opportunity for indirect fire controlled by forward observers and much firing was direct and over open sights.

In 1928, the manoeuvres of the EAF

3 FIELD ARTILLERY EXPERIMENTATION, 1920-30

gave the Birch Guns a similar role, quoted in the battery diary as, 'the usual role of close support of tanks by direct fire'. But after two seasons of exercises, an element of doubt is detected in the reports of the exercises. The value of the close support of tanks was being questioned. The battery diary records, 'the use of AFV's to immobilise the enemy formation and then to shell it at leisure with artillery, has received favourable notice. The close support of tanks remains in a considerable fog. To support tanks with what are, or should be, themselves tanks seems as much as if we had supported infantry in the last war with rifles.'

There also appeared to be mechanical problems. It is not clear why a vehicle, which was basically the same as he well-proven Mark II Dragon, was acquiring a reputation for unreliability. In 1928, it was recorded that two of the SP guns had to go to Woolwich for overhaul and were unlikely to be seen again for six months.

Finally, on 1 February 1929, the EAF was disbanded for reasons that will be discussed later. The problem now was how to employ the battery of Birch Guns. The official training manual, which summarised the lessons of the past three years of experiments, 'Mechanised and Armoured Formations', spoke of 'a close-support tank whose function was to accompany medium and light tanks in battle and provide heavier covering fire than that provided by machine-guns. A Royal Artillery weapon to be armed with a gun or howitzer and firing smoke and HE and a discharger tube for smoke bombs. Armour and mobility as for the medium tank with 3.7-inch howitzer.' This was a role that the mechanised Light Batteries experimented with over the next few years and, in the meantime, the planners looked for another role for the Birch Guns, one they were designed for, but which until now had not been taken too seriously.

The Birch Gun had been designed to have an anti-aircraft role. It was capable of elevating to 90° above the horizontal and was fitted with dials capable of receiving data from the Vickers predictor. In 1929, the official raining manual had pointed out the need for 'an anti-aircraft carrier' to give protection to armoured brigades and capable of engaging aircraft up to 12,000ft,

Two of the production Birch guns in action during an exercise on Salisbury Plain. Despite the shields fitted to the mounting, the gunners are very exposed. Notice that these units are also equipped with towing hooks.

'suitable existing equipment are the multiple Lewis guns and the 18pdr gun on SP mounting'.

It says much for the training and adaptability of the Gunners of 20 Battery that, in the space of one training session, they could convert from the unique pioneering role of manning self-propelled guns to become an anti-aircraft battery. Yet this was the task set by the War Office in March 1929 when the battery was ordered to train as an anti-aircraft battery using the self-propelled guns. Individual sections had undergone anti-aircraft training at Watchet in 1926 when a number of deficiencies were found with the equipment and several modifications were recommended but never implemented. The War Office warned the battery that it must be ready to attend practice camp in August in the new role, but that it did not intend to make any of the recommended improvements before then.

An officer who served in the battery during this period recalls that, when the Birch Guns were first issued, there were no technical manuals or drill books and everything had to be worked out from first principles. So, it was with the Vickers predictors and the height finders that formed vital components of the anti-aircraft system. The training of the specialists to man these vital items of equipment was crucial and courses were arranged at the School of Anti-Aircraft Defence at Biggin Hill for a limited number of detachments and officers.

Anti-aircraft gunnery depended on two methods of engagement: case one relied on the visual acquisition and engagement of the target aircraft by the gun layers; case two relied on the use of instruments to engage the target, whose future position was predicted automatically by the Vickers predictor and the information passed electrically to dials on the gun mounting.

The former case required considerable skill on the part of the gun-layers in estimating how much to 'lay off' for the future position of the target. In the latter case, the skill was required on the part of the predictor operators and the height finders, whereas the layers had the relatively simple task of following the pointers on the dials using the traversing and elevating handwheels on the gun mounting.

Although there is little doubt that the Gunners of 20 Battery acquitted themselves well both at Watchet and at practice camp, it is reasonable to question whether it would not have been more sensible to have used one of the more experienced batteries from an Anti-Aircraft Brigade to perform this role. A particularly strange decision was the issue of the standard 3in 20cwt anti-aircraft gun to the battery in June for practice purposes. In the space of a few months, an experienced mechanised battery with revolutionary equipment was transformed into another role that could probably have been done more effectively by the Gunners of an Anti-Aircraft Brigade. Even more incredibly, the battery practised anti aircraft gunnery using the split-trail Mark IV 18pdr QF field gun. A more unsuitable role for this gun is hard to imagine and it is not surprising that the idea was quickly abandoned.

Before leaving the Birch Gun, it must be recorded that a turreted version of the gun was produced. Two vehicles were made with enclosed turret mountings for the gun, presumably to counter criticisms that the earlier design of gun left the crews exposed and vulnerable. The turret, however, restricted the elevation of the gun and further reduced its maximum range. There is no record that the turreted guns were ever issued to a service unit although the remaining Birch Guns served on in 20 Battery for two years before being replaced with Light Dragons in June and July 1931.

Half-track tractors

The third type of cross-country vehicle that the army experimented with was the half-track vehicle. The half-track evolved as a means of overcoming the problem of wheel sinkage in boggy ground. The rear axle weight was transferred onto a larger ground contact area of track than that provided by a conventional rear wheel. Ground pressure was therefore reduced and the problem of sinkage considerably lessened. In addition, the enlarged ground contact area gave better adhesion and hence better traction. All this could be achieved in a half-track vehicle without the complication and expense of the differential steering mechanisms necessary in a fully tracked vehicle. Half-tracks used in the Army relied on conventional front-wheel steering. Most systems used were standard commercial chassis with the rear wheels replaced by track bogies. Half-tracks were inevitably a compromise combining the complications and expense of tracked vehicles while not really achieving either the good cross-country performance of a tracked vehicle or the good road performance of a wheeled vehicle. Until the advent of reliable low-pressure large-section pneumatic tyres, half-tracks provided a cheaper method of gun haulage than full-tracked tractors such as the Dragon.

There were two types of half-track bogie used by the Army during this period. The first was developed by Adolphe Kégresse while working as the Chief Engineer to the Imperial Russian Family. He used a system whereby a flexible track made of rubber vulcanised onto canvas was friction-driven by a rear driving wheel over a front idler wheel via a pair of small double-bogie suspension wheels. Drive was taken directly from the conventional rear axle of the vehicle. Kégresse converted a number of limousines belonging to the Czar for use over snow. After the Revolution, he returned to France and, together with an industrialist called Hinstin and the car manufacturer André Citroën, worked on a commercial version of his track-bogie system. The first Citroën-Kégresse was produced in 1921 and was tested in the Sahara and the Alps. In 1922 and 1923, five Citroën-Kégresse half-tracks achieved the first motor vehicle crossing of the Sahara and attracted considerable attention among the military authorities in Europe and the United States.

The other system was that designed by Roadless Traction Ltd of Hounslow, the firm that the tank designer, Colonel Philip Johnson, formed on leaving the Army. Their system used a toothed rear sprocket driving a track made up of jointed segments. The drive was positive, unlike the Kégresse system, and was therefore less susceptible to slippage. The firm produced 'Orolo' bogie units, which could replace a standard rear wheel with the minimum of conversion work. The system was fitted to various Morris tractors and some FWD lorries used for medium artillery haulage.

Citroën-Kégresse half-tracks

In 1923, the Army purchased a small number of Citroën 15cwt vehicles fitted with Kégresse half-track bogies for evaluation purposes. These were civilian Citroën 10CV Model B2 touring cars fitted with the Kégresse Hinstin half-track bogie. No 76 Battery of 9th Field Brigade received the first in January 1923 and a further three were received in May 1923 in time for the visit of the King and Queen to Aldershot on 24 May when a Citroën-Kégresse 15cwt of 20 Battery was used to transport Queen Mary during the inspection.

The Citroën-Kégresse 15cwts were used mainly as battery staff vehicles and, although they were designed to take three passengers, they were found to be too small and cramped for the amount of equipment that needed to be carried by the battery staff personnel. With a

MOVING THE GUNS

recorded road speed of 18mph they were considered to be somewhat underpowered and too slow to be able to move rapidly in advance of the main body of the battery.

The rubber track gave problems with slippage when it was either wet or worn and, in 1927, Kégresse evolved an improved design of track known as the P16. This employed a positive drive with steel projections rivetted to the circumference of the driving sprocket, which was meshed with blocks of rubber secured to the inside of the rubber track. A demonstration of this track was given at Farnborough in the summer of 1927, when the advantages were listed as: good ability to cross rough country, no joints or pins, lighter than a metal track, higher speeds than a metal track, silence, driving pads easily replaced and less damage caused to roads.

A photograph exists of a 15cwt Citroën-Kégresse fitted with a specially designed battery staff body with crew seating, cable winding gear and a collapsible hood. This is thought to be one of two vehicles issued to 28 Battery of 9th Field Brigade in June 1925 with 'special bodies to take four men besides the driver'. This improved version was designed to overcome the limitations of the original model, the fact that it could only carry three men and a limited amount of equipment. The Kégresse bogie of this vehicle is modified with the driving and idler sprockets raised off the ground, leaving the four small suspension wheels to carry the weight of the vehicle. The design of the bogie is reminiscent of the later American Cunningham bogies which were developed from the Kégresse system.

After 1926, the 15cwt Citroën-Kégresse was gradually replaced by the Crossley-Kégresse 15cwt. The Citroëns continued to be used, however, as staff vehicles in both 9th Brigade and 1st Brigade. Some Citroën-Kégresse battery staff cars accompanied 80 Battery to China when 1st Brigade was deployed there in February 1927, as part of the Shanghai Defence Force.

Queen Mary, looking slightly uneasy, riding in a Citroën-Kégresse staff car of 20 Battery during the Royal inspection at Aldershot, 24 May 1923.

3 FIELD ARTILLERY EXPERIMENTATION, 1920–30

Crossley-Kégresse half-tracks

When it became apparent that the Citroën was not really suitable for the task allotted to it, the Army turned to the Crossley Motor Company of Gorton, Manchester to produce a range of half-tracked vehicles. These were based on their existing 15cwt and 30cwt chassis with Kégresse tracked bogies fitted in place of the rear wheels.

Two 15cwt half-track staff cars were delivered by Crossleys to MWEE in 1926 for trials as battery staff vehicles. They had the Crossley four-cylinder 27bhp engine, which was considerably more powerful than its Citroën predecessor. The vehicle had a touring-type body specially designed to carry the battery staff and had lockers fitted above the mudguards to carry equipment. It is believed that these two vehicles were eventually issued to 20 Battery of 9th Field Brigade in July 1927 as battery staff cars. Subsequently, a quantity of these vehicles were issued to both Field and Medium Brigades. Two Crossley-Kégresse staff cars accompanied 52 Battery of 1st Field Brigade to China as part of the Shanghai Defence Force.

The 30cwt version was ordered from Crossleys in 1925 and the final production run came to over 40 vehicles, of which a small quantity was converted into field-artillery tractors capable of towing the 18pdr gun or the 4.5in howitzer. The artillery tractor body was fitted with crew seating for seven men plus a driver and had ammunition and equipment stowage. The vehicle had a chassis-mounted winch capable of being used from the front or the rear of the vehicle. The Crossley-Kégresse 30cwt artillery tractors were first sent to Woolwich Arsenal where it is likely that the special artillery bodies were fitted before the five vehicles were issued to 19 Battery of 9th Field Brigade on 10 June 1926 in place of Mark II Dragons. In July 1926, the battery reported

A Citroën-Kégresse battery staff vehicle issued to 28 Battery, 9th Field Brigade in June 1925. Part of the cable winding apparatus can be seen in the back but the most noteworthy feature is the modified form of suspension.

Two Crossley-Kégresse 15cwt halftrack staff cars form part of a convoy passing through Upavon in Wiltshire. The leading car mounts a Lewis gun for anti-aircraft defence while the second one has its hood up.

The battery of headlamps and large fluted radiator shell gave the big Crossley-Kégresse 30cwt Field Artillery Tractor an imposing appearance. This one carries the markings of 19 Battery, 9th Field Brigade; the War Department number H181 and Middlesex registration MK8210.

53

MOVING THE GUNS

The one and only Crossley-Kégresse portée halftrack at the Military College of Science, Woolwich. MK8205 was originally built with an open truck-type body.

The 3-ton Crossley-Kégresse only appeared as a prototype, with a simple box body and not even the comfort of a canopy for the driver. It was the only forward control halftrack in this series and it has the later P16 positive drive suspension system.

transmission breakdowns with the Crossleys at annual practice camp but thereafter the vehicles appeared to give little trouble. The Crossley-Kégresse tractors were used throughout the EMF and EAF exercises of 1927 and 1928.

At the mechanised vehicles demonstration given for the Dominion Premiers at Camberley in 1926, a 30cwt Crossley-Kégresse was shown with a body adapted for the portée of a 3.7in howitzer, a further system of gun haulage that was being experimented with at the time and which will be described in a later section. This vehicle had a sloping flat bed at the rear on which to carry the gun and such a vehicle is known to have been in use at the Military College of Science at Woolwich in 1927.

Finally, in 1928, the War Office ordered one Crossley 3-ton half-track vehicle fitted with the new Kégresse P16 type positive-drive track. This vehicle was given the number B3E1 and was supplied by the manufacturers with a basic wooden body. It remained on trial at MWEE being evaluated against a rival vehicle supplied by Burfords. It was originally supplied with a 30bhp four-cylinder engine giving a road speed of 28mph. A more powerful engine was later fitted but nonetheless its performance did not match that of the Burford. After completing more than 300 miles of trials, it was decided not to adopt it for military use. This vehicle was fitted with two experimental types of track: one with diamond-shaped and the

An early Burford-Kégresse 30cwt taking part in the 1925 Wool Trials. As with their lorries, Burfords always adopted a semi-forward control half cab layout for the driver.

other with rectangular-shaped patterns to the track. The diamond-shaped pattern, after modification to allow mud to be thrown off, was adopted as the standard track.

One of the claimed advantages of the half-track over the pneumatic tyre was that it was less susceptible to damage by small-arms fire. Exhaustive tests were carried out by the Directorate of Armaments attacking Kégresse tracks with a variety of small arms, and armour-piercing ammunition and grenades to determine how long the track would continue to function thereafter. Despite extensive grenade damage, the track being tested appeared to continue to function quite satisfactorily.

Burford-Kégresse half-tracks
The other firm to produce half-track vehicles for the Army using the Kégresse rear bogie was H.G. Burford and Company Ltd. They produced two types of vehicle, in the 30cwt and the 3-ton classes. The 30cwt type was also used by various other mechanised units apart from the Royal Artillery.

Twelve 30cwt chassis were ordered in August 1925, eleven of which were delivered to MWEE and numbered H157 to H167, while the twelfth was sent to Vickers Ltd to have an armoured body fitted to convert it into a machine-gun carrier. Five out of the eleven vehicles were sent to the Royal Ordnance Factory at Woolwich to be fitted with a special gun tractor body with crew seating, ammunition and equipment stowage. These five-gun tractors were issued to 80 (Howitzer) Battery of 1st Field Brigade in May 1926 and eventually went to China with the battery in February 1927. During manoeuvres in August and September 1926, 80 Battery reported that 'the Burford-Kégresses behaved splendidly on all occasions and gave practically no trouble at all'. Further Burfords of the same type were ordered and were issued to 52 Battery in April 1927 in place of their Mark II Dragons before the battery sailed to China to join the remainder of the brigade with the Shanghai Defence Force later in the year.

The Burford-Kégresse was apparently considered to be an adequate gun tractor by its users without it being so popular as the Dragons. When 1st Field Brigade left England to sail for China, a popular weekly called *Truth* reported, 'this fine artillery unit left this country with its guns towed by Bulford Negresses'!

When 10th Field Brigade was mechanised in 1928 in place of 1st Field Brigade, it received a number of 30cwt

MOVING THE GUNS

A Burford-Kégresse 3-ton Field Artillery Tractor of 30 Battery, 10th Field Brigade. It is fully stowed, with the canopies erected and the gun detachment in their places. Notice the raised, diamond pattern treads on the tracks.

Burford-Kégresses, 30 Battery receiving two during April 1928 and a further two a month later. The 30cwt chassis was also supplied with a modified body for the portée role to 9 Light Battery of 2nd Light Brigade in September 1927. This role is described in more detail later on and it is sufficient to mention here that five of these vehicles, with the sloping rear platform to carry the 3.7in howitzer, were drawn from the ROF Woolwich on 19 September 1927 and issued to 9 Battery during 1928. When the EMF and EAF experiments came to an end in 1929, two were converted into lorries and the remaining three became surplus to establishment and were finally disposed of in March 1929.

The half-track was originally developed as a cheaper alternative to the Dragon. The commentary for the demonstration to the Dominion Premiers in 1926 described the Burford-Kégresse as, 'a cheaper, less ambitious form of transport for our field guns'. It was claimed that savings of £5,000 a year could be made by adopting such a vehicle. One disadvantage, however, was the fact that the Burford could only carry 56 rounds of ammunition against the 128 rounds carried by the Dragon and that extra ammunition-carrying vehicles were required.

In 1928, the War Office issued a specification for a half-track vehicle in the 3-ton class. The Burford contender was known as B3E2 with a WD number of D988 and a vehicle registration number of ML8721. This vehicle had the more powerful Burford MA1 four-cylinder 54hp engine with a four-speed gearbox and a Kégresse twin-ratio final drive. The Kégresse rear bogie was of the new P16 pattern with the positive drive. The prototype was supplied by the manufacturers complete with a field artillery body, which included seating for a detachment of six and stowage for 72 rounds of ammunition. It was designed to tow the 18pdr QF gun and limber, though it seems to have been used mainly with the heavier 4.5in howitzer. The prototype was delivered to MWEE in March 1929 where it remained as a trials vehicle before being passed on to 10th Field Brigade in October 1931.

In July 1928, an order was placed for five production models, similar to the prototype but including some modifications. They were issued to 30 (Howitzer) Battery of 10th Field Brigade on 17 July 1929, and were used by the battery throughout the Divisional and Army exercises in 1929. In 1930, the battery took part in exercises on Salisbury Plain with the 1st and 2nd Cavalry Brigades and was attached to one of the brigades in place of a Royal Horse Artillery (RHA) battery. In July 1931, the Burfords appeared for the first time in a mechanised 'mock battle' at the Aldershot tattoo. Later in the year, the Burfords exercised with the 6th Infantry Brigade and it was reported that, 'no serious mechanical trouble was experienced with the Burford tractors during this period, but at times the number of tractors available was limited chiefly owing to trouble with the differentials. This was rectified by strengthening certain bolts.' The five tractors were handed over to 51 Battery of the same brigade in March 1933 to be replaced by the Light Dragon Mark II. Finally, in March 1934, the five tractors were handed on to the newly mechanised 20th Field Brigade at Catterick.

In November 1929, ten new Burford 3-ton vehicles were ordered, which embodied all the improvements made to that date to the prototype vehicle. They were fitted with the diamond-shaped track pads that gave greater traction. Five were issued to 76 (Howitzer) Battery of 9th Field Brigade in May 1930 replacing Mark II Dragons, which then went off to be converted for medium artillery haulage. In September 1930, the battery took part in a similar exercise as 30 (Howitzer) Battery, providing close support for 2nd Cavalry Brigade in place of a horse artillery battery. In March 1932, the five Burfords were handed on to 20th Field Brigade at Catterick, then in the process of mechanising. The Burfords were replaced by Light Dragons Mark II. The other five Burfords were issued to 19 Battery of 9th Field Brigade to replace Crossley-Kégresse 30cwt tractors. Where these tractors eventually went to is not known.

Morris-Roadless half-tracks

One of the half-tracked tractors to appear at the demonstration for the Dominion Premiers in 1926 was a curious little vehicle produced by Morris Commercial Motors Ltd. It appeared to be based on the Morris Martel tankette but with a reversed layout with a standard Roadless tracked bogie at the rear and conventional front wheels and steering. The engine was the standard Morris 15.9hp four-cylinder engine giving a top speed of 18mph and a cross-country speed of 10mph. At the Camberley demonstration, it was described as being suitable for use by Territorial Brigades. It seems that it was a commercial venture by Morris Commercial and was not built specifically with the Army in mind. At this time, various experiments were being carried out by Territorial Brigades

This Morris-Roadless – B14E1 to the Army – was a prototype for the Mark II series. At this time Philip Johnson had developed a form of rubber jointed track and, because the pitch changed when it stretched, the teeth on the large drive sprocket were adjustable.

MOVING THE GUNS

The original Morris-Roadless tractor had solid tyres on the front wheels and simple plate tracks. Designed by Colonel Johnson the Roadless system was a strong rival to Kégresse and, in the early stages at least, a good deal less complicated.

The second Morris-Roadless tractor had bench seats for the gun detachment, pneumatic tyres and a rack of ballast weights at the front to keep the nose down when towing. The Mark I Field Artillery Tractors (CT5 Type) were almost identical.

using commercial agricultural tractors, mainly Fordsons, and this vehicle may have been an attempt by Morris Commercial to enter the market. The prototype vehicle was sent to MWEE Farnborough in February for trials and was eventually passed on to the RTC Centre at Bovington in December 1932.

The next development was the production of the No 2 Tractor, which was delivered to MWEE in February 1927 and given the trials number 70. This vehicle was similar to the first except that the front axle was set further back and a rack was provided to carry ballast weights to counteract the tendency to rear up when pulling a towed load. The vehicle was fitted with a specially designed body with seating for nine men arranged in three rows of three seats. It was apparently designed to tow the 4.5in howitzer and was being considered as a possible tractor for the Territorial Army Artillery units. This vehicle took part in the War Office trials at Wool in 1927. It is known that six, numbered D376 to D381, were ordered and delivered in the latter half of 1927.

The version that appeared in 1929 was fitted with a special field-artillery body with stowage lockers immediately behind the driver's cab, and seating for four crew in the rear of the vehicle covered with a canvas hood. The driver's position was of the semi-forward control type and the front axle was placed well back under the engine. The 46 Battery of 10th Field Brigade reported receiving five Morris-Roadless tractors Type CT5 on 21 June 1929, 'to test their suitability as Artillery Tractors'. One section took part in the War Office Mechanisation trials at Wool in February 1930. It seems that track wear was a considerable problem with these vehicles for there are reports in July 1932 of tractors being left in camp to save expense and damage to tracks, and of guns being towed on exercise by six-wheelers. Similarly, during the 1934 training season, it was reported that the tractors were converted into four-wheeled tractors in order to reduce wear on the tracks.

The five vehicles were finally taken off charge at the end of March 1934 and were sent by rail to 1st Heavy Brigade in the Royal Citadel at Plymouth. What a Heavy Brigade wanted with field artillery tractors is not at all clear, although they may have been used by the 18pdr saluting battery stationed there. A photograph does exist of a Morris-Roadless tractor of the earlier pattern outside one of the buildings in

3 FIELD ARTILLERY EXPERIMENTATION, 1920-30

the Citadel towing an 18pdr QF gun. The vehicle carries the unit markings of 3 Heavy Battery.

Other versions of the Morris-Roadless tractor were produced. There was a semi-forward control version of the No 2 Tractor, which may have been trialled for use by the Royal Marine Artillery. The Royal Marines also trialled an all-wheel version, which was known as a 'Light Tractor'.

The Field Artillery Tractor Mark II had the ability to change its track bogie for wheels when required, but this obviously called for additional transport to carry the spare wheels or bogies. A version of the Mark II was supplied for use by artillery units in India with a slightly different body fitted with what appears to be additional crew seating at the expense of equipment stowage.

The development of the Morris-Roadless tractor is a confusing story and one for which all the facts are not yet known. What is recorded, however, is a comment from a Gunner who served in 46 Battery who claimed that the tractors were so under-powered that they were only just able to get up the square at Deepcut in low gear!

Data sheet for the Morris-Roadless FAT Mk II.

The portée experiments

Some of the more interesting and unusual experiments were those carried out by 54 Battery of 10th Field Brigade into various ways of transporting the gun and carriage on a vehicle or trailer. It seems from the commentary that accompanied the Dominion Premiers Demonstration in 1926, where an 18pdr

A Morris-Roadless Field Artillery Tractor Mark II of 46 Battery, 10th Field Brigade, posed for its official photograph with an 18pdr and limber in tow.

MOVING THE GUNS

and limber appeared carried on a First World War-vintage Peerless lorry, that the method was trialled largely as a means of transporting the guns of the Territorial Army Artillery Brigades. The method had been used successfully by the French Army in the First World War. The principle was that the gun and carriage could be carried more rapidly on a conventional lorry to a point where it was needed, where the gun was dismounted and brought into action. This method overcame the problem of damage being done to the gun carriage and equipment when it was being towed behind a mechanical vehicle at speeds greater than would be normal behind a horse team. Before the advent of sprung carriages and pneumatic tyres, it was found that considerable damage ensued when guns were towed at speeds greater than 5mph for any length of time. Later methods of portée also allowed the gun to be fired in an emergency from the back of the portée vehicle without first being dismounted, although this presumably was at the expense of accurate laying.

There were two possible ways of employing ported artillery. The one already mentioned was with the artillery units of the Territorial Army, where the problem of acquiring and managing teams of horses was becoming more acute as time went by. The other way was to use a portéed battery in a role which required rapid deployment to a flank or to another threatened area of the battlefield. There remained the problem of manoeuvring the gun into a firing position once it had been dismounted from the carrying vehicle. In general, the four- and six-wheeled vehicles of the time did not have the cross-country performance to carry the gun right onto the firing position.

The Army experimented with various small agricultural tractors capable of moving the gun onto the gun position, before settling on the Cletrac full-track tractor produced by the Cleveland Tractor Company. This tractor was small enough to be carried either on to a trailer or on the vehicle itself. In the early experiments with the Peerless 3-ton 4 x 2 lorry converted to carry an 18pdr gun and limber on the rear, a hole had to be cut in the back of the cab of the lorry to accommodate the muzzle of the gun. The limber was then loaded after the gun and stowed straddled across the trail pole. A similar

The Burford Cletrac tractor tested by MWEE is shown at Aldershot on a two-wheeled transporter trailer.

3 FIELD ARTILLERY EXPERIMENTATION, 1920-30

One of the two big Thornycroft XB transporters of 54 Battery, 10th Field Brigade, with a Cletrac and 18pdr aboard. The gun detachment prepares to hang on like grim death in acute discomfort. Note the loading ramps stowed beneath the body.

vehicle carried the Cletrac and so a complete sub-section of gun, limber and tractor could be carried in two portée vehicles, although there did not appear to be much room left to carry the detachment as well. This was the combination shown at the Dominion Premiers Demonstration in 1926. There is no evidence of a winch or other mechanical aid to haul the gun onto the vehicle and it seems likely that it had to be manhandled on and off. The Peerless combination was entirely experimental and was never trialled by a service unit.

In early 1928, the Army decided to extend the experiment with the use of commercial load-carrying vehicles. Early in the year, two standard Thornycroft XB heavy six-wheeled chassis with the long wheelbase of 15ft 9in were purchased. Both were fitted with power-driven capstan winches to assist in loading the vehicles. Each carried a Cletrac tractor and gun and towed an ammunition limber behind. As each vehicle could also carry the entire detachment, it was possible to transport a complete section of two guns, limbers and Cletracs on two Thornycrofts.

Although the capstan winch was provided, it seems that the most common way of loading the vehicle was to drive the Cletrac up the ramps of the vehicle under its own power then, when it was clear of the ramps, they would be adjusted to the width of the gun, which would then be drawn up onto the lorry by the Cletrac as it moved forward into its parked position. The gun and tractor were then secured in position and the ramps stowed along the side of the vehicle. The ammunition limber was hooked into place in the rear and the detachment occupied seats along the side. The combination was apparently capable of achieving 30mph along the road, though presumably not when towing the limber. There was additional ammunition stowage on the vehicle itself. The crew seating looked most precarious and the whole outfit must have had a 'Keystone cops' look about it when travelling the roads. One of the Thornycrofts had a half-cab fitted to it purely for the benefit of the driver, which only served to add to the curious appearance of the outfit.

Experiments were also made using a low-frame chassis vehicle designed for passenger carrying, with a view to side-loading the vehicle while reducing its overall height. However, owing to the great width of road needed to load from,

61

MOVING THE GUNS

One of the pair of Guy 6 x 4 portées of 54 Battery in unladen state. The special tracks, stowed on a platform beneath the chassis, could be wrapped around the tyres of the rear bogie to improve traction on soft ground.

The two Guy 4 x 2 portées which formed a sub-section of 54 Battery in 1929. The gun lorry carries the 18pdr, muzzle first, and tows a small, pneumatic-tyred limber. The Cletrac lorry also carries the gun detachment. Notice the hand-operated winch on each vehicle.

3 FIELD ARTILLERY EXPERIMENTATION, 1920-30

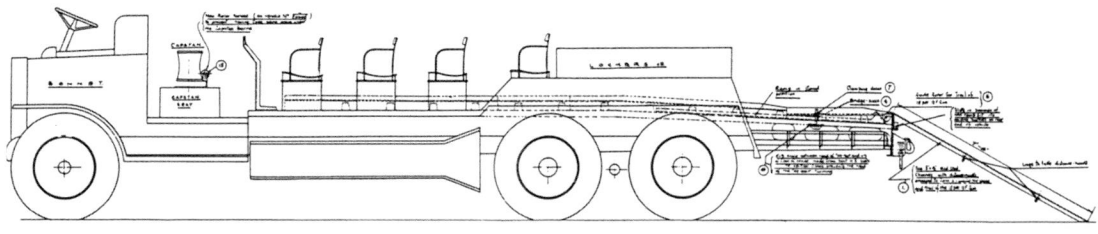

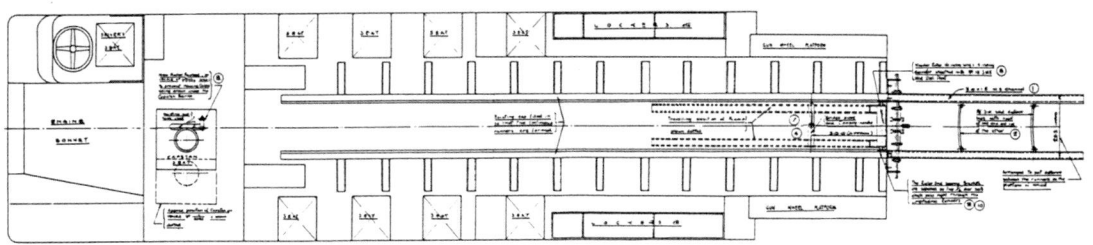

The RAOC outline diagram for a Thornycroft XB portée.

the scheme was abandoned. Later, in June 1928, it was decided to experiment using commercial Guy vehicles. In this case, two were used for each gun sub-section: one lorry carrying the gun and limber with half the detachment, the other carrying the Cletrac tractor and the remainder of the detachment. Each lorry could tow an additional ammunition limber. Two six-wheel 3-ton lorries were used for one sub-section and two four-wheel 3-ton lorries for the other sub-section. Loading trials were carried out at MWEE in 1929 and the vehicles were issued to 54 Battery on 4 July 1929 in time for the 1929 collective training season, which began in September of that year.

In 1930, the Mechanical Warfare Board reported, 'of the three types of vehicle employed, namely, the Thornycroft XB six-wheeled long chassis, the Guy six-wheeler and the Guy four-wheeler, the Thornycroft is considered to be the most suitable owing to the fact that with this outfit, only one vehicle per gun is required whereas with the others, two vehicles per gun are required.'

Exercises and demonstrations continued through 1930 and 1931 and, in 1931, the Board reported, 'although no decision has yet been made to extend the use of this method of transportation, sufficient experience has been gained up to the present to serve as a valuable guide in any contemplated future development where questions of rapid movement of gun sections from one area to another call for special consideration.' In fact, shortly after this, two developments rendered this method of transportation unnecessary, although it is interesting to note that when a similar requirement to move guns rapidly about the battlefield occurred with the anti-tank guns in the Western Desert in the 1940s, the portée idea had a brief resurrection.

The first development was the decision made in 1930 to mechanise field batteries of the Territorial Artillery using standard Morris Commercial 6 x 4 D Type 30cwt trucks as gun tractors, a cheaper solution made at the expense of good cross-country performance. This rendered the portée idea redundant as far as the Territorial Army was concerned. Secondly, after 1930, the advent of reliable low-pressure cross-

A Morris Commercial D Type 30cwt lorry towing an 18pdr on a special two-wheeled transporter trailer.

country tyres and the tandem rear bogie gave six-wheeled vehicles a cross-country performance almost as good as the existing half-tracks at far less expense. Thus, the portée method became a victim of technological advance and vehicles in 54 Battery were handed back to Ordnance in March 1932 to be replaced by the newly developed Light Dragon Mark II.

At the same time as the portée experiments were proceeding, trials were conducted carrying the gun on a special trailer behind a standard medium six-wheeled lorry. Two methods of haulage were investigated. In July 1928, an 18pdr gun was adapted so that it could be loaded on to a small-wheeled undercarriage produced by Citroën. The carriage could be fitted to the gun in about 3½ minutes but it needed the permanent removal of the brake mechanism from the gun carriage, which was not acceptable. The carriage apparently towed well behind the lorry but it was not possible to manhandle the gun with the undercarriage fitted.

By 1930, 1,000 miles of endurance tests had been completed and certain defects had become apparent. An engineer from Citroën modified the design and four carriages of the improved pattern were ordered in 1930 and delivered to 48 Battery for trials in 1931. The battery reported a problem with the carriages swaying some 10in to the left and right behind the towing vehicle. They also suggested that it would not be practical to use the carriages if there was any threat from hostile AFVs because of the time it took to get the guns off the carriages and into action. The second method of haulage was the use of a specially designed two-wheeled pneumatic-tyred trailer capable of carrying either the 18pdr gun or the Cletrac tractor. Trials proved the system to be satisfactory particularly after 9.00–22 low pressure tyres were fitted to the trailer in 1931. Service trials of the two trailers were finally suspended in 1932, 'pending a decision as to the suitability or otherwise of this form of portée from the tactical point of view'.

Another type of undercarriage for the 18pdr was known as the 'Egypt' undercarriage and consisted of pneumatic tyres and wheels mounted on a sub-frame. Its name implies that it was either developed in Egypt or was designed for the use of the Field Artillery Brigade stationed there.

One further development was the provision of detachable pneumatic-tyred wheels, which were bolted to the wooden-spoked artillery wheels. These were known as 'Stepney' rims. It seems that there was a reluctance to take the obvious step of fitting standard pneumatic tyres and wheels to the gun carriages because of the difficulties in manhandling and traversing them, and because the reduced height of the carriage would limit the elevation of the piece. In 1932, a specially sprung carriage for the 4.5in howitzer was introduced which partially solved this problem.

The third portée scheme was the carriage of the 3.7in howitzers on specially modified Burford-Kégresse 30cwt half-track vehicles. An example of the equipment was shown at the Colonial Premiers Demonstration in

1926 and five vehicles were issued to 9th Pack Battery in September 1927. In place of the normal gun tractor body, a sloping rear platform was fitted. The 3.7in howitzer was manhandled onto the platform via ramps and carried muzzle forward with its trail legs folded back over the gun. A box of 'ready' ammunition was carried between the trail legs of the gun. A disadvantage of the system was the lack of ammunition stowage and lack of detachment seating, who travelled separately in the 15cwt Crossley-Kégresses also used by the battery.

The idea in this case seems to have been not so much the rapid movement of the guns around the battlefield, as the speed of the half-tracks was limited anyway, but rather the need to prevent damage to the lightly constructed 3.7in pack howitzer. This gun was primarily designed as a mule-transportable light howitzer for use in mountainous regions and its carriage was not robust enough to be towed behind a tractor. With this equipment there was no need for an auxiliary light tractor to move the gun into its firing position as, firstly, the half-track vehicle itself had a reasonably good cross-country performance and secondly, the 3.7in howitzer was light enough to be readily manhandled into position.

It is worth, at this point, digressing slightly on the way that the close support role of the Light Batteries developed after the demise of the EAF in 1929. The reason for the disbandment of the EAF is discussed later and it is sufficient to recall here that, after 1929, experiments were conducted using the two Pack Batteries into ways of providing close support for the infantry and cavalry brigades. Each battery had its establishment increased by four officers and 55 other ranks and each battery was organised as two separate experimental batteries. In addition to the four 3.7in howitzers already held, a further six 3in mortars were issued. The 3.7in howitzer battery produced two sections of two guns to work with the 2nd Cavalry Brigade at Tidworth, while the 3in mortar battery formed three sections of two mortars each to support the experimental 7th Infantry Brigade also stationed at Tidworth.

Experiments had begun in 1928 into the most suitable means of transporting the 3in mortars and the 3.7in howitzers. The earlier use of the Burford-Kégresse half-tracks had a number of disadvantages, particularly the conspicuousness of the outfit and the time it took to load the gun onto the vehicle. Four criteria were laid down for an improved method of carriage:

a – the mortar was to be dismounted from the carrier for action
b – the 3.7in howitzer was to be dismountable or not – whichever was found to be the most convenient
c – as much protection as possible was to be given to the driver and crew during movement
d – the carrier was to be as inconspicuous as possible having regard to efficiency.

By 1929, the following methods of transportation had been experimented

An 18pdr gun mounted on the Citroën sprung undercarriage, photographed at MWEE.

MOVING THE GUNS

Although the 3in mortar could be fired from the Carden-Loyd carrier, it was also designed to be dismounted, complete with its baseplate, and fired from the ground. In this case an extension tube, normally stowed across the rear of the vehicle, could be added to the barrel, presumably to increase the range. The four-man detachment, belonging to 9th Light Battery, who tested the equipment in 1929, required two Carden-Loyds to bring them into action, so at least two men had to be trained as drivers.

A Carden-Loyd towing the Kégresse transporter trailer with a 3.7in howitzer aboard. Notice that this carrier also has a machine-gun mounting at the front and ammunition lockers on each side.

with: for the 3in mortar, a Carden-Loyd Mark VI carrier was adapted with a special heavy-duty axle, and a drawbar and towing hook. The mortar was mounted on the front of the top plate and was fired from the vehicle. The carrier towed a small Carden-Loyd tracked trailer capable of carrying four men and ammunition. For the 3.7in howitzer, two alternative methods were tried. In the first, a Carden-Loyd Mark VI carrier towed a small Kégresse tracked trailer on which the 3.7in howitzer could be loaded in about 45 seconds. The second method used a Carden-Loyd tracked trailer weighing about 7.5cwt, again towed by a Mark VI carrier. This trailer was less handy than the first and took about 1½ minutes to load. The Carden-Loyd trailer had actually been designed with a number of uses in mind: as a possible carrier for the 3in mortar, already described, for the 0.8in anti-tank machine-gun and, with a box body fitted, as a carrier for an anti-tank gun and detachment.

By 1930, it was reported that the future policy with regard to the transportation of the 3.7in howitzer was undecided. Experiments were tried replacing the wheels of the gun carriage with tracks, but the problem was that the 3.7in howitzer was never designed for mechanical traction in the first place and the basic carriage was unsuitable for this kind of use anyway. At the end of 1930, it was decided to fit larger diameter pneumatic tyres and wheels to a specially designed sprung carriage, making it more suitable for towing by the carriers.

Despite a delay in the issue of the new equipment, both batteries began exercises with their respective brigades in September 1929. Experiments continued in the use of close support batteries until the issue of 3in mortars to infantry battalions in 1934 and the mechanisation of the RHA with the 3.7in howitzer in 1936, rendered them unnecessary. About the same time the RTC adopted the 3in mortar-armed medium tank as their close support weapon and the Royal Artillery effectively lost their claim to be the providers of close artillery support for armoured formations.

Pavesi 4 x 4 field artillery tractor

The last of the gun tractors trialled by a service unit during this early period was a rather curious vehicle developed in Italy in 1914 by Ing Pavesi and produced by SA La Motomeccanica. The Pavesi was unique in that the body

3 FIELD ARTILLERY EXPERIMENTATION, 1920-30

One of the Italian-designed Armstrong Siddeley Pavesi tractors of 51 Battery, 10th Field Brigade, with the detachment on board and an 18pdr in tow. The solid-tyre wheels, with their special traction spuds folded inboard, can easily be seen and it is not difficult to imagine how the sharp blades would cut into the ground and tear it up.

of the vehicle was in two parts, which articulated in all planes, thus enabling the four wheels to remain in contact with the ground at all times.

Armstrong Siddeley bought the right to manufacture Pavesis in Britain although they replaced the original flat twin-engine with their own air-cooled engine and a five-speed Wilson epicyclic gearbox. One vehicle was demonstrated to the Army in May 1929 and on the strength of its performance, five were ordered to be trialled by 51 Battery of 10th Field Brigade who received them in place of Burford-Kégresse tractors.

The Pavesis were never really satisfactory – one peculiar feature was that the wire-spoked wheels had solid rubber tyres and hinged spuds, which could be swung into place in soft going. In 1930, the Mechanical Warfare Board reported, 'without spuds, the performance is poor as wheelspin takes place at the least sign of clay or bog. In sand, the fitting of spuds does little to improve the performance as they excavate the sand from under the wheels and the vehicle gradually sinks onto its belly. The spuds themselves become clogged with sand and mud and under such conditions are very difficult to engage or disengage. It is impossible to run on hard ground with the spuds fitted without causing damage to the vehicle so that on a route with varying natures of terrain, the vehicle would constantly have to stop in order to engage or disengage the spuds.' It was also reported that the spuds had a 'milling-cutter' action and tore up the track and road so badly as to render it impassable for following vehicles. Trials were also carried out with 44 x 10 single

The transporter trailer designed by Carden-Loyd carried the 3.7in howitzer pointing rearwards. Notice how the trails are folded. This early model of the Mark VI carrier does not have any side stowage lockers.

Trakgrip tyres, which gave a superior performance and a vehicle fitted with these tyres was briefly trialled as a four wheeled vehicle.

Generally, the performance of the vehicle was regarded as disappointing. It was slow and noisy and very heavy compared with the load it was designed to tow. The driving position was described as one of 'acute discomfort' and, in an age when crew comfort was low on the list of designer's priorities, this comment must have been heartfelt.

The engine gave problems throughout. It was a 45hp vertically-aligned suction-cooled four-cylinder engine specially designed for the tractor by Armstrong Siddeley. Initial design work was considered to be faulty as cylinder cooling was inadequate and resulted in a very high rate of cylinder wear. The fan drive and timing gears also produced a very noisy engine. In 1931, the manufacturers modified the engine with a view to obtaining better cooling and improved volumetric efficiency. Nonetheless, the Mechanical Warfare Board had to report that, 'in its present form, the engine cannot be regarded as being suitable for adoption in the Service'.

The Pavesis were used by 51 Battery throughout the 1930 and 1931 exercise seasons but their unreliability made them unpopular with their users. In July 1932, for instance, it was reported that two of the tractors failed to make a 63-mile march to Practice Camp.

In September 1932, the battery diary records that the 'Pavesi tractors have been adjudged unsuitable in type and reliability and are to be replaced when the new 2-ton tractors (Light Dragons) are available'. Finally, in March 1933, the Pavesis were handed back to Ordnance, 'a fact much appreciated by all ranks because of the unreliability of these vehicles'. The 51 Battery did not, in fact, get the new Dragons straightaway. They went to 30 Battery and 51 Battery had to be content with a reissue of five Burford-Kégresse 3-ton half-tracks for a year before they too were issued with Light Dragons.

This saw the end of the Royal Artillery's brief flirtation with 4 x 4 tractors, a system which lapsed until the emergence of the Guy and Morris 4 x 4 tractors in the late 1930s.

Other experimental work
Alongside the mainstream development of mechanised artillery traction there was a fascinating sub-stratum of experimental work. The years between the wars were particularly fertile in engineering technology and ideology, which did not always produce entirely practical results but they deserve a brief study nonetheless.

In 1922, the War Office sanctioned a trial, the purpose of which was to find a suitable wheeled field-artillery tractor capable of accompanying motorised troops. The ability to keep up with the new subsidy 30cwt lorry was a prime consideration but tests were also carried out over rough country since, unlike the infantry who could dismount and move forwards on foot, the artillery had to be hauled right up to the fighting line.

The competing vehicles were mostly of wartime vintage, a motley collection from five nations. The British entries were a Foster Daimler tractor, which looked positively archaic, and a tiny Glasgow tractor, which just looked silly. The former was not only huge and clumsy by postwar standards, but was also painfully slow and no doubt over-powered for the job, since it had been designed for hauling much heavier equipment. The Glasgow, on the other hand, was remarkably small though hardly any quicker. Designed for agricultural work and built by a consortium in a redundant munitions factory at Cardonald, it was powered by an imported Waukesha four-cylinder engine. It was a three-wheeler, with a single wheel at the back, and all three wheels were driven. It ran on solid rubber tyres and, to avoid the complications of a differential on the front axle, the designers opted for a simple ratchet system to vary the speed of each wheel when turning. Its main handicap as a gun tractor was the minimal ground clearance. The narrow, smooth tyres did not help much either and it was quickly rejected.

The French vehicle was a four-wheel drive Latil that had earned a fine reputation during the war but, by now, it was beginning to look a little dated. The curious Italian Pavesi tractor, which steered with an articulated chassis, showed some promise, but one turned over killing the driver, which hardly endeared it to the military. Another wartime type that had given good service, was the American FWD 3-ton truck, which entered this trial under the name 'Clintonville', the town where it was built, which appeared on the radiator. It was in the same league as the Latil. Finally, three German tractors were entered, drawn from a huge pool of captured vehicles stored at Aldershot. Both Germany and Austria had produced many excellent heavy artillery tractors during the war and had used them extensively. The speedy reduction of the Belgian forts around Liège was as much due to the heavy tractors that hauled the heavy guns forward as to the guns themselves. Two of these, the Lanz and the Benz, were little better than the Foster Daimler, though they looked a lot more modern. The Mercedes Daimler was a real eye-opener. It was a large and powerful four-wheel drive machine and it hardly noticed when an 18pdr gun and limber were hitched on to the rear.

All that the trials really proved was that there was, at the time, no such thing as a field-artillery tractor to meet modern

The little Glasgow tractor undergoing a stability test. All three wheels can be seen along with the ratchet device built into the front axle that served in place of a differential. Smooth solid tyres and low ground clearance were against it from the start.

requirements. Apart from the obvious fact that four-wheel drive was essential, together with a powerful winch, the wartime vehicles were all too large and heavy for the job.

Britain had failed to produce any effective four-wheel drive vehicles during the war and had had to rely extensively on American-produced vehicles. Even after the war, no British manufacturer took up the challenge, presumably because there was no demand for such a vehicle in commercial circles and the Army was forced to look to its own resources. The Royal Army Service Corps (RASC) decided to produce a machine of their own design, based on some of the captured German tractors. The result was the Hathi tractor, which appeared in prototype form in 1923 and which is described

MOVING THE GUNS

The four-wheel drive Latil, a wartime French model, photographed during the 1922 tractor trials. Although fine across country the steel strakes, fitted to the heavy cast wheels, did not behave so well on a hard road and set up vibrations that could shake a less sturdy chassis to pieces.

An ex-German Army Krupp-Daimler KD1 tractor taking part in the 1922 trials. This, the best among all the tractors tested, managed an 18pdr with such ease that a 6in howitzer replaced it. However, the machine was designed for much heavier loads.

more fully later on. One of the main drawbacks of all the wartime vehicles was their wheels. A large diameter was considered essential to provide adequate traction, but steel rims or solid rubber tyres set up severe vibration which dictated a substantial chassis. The result was that all such tractors were not only unacceptably large but they were of quite massive construction and excessively heavy. Recent developments in large-section, low-pressure pneumatic tyres solved both these problems: wheels could now be a lot smaller and the smoother ride permitted much lighter chassis construction. On the road the Hathi was relatively fast and quiet, and across country its low ground pressure gave it a considerable advantage. Even if it did get stuck while towing, all that was needed was to unhitch the gun, move the vehicle on to firm ground and then winch the gun forward. Negotiations with Thornycrofts soon resulted in orders being placed for a production model, which was also advertised as being suitable for commercial use in under-developed countries; not, in the event, that this led to any great interest.

The failure of the Glasgow tractor did not deter the War Office from wanting to try other ones, though there were not many to choose from. A traditional preference for steam tackle on the part

3 FIELD ARTILLERY EXPERIMENTATION, 1920-30

of Britain's farmers had inhibited tractor development until wartime demands put a lot of pressure on agriculture, but by then it was too late to design and build tractors in sufficient numbers. As a result, the Ford Company of America built a factory in Cork where the famous Fordson was built from 1919 onwards. Two Fordsons were acquired for trials by the Tank Testing Section at Farnborough in 1923 and one was converted into a tracklayer by the fitting of a modification kit known as the 'Trackson' system. They were tested in a variety of roles and, although artillery haulage is not specifically mentioned, both tractors were tested in this role by the Royal Marine Artillery at Fort Cumberland at Portsmouth. Wheeled Fordsons were also trialled in India and were used by the Territorial Artillery, a use which is described more fully later on.

The Austin Motor Company also entered the tractor business. One of their 20hp models was trialled in 1924 and an imported McCormick Deering was tried in 1926. This was the Model 10/20 that ran on solid rubber tyres. It was tested towing an 18pdr gun, a 4.5in howitzer and even a 6in gun, but it failed miserably on all counts. This seemed to blight the cause of the wheeled tractor and attention turned to tracked types. The Royal Marines trialled two versions of the Fordson using the Roadless and Trakpul systems, while the Army took another look at the Clayton. An earlier model of this full-track type had been used extensively during the war by the Royal Flying Corps (RFC) and the Royal Air Force (RAF) for aircraft handling and general duties, and the version tested in 1927 was little different from the wartime tractor. It was available with either a Dorman petrol or Aster paraffin engine. MWEE tested the latter version towing a 6in gun but it did not come up to expectations. It was tested again in 1929, after going back to the makers for modifications, but it still appeared to be unsuitable for the role.

The prototype Hathi, perched on a pair of improvised scotches, demonstrates its winch. Spartan as it was, it showed much promise and was a great tribute to the innovative Royal Army Service Corps (RASC) design team.

The Austin farm tractor tested for gun haulage at Farnborough. The extra seats were fitted specially for this trial.

The original Cletrac demonstrator showing off its powers as a gun tractor. Notice the transverse front spring, and the power take-off ahead of the radiator.

71

MOVING THE GUNS

The old 32hp Albion three-tonner converted to a halftrack by Armstrong Siddeley Motors. The original chain final drive was retained while the tracks were Philip Johnson's highly flexible 'snake' type.

The first Armstrong Siddeley Dragon B1E1. This was the amphibious version, which was also tested as a gun transporter; it, too, is equipped with snake tracks.

Ultimately, the most successful contender was the Cletrac, built by the Cleveland Tractor Company of Ohio. It was marketed in Britain by Burfords and the version tested was the Model K. It employed a simple but effective regenerative steering system, which was adopted for use in a number of AFVs and has been known as the Cletrac steering system ever since. A number of these tractors were supplied for the use of the Royal Artillery in their portée role already described.

Another favourite solution to the problem of road and cross-country movement was the half-track, which combined some of the qualities of both means of traction – or dispensed with half the advantages of each, depending on your point of view. As we have seen, half track production was dominated by the Kégresse and Roadless systems, but other firms tried their hands at experimental prototypes. One was Armstrong Siddeley who converted a wartime Albion lorry by fitting a track bogie of their own design to the rear axle. It employed Johnson's snake track to make turning easier, and what was described as synchronised steering, which appears to have been a method of linking the track brakes to the steering wheel. A year later, in 1924, Vickers offered a version using a Peerless lorry. In this case, the track and suspension system derived from

3 FIELD ARTILLERY EXPERIMENTATION, 1920-30

the type fitted to their medium tank, but it was prohibitively heavy for a lorry and both experiments failed to develop beyond prototype stage. Roadless, in addition to producing a range of commercial half-tracks and artillery tractors, also produced a few speculative prototypes, mainly with a view to producing small half-track tractors for the Territorial Army. Some of these could be converted from half-tracks to wheeled tractors as the situation demanded.

In exactly the same way, the mainstream Dragon development was complemented by a series of experimental prototypes, which never progressed beyond that stage. Three were produced by Armstrong Siddeley for a variety of roles, but with one thing in common – the system known as 'horn steering'. This was a system invented to ease the ever-present steering problem by causing the front end of the track frames, the horns, to move laterally, curving the tracks as they moved. This would cause the tracks to lay down in a curve and enable large radius turns to be achieved without using skid steering. The first of the experimental Dragons, B1E1, appeared in 1923. It was an amphibious load carrier, which was also looked at as a potential gun carrier. B1E2 appeared in the following year. It was originally designed as a gun tractor or transporter but was later converted into a machine-gun carrier. The third and last model was B1E3, a very much larger model dating from 1925. It appears to have been a cross between a personnel carrier and a gun tractor. These last two models were not amphibious but all three used the same system of flexible track.

Meanwhile, a Mr Ingoldsby from one of Vickers' subsidiary companies was working on a scheme of his own that evolved into two prototypes, the Ingoldsby Transporters. The designer's aim was to produce tracked machines,

The Vickers-Peerless halftrack was nothing if not substantial. Indeed, probably much too solid for the work it had to do since all the suspension items were designed for a Medium Tank. Just beyond it can be seen the Fordson tractor with Trakson crawler tracks fitted, which was under test by MWEE at the same time.

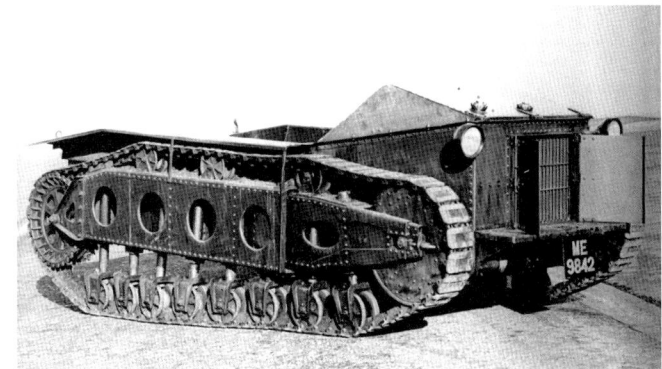

B1E2, the second Armstrong Siddeley Dragon, was the lightweight model. It has conventional tracks but also uses the horn steering system, which shows up clearly in this view. Later, the vehicle was fitted with a high-sided body and demonstrated as a machine-gun carrier. In this unladen state the action of the suspension is quite obvious.

The third Dragon in this series, B1E3, was much bigger. The driver sits to the right, alongside the engine, but the rear section is nearly all seating, running down both sides of the body.

73

MOVING THE GUNS

This is the only photograph of the machine known as the Protected Track Dragon, designed and built at Woolwich. This view clearly shows the free-rolling front rollers and the casing that shrouds the chains carrying drive to the spudded rear rollers.

which could be easily driven by the ordinary MT driver without the need for specialised training. His first model, which appeared in 1924, used a Lanchester engine, although details of the transmission and suspension are not known. However, the track used was Balata belting, a sort of rubberised conveyor belt, which would have had a degree of lateral flexibility. The 1925 version was altogether more bizarre. It ran on ten enormous disc wheels, five on each side, and the track consisted of circular, hardened rubber beads threaded onto a core of wire rope. The object was to reduce lateral resistance during turning but it also caused excessive wear. Beyond the fact that it was powered by an AEC engine, little more is known about it.

Finally, mention must be made of a Dragon made by the Royal Ordnance Factory in 1924. Known variously as the Woolwich, or PT ('protected track') Dragon, it had side skirting plates to protect the running gear. However, this was not the most interesting aspect of the design. Extensions of the track frames at each end culminated in heavy-duty rollers. Those at the front spun free on stub axles but the rear pair were driven by chains from each final-drive sprocket. The object can only have been to help the machine over extra wide trenches assisted by the rear roller, which was fitted with projecting spuds. How a wheeled gun or limber was to follow behind is not clear, and the whole object of the exercise is a mystery.

The first Ingoldsby Transporter employed a Lanchester engine. The tracks were made from industrial conveyor belting, studded with metal guide links and rubber blocks.

Legend has it that the French inventor of the half-track system, Adolphe Kégresse, threw his hat in the air and exclaimed, 'la mort de la roue!' when one of his vehicles beat all the wheeled contenders attempting to climb Gallows Hill during the Wool Trials at Bovington in February 1925. Had he attended the 1927 trials at the same place, he might have had to eat his words, if not his hat, for wheeled vehicles were making a determined comeback. In addition to the Hathi, another four-wheel drive vehicle, the Vulcan-Holverta, took part, and it was of such a sophisticated design that it terrified most of the mechanics present who saw it. At the time, the future seemed to lie with multi-wheelers. In 1928, Armstrong Siddeley Motors built a most unusual vehicle on the Pavesi articulated chassis principle, which had eight wheels instead of four. In a sense it had sixteen since, at the end of each axle was a pair of narrow wheels fitted with slim, high-pressure tyres. It was powered by a Genet radial aircraft engine mounted in a bullet-shaped bonnet, which gave it a potential top speed of 40mph. In practice, it was considered lethal at anything over about 20mph. It was tested in a variety of roles including that of a gun tractor, but it was generally agreed that it would perform a lot better, and a great deal more

The strange-looking Ingoldsby No 2 Transporter and its curious round section tracks. Both vehicles appear to have had layshaft drive to all wheels and an ability to steer by turning all the wheels, hence the need for laterally flexible tracks. They were designed to be easy to drive although the transmission was incredibly complicated.

This Armstrong-Siddeley Pavesi-type eight-wheeler was the second prototype and it is shown at MWEE with an 18pdr and limber hooked up. Steering was by chassis articulation while each pair of wheels also pivoted in the vertical plane to accommodate rough ground.

MOVING THE GUNS

The Leyland and AEC eight-wheel drive tractors designed and built for colonial transportation. Both are shown during gun towing trials with the Royal Marines. The Leyland tows a 60pdr while the AEC hauls the barrel of a naval gun on a special solid-tyre transporter.

safely, if it were fitted with large section, low-pressure tyres instead. A modified second model appeared in 1929, which had the low-pressure tyres and a four-cylinder air-cooled engine beneath a conventional bonnet. This model, too, was tested for various purposes including that of artillery tractor.

Three more eight-wheel drive tractors appeared over the next few years and, although they go beyond the timespan of this section, they may be dealt with here for convenience. The first dates from 1931 with an impressive looking tractor produced by Guy Motors. Fitted with an artillery tractor body and powered by a six-cylinder engine, it produced an amazing performance, especially during the trials in North Wales, but it was never adopted for service use and the prototype was later converted into a six-wheeler. At this time, MWEE also tested vehicles for the Colonial Office and one of these was a large eight-wheeled tractor built by Leylands from funds supplied by the Colonial Office Council and the Empire Marketing Board. It was a forward control machine with a six-cylinder, 80hp engine located behind the cab. It ran on four, close-coupled axles, all of which steered as well. The idea behind the design was to produce a vehicle capable of hauling two eight-wheeled Dyson trailers with a payload of 15 tons as a road train for use in those wilder parts of the Empire where good roads did not exist or where the railway had yet to reach. During the trials, the Royal Marines got hold of it and used it to tow a 60pdr gun, but it was later sent to the Gold Coast and never heard of again. However, in 1933, the idea was revived and this time AEC produced an even bigger version with a diesel engine that could handle longer trains with a gross payload of 30 tons. This model had wider spaced axles with the steering only operating on the front and rear wheels. It, too, spent a brief time with the Royal Marines and enjoyed some modest commercial success.

The four-wheel-drive, four-wheel steer Latil model TL tractor running on trade plates at MWEE with a Royal Tank Corps driver at the wheel.

Four-wheel drive reappeared again in 1929 when MWEE tested a Latil Model TL designed mainly for light commercial

MOVING THE GUNS

An early example of the FWD six-wheel drive tractor gives a cross-country demonstration. The covers for the epicyclic hub reduction gears show up plainly on the wheels.

and agricultural work. Unlike its wartime predecessor, this version ran on pneumatic tyres. Although it seems to have turned in a very impressive performance, it was never adopted by the British Army, though it was built under licence by Shelvoke and Drewry for a while in the 1930s.

Turning to six-wheel drive, a six-wheeled version of the Hathi was produced but it never really caught on. The Royal Marines, with their rather specialised requirement for tractors to tow the medium guns of the Royal Marine Artillery, appear from time to time in the story, and indeed, at some stage, they fielded a Roadless half-track version of the Hathi. This was a most impressive looking machine, which served with

the Mobile Naval Base Defence Organisation for a while. FWD Motors of Slough was an offshoot of the American company, which, by 1929, was a totally independent concern. In that year, they produced a handsome semi-forward control six-wheel drive tractor for the Army powered by a Dorman engine. Tested against a Roadless half-track version on the same basic chassis, it was found to be less effective towing the 60pdr gun, but was adopted instead as a tractor for the 3in 20cwt anti-aircraft gun and as a recovery tractor for the RAOC. It is described in more detail later on.

Scammell Lorries also entered the 6 x 6 field at the same time with a modified version of their famous Pioneer lorry.

3 FIELD ARTILLERY EXPERIMENTATION, 1920-30

The impressive Hathi-Roadless tractor belonging to the Royal Marines, which was tested at Fort Cumberland near Portsmouth.

In view of the firm's expertise in producing heavy off-road trucks, it is curious that the War Office took so long to show any interest in their products. A conventional 6 x 4 Pioneer had been tested in 1927 and the type began to enter service in the late 1930s, but the six-wheel drive version remained a one-off as far as the War Office was concerned. It remained for years as a recovery tractor and the Indian Army examined it as a potential road train tractor but nothing more came of it.

Finally, it was Indian Army interest that prompted Guy Motors to produce a six-wheel drive tractor at the same time as their eight-wheel version. They had already supplied some 6 x 4 trucks as ammunition vehicles and gun towers, and the 6 x 6 was almost identical except for the provision of a layshaft drive to the front axle. It was tested in India but never entered service. Leyland also produced a conventional-looking forward-control 6 x 6 tractor in 1930 and all four vehicles were tested against each other in trials to find a suitable medium-artillery tractor. These trials and the results are described more fully in the section dealing with medium artillery.

Another most impressive vehicle was the six-wheel drive Scammell offered to India, but tested originally by the British Army as a gun tractor. The front axle, with its bulbous differential casing, had to be located ahead of the radiator but this would have improved its potential cross-country performance.

79

4 THE ARMOURED FORCE EXPERIMENTS, 1925–29

The EMF and EAF exercises in the late 1920s gave Gunners the opportunity to prove the value of mechanised artillery support for armoured formations, as well as gaining useful experience in tactical handling. It also enabled them to try out all the various methods of mechanised gun haulage in conditions as close to actual battle as it was possible to achieve.

4 THE ARMOURED FORCE EXPERIMENTS, 1925–29

A Birch Gun of 20 Battery rolls through a Wiltshire village on an overcast day. Crew comfort was hardly a consideration in the design.

reactionary indifference and hostility of some of the military establishment. Until 1927, units of the RTC remained firmly under infantry control, the tanks being seen merely as weapons to be used in support of infantry attacks. Other views, of course, were held by such as Fuller and Liddell Hart who saw the tank as the ultimate war-winning weapon capable of all military activity from reconnaissance through to final victory.

The mechanised vehicle demonstration held at Camberley in October 1926, in which 9th Field Brigade took part, may have been instrumental in persuading the Chief of the General Staff, General Sir George Milne and Winston Churchill, the Secretary of State for War, to press ahead with experiments in mechanised warfare. Owing to the financial strictures of the time, Churchill insisted on a limited small-scale experiment to resolve some of the problems of handling mechanised forces.

In May 1927, the Force was created and consisted of the following units, which were divided into the tactical groupings as shown below:

> Flank Reconnaissance Group provided by armoured cars of the 3rd Bn RTC
> Main Reconnaissance Group provided by tankettes of the 3rd Bn RTC.

The Main Force consisting of:

> Medium tanks of 5th Bn RTC
> Mechanised infantry machine-gun battalion provided by 2nd Bn Somerset Light Infantry
> Mechanised field company of the Royal Engineers (RE)
> Mechanised Field Brigade Royal Artillery
> Mechanised Light Battery Royal Artillery.

The four batteries of 9th Field Brigade supported the Main Force and the Light

The Experimental Mechanised Force (EMF), which was formed on 1 May 1927, had its origins in the mobile column formed by the 7th Infantry Brigade during 1925. The artillery support for this column had been provided by 9th Field Brigade RFA, and much preliminary work evolving basic battle drills using mechanised units was done during the exercises of 1925 and 1926. The formation of the Tank Corps itself was beset with much intrigue and infighting within the Army as the new arm sought to establish itself against the

81

MOVING THE GUNS

19 Battery, 9th Field Brigade, with 18pdrs and Crossley-Kégresse 30cwt towing vehicles, prepare to move off during an exercise with the Mechanised Force, 1927.

Battery supported the Reconnaissance Group. The Main Force was split into two groups for movement because of the variety of types of vehicle and their differences in speed. The fast group consisted of wheeled vehicles and the slow group of tracked vehicles. The batteries of 9th Field Brigade were allocated according to the various vehicles they had. Thus, the 18pdr guns towed by Crossley-Kégresse half-tracks tended to move with the fast group, while the Dragon-towed 18pdr guns and the 4.5in howitzers of 28 and 76 Batteries together with the Birch guns of 20 Battery tended to move with the slow group. The Light Battery had 3.7in howitzers portéed on Burford-Kégresse half-tracks. The composition of the Force was designed to be flexible, with artillery batteries and machine-gun companies of the infantry battalion being allocated to parts of the Force as the tactical situation developed.

The Force was given the task of experimenting with the theories already largely proposed by Fuller and Liddell Hart except that the Force was not completely armoured. The machine-gun battalion and the Royal Engineer company, for instance, were transported in Crossley-Kégresse half-tracks and Morris Commercial 6 x 4 trucks. The Force was formed in order to evolve a fixed organisation for a mechanised division of all arms. It was given three specific roles to experiment with during 1927 and 1928:

- strategic reconnaissance in place of cavalry
- cooperative action with conventional forces
- independent action sustained over 24 hours.

The artillery batteries took part in all the major exercises of the Experimental Mechanised Force in 1927 and the Experimental Armoured Force (EAF) in

82

1928. The exercises followed the usual progression of battery, brigade, division and force training carried out largely on Salisbury Plain.

The aspects of mechanised training that were carried out during 1927 were as follows:

- Firstly, a day's march of approximately 30 miles was carried out in two groups. The fast group consisted of six-wheelers and half-track vehicles moving at an average speed of 10mph and the slow group of tracked vehicles moved at about 7mph. This march demonstrated the vulnerability of the Force to attacks from the air. It also showed that the clearance of road blocks would not normally delay a column in which march discipline was good and in which the passing and acknowledgement of signals had been practised.
- Secondly, a night march of approximately 25 miles was practised, mostly across country, at the same speeds as the day march, demonstrating that the same speeds could be maintained cross-country using rear lights only, except for the leading vehicle in each group.
- Thirdly, the vulnerability of the Force to attack by conventional forces was tested in two situations: when the Force was on the move and when the Force was in night bivouac. The Force proved to have insufficient protection when on the move but was able to protect itself when in bivouac.
- Fourthly, the ability of the Force to envelop a larger conventional force on the move was tested. It was shown that this was possible but there was difficulty in maintaining the cordon thereafter.
- Fifthly, in attempting to harass and check a larger force moving across its front, the Force did not use sufficient speed and allowed the conventional force to escape.
- Sixthly, the Force was used to carry out an attack on a strongly held defended position and it was shown

The Burford-Kégresse half-track portée vehicles of 9th Light Battery take a breather by the roadside. The 3.7in howitzers are carried complete with their extra-wide shields. The loading ramps can be seen stowed on the sloping rear deck.

- that success depended on how well the defending anti-tank weapons were handled.
- Seventhly, the Force was assessed for its value as a rear guard. It was discovered that the Force could cause early enemy deployment and could choose its own time for breaking off an engagement.
- Lastly, the ability of the Force to check the advance of a larger conventional force with cavalry was tested. The conventional force was found to be vulnerable except when it was 'lying-up' in a tank-proof locality.

On 31 August 1927, the batteries took part in an inspection and tactical demonstration at the conclusion of the exercises for Winston Churchill, then Chancellor of the Exchequer, which included a tactical river crossing of the River Avon under simulated gas attack.

River crossings were a particular responsibility of Major Martel who commanded the Royal Engineer Company. A noted tank enthusiast who designed and produced the prototype Morris Martel one-man tank at his own expense, this Sapper conformed to the stereotype eccentric mould in which the Gunners viewed most officers of their sister regiment. It is recalled by an officer who served in the EAF that, after a number of Dragons had actually or nearly drowned on Martel's various river-crossing exercises, they refused his further invitations to take part on the grounds of 'previous engagements'.

So ended the first year of experimentation of the Mechanised Force, during which the Gunners in particular had gained valuable experience in the tactical handling of mechanised artillery. Critics abounded, however Liddell Hart, now writing as the Military Correspondent of the *Daily Telegraph*, was scathing in his criticisms of the EMF's achievements. The first exercise he described as 'an attempt to drill a mechanised menagerie into a Noah's Ark procession carried out in slow time'.

During 1928, the EMF was renamed the Experimental Armoured Force (EAF) and it exercised throughout the year. In June, there was an administrative exercise to sort out the logistic side of maintaining the Force. Later in the month, a demonstration was given for the Imperial Defence College, which consisted of a tactical river crossing of the River Avon at Amesbury. During this exercise it is interesting to note that the spare Dragon of 28 Battery was used as a standby recovery vehicle should any tanks fall into the river during the crossing, there being no other vehicle suitable for this task. In July, the Armoured Force gave a demonstration of an attack for observers from the Indian Army and the Staff College and later in the month was inspected by 400 Members of Parliament. In late July, 9th Brigade went to Practice Camp at Larkhill where anti-tank shooting 'over open sights' was practised. Then, at the end of August, Armoured Force training recommenced with the Force being constituted the same as in the previous year with the addition of one company of mechanised infantry from the 2nd Battalion the Cheshire Regiment.

A Carden-Loyd Mark VI carrier, towing the same maker's tracked undercarriage for a 3.7in howitzer, crosses a pontoon bridge. Just visible beneath the head of the horse at the right of the picture is a small tracked trailer, towed by another Carden-Loyd and presumably containing the gun detachment belonging to 9th Light Battery.

The Armoured Force exercises in 1928 placed more emphasis for the artillery on the support of attacks onto prepared positions rather than the close support of the attack itself. There was increased emphasis on anti-tank shooting, a job for which the 18pdr gun was not suited with its low muzzle velocity and the slow gearing of the traverse mechanism.

The exercises came to a conclusion at the end of September and 20 Battery reported that the Birch Guns had done an average of 850 miles each and that, 'it is a great fight to keep them running, and their armouring and general inaccessibility adds considerably to the time required for nearly all repairs.' The main lessons that came out of the 1928 manoeuvres seem to have been the vulnerability of the Medium tanks in action and the general sensitivity of armoured vehicles to ground.

In February 1929, the Armoured Force was dispersed. This was not apparently due to a lack of faith in the concept of an independent armoured force as such, but rather to a desire to study more closely the cooperation of AFVs with conventional formations, particularly infantry. To this end, two experimental brigades were formed – the 7th Infantry Brigade at Tidworth and the 6th Infantry Brigade at Aldershot.

It is clear that a fixed organisation was not suitable for the variety of roles that had been envisaged for the Armoured Force. The reconnaissance role required highly mobile AFVs such as light tanks and armoured cars. In the cooperative role, the Armoured Force clearly had an important function but in the days of unreliable, insufficient and short-range wireless sets, there were considerable practical problems in coordinating armoured flank attacks with the main force. The third role of the independent task was never really defined, although a number of possibilities were experimented with.

At the end of two seasons of exercises, it was clear that a fixed organisation of all arms was not what was required and it was mainly for this reason that the Experimental Armoured Force was disbanded in 1929. It was also, of course, the time of financial collapse in the USA and of worsening economic depression at home.

From the Gunners' point of view, the period of the EMF and EAF exercises was the opportunity to prove the value of mechanised artillery support for armoured formations. Unfortunately, they were battling against a number of obstacles. Firstly, there was a strong lobby of influential RTC officers and supporters anxious to prove the worth of the newly formed branch of the Army. Before the inevitable emergence of effective anti-tank weapons, the tank was seen by many as virtually impregnable and this was a view much encouraged by the popular press of the day. The tanks were undoubtedly ahead in the popularity stakes and the Gunners suffered as a result.

Secondly, the role that the Gunners were allotted – that of the close support of the armoured force – was rather ill-defined and (it was argued, with some justification) could be as adequately or better performed by the RTC themselves, given the right weapons. The Gunner interpretation of the role was based on the well-tried method of close support of the cavalry by the RHA, of field artillery brought quickly into action to protect a flank or give covering fire onto an objective or to exploit a tactical situation. It was a role that relied largely on fairly close-range direct fire generally without the use of observers.

The Armoured Force required a different type of support. It had its own integral fire support almost as powerful as that which the Gunners provided. The mobile nature of the Force demanded artillery support as mobile as the force it was supporting or, alternatively, the means to bring observed indirect fire down rapidly in support of the mechanised force. The ability to do that latter depended on reliable longer-range wireless sets and rapid and accurate survey methods, neither of which were available at the time of the EAF manoeuvres.

Thirdly, the weapons available to give support to the Force were inadequate for the job they were given. The 18pdr gun was a single-charge weapon and was therefore not flexible enough to be a good close-support weapon. If the mechanised force experiments had happened a few years later when the 25pdr howitzer had been available, the Gunners would have had the ideal close-support weapon. Another clear requirement for the Armoured Force was a good anti-tank weapon and, in this role, the 18pdr was unsuitable with its inadequate muzzle velocity. The gun used by the Light Batteries, the 3.7in howitzer, was designed as a pack howitzer for mountain use. Although it was more suitable as a close-support weapon, it lacked the weight of shell and range necessary for the job it was given. Lastly, the Birch Gun, in particular, acquired a reputation for being unreliable.

The net result of these difficulties was that there seemed to be a general lack of confidence among the Gunners about their ability to provide the necessary degree of support for a mechanised force. In a sense, the Gunners lost the propaganda war in the debate as to whether artillery support for a mechanised force should be provided by the Royal Artillery or by the RTC itself. Some elements in the RTC were only too keen to take over this role themselves. As early as 1925, Colonel Percy Hobart, then an Instructor at the Staff College and later to be the commander of the famous 79th Armoured Division, wrote to Colonel Lindsay, the Chief Instructor at Bovington, asking about 'the consummation of our accompanying guns to form a "Royal Tank Artillery"'.

The final blow must have come with the publication of the tactical doctrine, which emerged from the experiments, the training manual called *Mechanised and Armoured Formations*, published in 1929, and its revised version called *Modern Formations*, published in 1931. In these publications, popularly known collectively as the 'Purple Primer', there is no mention at all of the need for artillery in the close-support role, this role being allotted to a 'close support tank battery'. The 'close support tank' is described as being able to provide 'heavier covering fire than that given by machine-guns. Its primary task is to deal quickly during the progress of an attack with unexpected targets, which would normally be beyond the vision of the ordinary supporting artillery or which could not be dealt with by such artillery in the time available. This tank will frequently be the only artillery support available to attacking tanks and it is, in fact, the only type which can accompany other AFVs in action.' That such a vehicle did not exist in 1929, or even in 1930, is not mentioned, but the implication was clear – when such a vehicle did become available, it was to be manned by the RTC not by the Royal Artillery.

The description of the proposed 'close support tank' effectively summarises all the limitations of the weapons that the Gunners had available in 1927. They were restricted in range, did not have the signals or survey resources to give quick, accurate indirect fire support and were insufficiently mobile to keep up with the bulk of the mechanised forces. So, after 1930, the RTC experimented with a variety of close-support tanks to fill a role that the Royal Artillery found itself unable to do, although the Light Batteries did continue to support the two experimental brigades using 3.7in howitzers and 3in mortars.

The Birch Guns, probably the first serious attempt in the world to produce a battery of specifically designed self-propelled guns, lingered on for a couple more years. The authorities played around with an anti-aircraft role for which the guns were clearly unsuitable until they were finally withdrawn in January 1931 to, it would seem, everyone's relief, as the entry in 20 Battery diary records: 'no-one will mourn the loss of the SP mountings'.

The unhappy experience of the EAF probably prejudiced the minds of many Gunners for a considerable time against the practicality of mechanised artillery and of self-propelled artillery in particular. Certainly, no further attempts were made to produce a self-propelled gun until events in the Western Desert in the early years of the war made such a gun necessary. It is interesting to speculate what the outcome of the battles in Northern France and Belgium in 1940 and in the early years in the Western Desert might have been, had the Gunners emerged from the 1928 and 1929 experiments with more confidence in their ability to provide close support for mechanised formations.

The lessons of the EAF for the Gunners were not all negative, however. Further valuable experience was gained in the handling of mechanised vehicles. Tactics and battle drills were evolved, convoy drills, track discipline, concealment and camouflage, maintenance and servicing were all valuable lessons that were learnt. More importantly, it gave the Gunners the opportunity to try out all the various methods of mechanised gun haulage in conditions as close to actual battle as it was possible to achieve. As a result, ideas as to what was required began to polarise and, after 1931, the period of experimentation practically came to an end. From 1931 onwards, the Gunners pursued two main ways of hauling artillery – tracked tractors and wheeled tractors. By and large, these were the two main lines of development that continued through the period of total mechanisation, which began in 1935 to the outbreak of war in 1939.

HM King George V (with the stick) watches as a battery of 18pdrs of 9th Field Brigade moves across the Plain in extended order, towed by Mark II Dragons.

MOVING THE GUNS

5 FIELD ARTILLERY – CONSOLIDATION, 1930-39

The 1930s saw the emergence of the fully tracked Light Dragon gun tractor as the main means of traction for Field Artillery batteries. Mechanisation of the new armoured formations was partly with light tanks, so it was inevitable that artillery tractors should also be obtained from the same source. Light Dragons provided a successful means of gun haulage for nearly a decade.

5 FIELD ARTILLERY - CONSOLIDATION, 1930-39

A manufacturer's photograph of a Light Dragon Mark I with its canopy erected, prior to delivery. A form of horizontal coil-spring suspension was introduced at this stage, which gave a much easier ride.

Following the demise of the EMF and its successor, the EAF, in 1929, there was a general feeling that the period of experimentation should come to an end and that, from the huge variety of vehicles tested, a choice should be made of the most suitable tractors for the future. The future role of the self-propelled gun was so much in the balance that no further development proceeded along this line. The Dragons were considered to be good vehicles but expensive and really too powerful for the field role. Existing Mark IIs were converted for medium-artillery haulage and future marks were designed specifically for the haulage of the 60pdr gun and 6in howitzer. Half-tracks fell from favour as a civilian market failed to materialise and rigid six-wheelers with comparable cross-country performance were developed. The Pavesi 4 x 4 tractor was an 'oddity' that never progressed beyond the trials stage. The various portée experiments did not proceed beyond the prototype stage once the decision was taken to equip the Territorial Army with standard 6 x 4 tractors and once it became apparent that it was possible to achieve fast towing speeds with improved tractors, pneumatic tyres and sprung carriages.

For the Field Artillery, the Army required a smaller, lighter tractor that could also be used in the Battery Staff and Artillery Observer role. It is surprising that the vehicle which emerged, and that was to become the main means of traction for the regular batteries during this period, was a fully tracked Light Dragon. This was because reliable 6 x 4-wheeled vehicles were beginning to emerge at this period which, fitted with the standard War Office tandem rear bogie and modern pneumatic tyres, were able to achieve a cross-country performance only marginally less than that of tracked vehicles at a fraction of the cost. The Light Dragon was one of many offshoots from the light tanks of the period. These, in turn, had developed from the Martel one-man 'tankettes' on the one hand, and the Carden-Loyd machine-gun carriers on the other. At a time when it was financially expedient to mechanise the new armoured formations partly with large quantities of light tanks, it was inevitable that the artillery tractor should also be looked for from the same source. It was a happy choice as the Light Dragon series of gun tractors proved to be a very successful means of haulage for nearly a decade.

The Light Dragon

The Light Dragon, which was to provide the main means of artillery traction for the Regular Army in the remaining period up to the beginning of the Second World War, was one of many vehicles that owed its origins to the various 'tankette' and light tank developments of the period. It derived from the Vickers 2-ton tractor and the Artillery Observer's vehicle ordered from Vickers Ltd in October 1929. The Artillery Observer's vehicle was used in the 1930 exercise season by 20 Battery of 9th Field Brigade. Special experimental training was carried out with the 5th Battalion RTC to evaluate the artillery support of tanks before the opening of a timed artillery programme following the capture of the first objective. The idea was to have an artillery observer mounted in an armoured vehicle with wireless communication to the battery. The initial experiments were not successful because, as the battery diary records, 'Fire comes down too slowly by this means to be of influence in the very rapid and scattered anti-tank engagement which would occur. Also, the attack covers too much ground for one travelling observer to be alive to more than one corner of the situation.' Nonetheless, this was a very significant development in that it heralded the concept of a Forward Observation Officer (FOO) travelling in support of an armoured formation in direct

89

MOVING THE GUNS

The Artillery Observer's Vehicle D5E1 posed for the official photographer at MWEE. The driver sits to the left of the engine, while an elevated seat is provided for the observer at the back. These early Vickers-Carden-Loyd vehicles used a leaf-spring suspension which, in practice, proved too unyielding on rough ground.

communication and control of his battery of guns. It was a concept that required improvements, particularly in wireless technology, before it developed into the reliable system used some 12 years later in the Western Desert, where a single FOO was able to call on the instant support not only of his battery, but of every other battery in range.

The vehicle used for this experiment was a fully tracked machine weighing two tons and based on Vickers' newly designed Light Tank. It had the same Meadows 30hp engine, transmission and suspension as the Light Tank. It was capable of carrying three men together with their necessary wireless

The prototype 2-ton tractor was basically the same as D5E1, without the high-sided body. It participated in the 1930 Wool Trials but is shown here with a field gun and limber in tow.

and technical equipment. The vehicle was delivered to MWEE in June 1930 and used in exercises in August and September of that year.

Carden-Loyd mortar and machine-gun carriers had been used by the experimental Light Batteries in the close support role during and after the EAF exercises. This experience may well have persuaded the authorities of the suitability of light tracked vehicles for gun haulage. It was immediately apparent that the Light Tank could be adapted as a gun tractor. In addition, there were obvious advantages in having the same basic vehicle used in a number of different roles. A tractor version, known initially as the 'two-ton tractor', was ordered in 1929. It was essentially the same as the Artillery Observer's vehicle with the addition of a towing hook and the removal of the wireless equipment. A vehicle was delivered in early 1930 and first demonstrated at Bovington in February.

The prototype tractor had an open hull manufactured of 1/8in mild steel plate and provided seating for four men in addition to the driver. It had a low profile, being only 3ft 8in in height, and was capable of towing an 18pdr gun and limber at 25mph. The initial trials were very promising and the

Mechanical Warfare Board reported, 'it has far better performance than any existing tractor except possibly the Mark II Dragon'. As a result, an order was placed in December 1930 for 14 tractors, which were to incorporate a number of improvements. The tractor was based on the new Light Tank Mark II with the Meadows EPC engine and Horstmann suspension with bell-crank levers and coil springs. The track was of a new pattern and 10½in wide. Two specifically designed ammunition limbers were ordered at the same time, although there was provision for the stowage of 16 rounds of 18pdr ammunition on the tractor itself. The tractors were designed to tow a combined gun and limber weight of 2 tons 6cwt and produce a maximum road speed of 20mph. The vehicle was also capable of negotiating rough country at 6mph, of climbing a 45-degree slope and fording water to a depth of 2ft.

The 14 vehicles were delivered by Vickers-Armstrong at the end of May 1931 and were issued to 20 Battery of the 9th Field Brigade in place of the Birch Guns. The scale of vehicles authorised initially was ten tractors, of which three were allocated to the Battery Staff together with three specially designed two-wheeled trailers to carry wireless equipment, eight Austin Seven two-seater cars and three motor cycles.

The new tractors were favourably received and the battery reported, 'the tractors have great possibilities. They have ample power and are very inconspicuous. The first ones though, suffer from defects of design, great difficulty in changing gears and a tendency to skid when braked with a gun behind. All who have seen them are favourably impressed but they appear to be costly.' During September, the battery took part in manoeuvres with the 2nd Cavalry Brigade and it was reported that, 'the Battery was a remarkably handy and flexible fire unit, the R/T conferring powers of support impossible hitherto. There is less need for movement of the guns on the battlefield and consequently there is greater continuity of support and more concentration of fire power.'

Training continued throughout 1932 with the Light Dragons Mark I (as the 2-ton tractor was now known) being trialled with various combinations of trailers, Austin Sevens and motorcycles, to arrive at the best organisation for the Battery Staff. The two-wheeled trailer was replaced by a four-wheeled version with wire wheels and a folding hood, rather reminiscent of an overgrown perambulator. This was used to carry four Battery Staff personnel and equipment and was towed behind one of the Battery Staff Dragons. The No 1 wireless sets were carried in the Austin Sevens.

Four of the Light Dragons Mark I were retained at MWEE as trials vehicles and experiments were carried out to

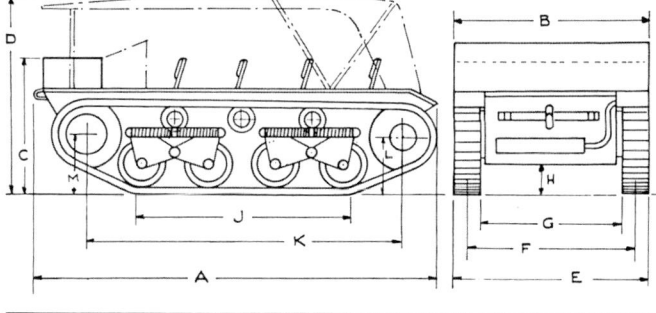

Data sheet for the Dragon, Light Mark I.

MOVING THE GUNS

determine the best combinations of springs in the suspension, and of various types of track.

The 3-Ton Tractor and the Vickers Tractor Truck

It is worth digressing at this point to describe two further vehicles that form part of the Light Dragon story. Vickers-Armstrong also produced a heavier and more powerful version of the 2-ton tractor, known as the 3-ton tractor. It appears to have been produced as a contender to General Staff Specification B3, its rivals being the 3-ton Kégresse half-tracks produced by Crossley and Burford, the latter being accepted for service. Under the designation B3E3, the vehicle was fitted with a high-sided steel body giving protected seating for six men. It was fitted with the same Meadows engine developing greater tractive effort through increased gear reduction and strengthened tracks and suspension. The vehicle was delivered in early July 1930 and subjected to comparative trials with the 2-ton tractor during 1931 and 1932. In 1931, the Mechanisation Board reported that comparative trials had not established any marked superiority in the 3-ton tractor's performance and that its suspension was markedly inferior. It was also found that there were weaknesses in the hull and that constant adjustments were needed to the steering mechanism. In 1932, it was decided to discontinue any further trials with the vehicle.

The Vickers Carden-Loyd Tractor Truck was a commercial design using a 30cwt lorry body fitted to a full-tracked chassis based on the 2-ton tractor. Three vehicles were purchased by the Army and were trialled by various units in Aldershot and Southern Command to test their suitability as first-line transport vehicles for tank battalions. They were never intended for artillery use, although photographs do exist of one vehicle being used to tow an 18pdr gun on an 'Egypt pattern' undercarriage. There were problems with the suspension and the vehicle tended to slew when turning with a trailed load attached. The vehicles never went beyond the trials stage and no more were ordered from Vickers.

The Light Dragon Mark IA

In February 1932, a contract was placed with Vickers-Armstrong for the supply

B3E3, the experimental 3-ton tractor built by Vickers-Armstrong was also similar to the Artillery Observer's vehicle, but the driver was positioned in the centre.

of four improved-design tractors, which became known as the Light Dragon Mark IA. The design, which featured a high-sided body with modified seating and locker arrangements that had been foreshadowed, late in 1931, by the conversion of one of the original Mark Is (D898) to approximately the same appearance. The redesigned body had seating for seven men including the driver, and the new model featured the Wilson epicyclic transmission and front axles similar to those fitted to the latest pattern of Light Tank. Twin levers replaced the unpopular steering tillers fitted to the earlier models. Three of these new pattern tractors were issued to 76 Battery of 9th Field Brigade in June 1932 and one was retained at MWEE for trials on an improved oil-cooling system.

The Light Dragon Mark II

In June 1932, an order was placed with the Royal Ordnance Factory for 14 new Light Dragons (increased to 15 in September) and in August, 26 were ordered from Vickers-Armstrong. The Vickers machines were designated Light Dragons Mark II while the ROF version became the Mark IIA. They were similar to the Mark IA but had a number of improvements and modifications. The Meadows EPT six-cylinder engine was fitted, with twin Zenith carburettors, and the latest design of Wilson epicyclic pre-selector gearbox.

The only major difference between the two marks lay in the design of the steering levers. On the Mark II they were fitted with a pawl device, which locked them in the 'on' position for parking, with a button release on the head of each lever. On the Mark IIA and all subsequent models, the pawls were eliminated in favour of a separate handbrake lever.

A Mark IIB model appeared in 1933 with 31 being ordered from Vickers-Armstrong and 21 from the Royal

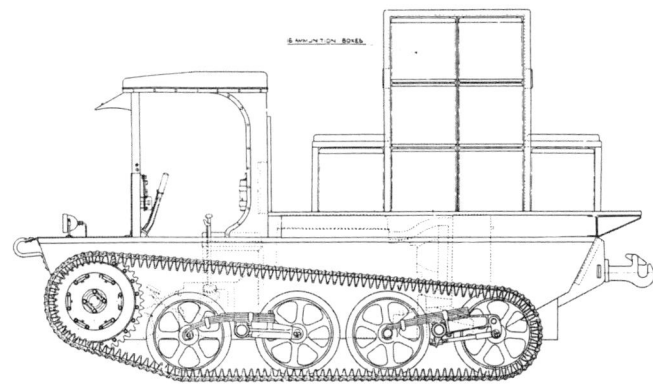

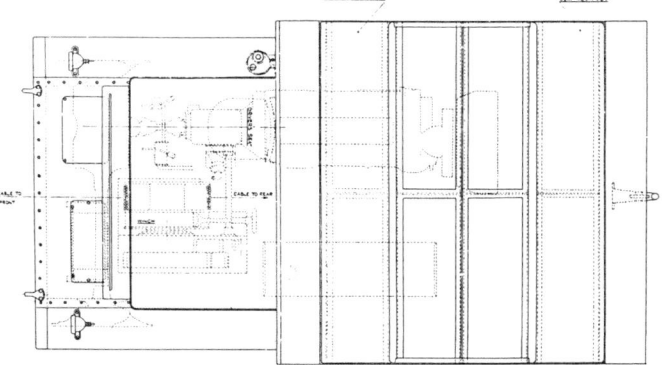

A drawing by Vickers showing the Tractor Truck adapted for use by an artillery unit, with seats for nine men and stowage for sixteen boxes of ammunition.

This 18pdr is protected by a timber cover over the breech. It is riding on the pneumatic-tyre 'Egypt' carriage, towed by a Vickers Tractor Truck. Although they enjoyed some commercial success, these little vehicles were not judged suitable for service use.

MOVING THE GUNS

A Mark I Light Dragon was fitted with a high-sided body and revised seating arrangements. In this form it served as the prototype for the Marks IA and II models.

Ordnance Factory. The main difference was the fitting of an improved pattern of Vickers angled double-spring suspension. The original Horstmann type, with its bell crank arms and horizontal springs, was found to be very susceptible to wear caused by the ingress of mud and dust. Captain Payne, an expert in engine cooling was called in by MWEE to design an improved cooling system. As a result, radiators were fitted with pressure vacuum-release valves, which pressurised the system and made it more efficient, especially in hot conditions. The standard oil cooler fitted to all Light Tanks was also fitted to the new pattern Dragons. The side plates of the vehicles, designed with economy of weight in mind, were found to distort badly around the front cross-shaft and at the return roller locations. The front of the hull was reinforced to deal with the cross-shaft problem and small triangular plates were bolted to the sides of the vehicles to support the outer ends of the top roller spindles. These plates were retrospectively fitted to all marks in due course. The 10½in cast manganese tracks were replaced with 9½in-wide malleable cast steel tracks and moulded rubber track guards were fitted to the rear of each vehicle. Fittings were also provided to accept cable-reeling gear that permitted the Dragon to lay and recover the telephone cable used on the gun position. Some difficulty was experienced with the hand-cranking starting device at the rear of the Dragon since it was necessary to unhitch the limber or gun to gain access

A Light Dragon Mark IA of 28 Battery, 9th Field Brigade, about to move off with an 18pdr and limber in tow.

5 FIELD ARTILLERY - CONSOLIDATION, 1930-39

to the starting lug and an attempt was made to design an internal hand-starting device.

The steadily increasing number of tractors produced reflects the decision to mechanise increasing numbers of regular Artillery Brigades from 1935 onwards as the government implemented its policy of rearmament in the face of increasing German militarism. Mark II series Dragons were issued to 20 Battery of 9th Field Brigade in April 1934 and took part in the 7th Infantry Brigade exercises, which ranged from Gloucester to Salisbury in September. The battery commented that the performance of the vehicles was very good, although there was obviously still a problem with the steering mechanism.

No 76 Battery of 9th Field Brigade started to receive Light Dragons from April 1932 in place of the Burford-Kégresse half-tracks. A Mark I Battery Staff Dragon was joined by four Mark IAs in May, three of which were distributed to the gun sections and one to the Battery Staff. In the following year, there was a further issue of four Mark IIs so that when the battery went to Practice Camp at West Down in May 1933, the vehicle establishment was:

- 4 two-seater Austin Sevens
- 6 Light Dragons
  (4 gun, 2 ammunition)
- 3 staff cars
- 3 motorcycles
- 3 Crossley 30cwt lorries
- 1 Crossley 3-ton lorry

It is also recorded that the battery had three experimental wireless sets on issue together with the new 0–360° dial sights for guns and directors. In October 1933, the remaining Marks I and IA Dragons were returned to Woolwich for upgrading and modification, including the fitting of Wilson gearboxes as fitted on the Mark II series. The new models were issued from February 1934 onwards in time for the Southern Command exercises.

The 9th Field Brigade formed part of the 'Westland' mobile force, which was the largest mechanised formation ever assembled and consisted of:

1st Tank Brigade:
- formed by three Mixed Battalions and one Light Battalion RTC.

7th Infantry Brigade, comprising:
- 1st Bn Royal Welsh Fusiliers
- 2nd Bn The Loyal Regiment
- 1st Bn King's Own Yorkshire Light Infantry
- The 11th Hussars in armoured cars
- 9th Field Brigade RA with three 18pdr batteries and one 4.5in howitzer battery.
- Plus, supporting services.

In what became known as the Battle of Hungerford Bridge, 9th Field Brigade took part in an operation to secure bridges over the River Kennet. A lot of valuable experience was gained during the exercise of long marches with mechanised forces, the longest being 90 miles in one day.

In the 10th Field Brigade the issue of the Light Dragons began in March 1933 with the receipt of the first two

A Light Dragon Mark II, with all its weatherproof covers in place, photographed at the Vickers-Armstrong works at Newcastle. The Mark IIA was virtually identical.

Light Dragons Mark IIB, IIC and IID featured another new type of suspension designed by Horstmann, which employed sloping springs. BMM66 was a Mark IIC and the picture also shows the shield fitted over the exhaust pipe and the external brackets that supported the spindles of the return rollers.

Light Dragons Mark II. By early April, 30 Battery was up to strength with eight Light Dragons, six for the guns and two for Battery Staff. In 51 Battery the issue of Light Dragons began in March 1934 and by June the battery was up to full vehicle strength. The 54 Battery received its complement of Light Dragons in February and March 1934 in place of the Guy and Thornycroft portées. The Light Dragons remained with the batteries until 1936 when they were gradually replaced by the new Morris Commercial CDSW 6 x 4 gun tractors.

The Light Dragon was a popular vehicle with the detachments, its only major problem was the peculiarity of the differential steering mechanism, which tended to oversteer when braking downhill. In 1933, the Battery Commander of 30 Battery reported, 'After one year's work with the Light Dragons it is quite apparent that, with a few minor alterations, its adoption as the universal light artillery tractor is well justified. The chief drawback at present is the tendency of the gun to overrun the vehicle going downhill. This has caused a few nasty skids on macadam roads with some damage to equipment. All the drivers, experienced as they are, slow down to between 5 and 8mph going downhill. This is very exasperating from the Battery Commander's point of view, but understandable to anyone who has seen one of these overrun skids.' The problem was compounded by the fact that the gun carriages were not fitted, at this time, with any type of vehicle actuated overrun brakes.

A gunner who served in 54 Battery at this time recalls a Light Dragon going out of control in Exeter, on the way to Practice Camp at Okehampton, which nearly ended up in the River Exe. The local press recorded a similar incident on the same journey when a Light Dragon finished up in the front of a wine and spirit shop in South Street, Exeter. These tracked vehicles were a novelty to the civilian population at the time and were variously described as 'War Machines' or 'Tanks'. The ability of the vehicle to turn around on the spot apparently dumbfounded a local Devon police constable who had laboriously mapped out an alternative route for a battery that had taken a wrong turning, only to find the tractors could easily turn in the width of the lane and continue their journey.

Modifications to existing vehicles and the introduction of new marks continued throughout the life of the Dragons. In 1935 it was reported by the Mechanical Warfare Board that the existing Marks I to IIB were giving satisfactory service and that the majority had completed approximately 1,000 miles each, without appreciable mechanical trouble. Earlier models were being brought up-to-date and attempts were being made to improve the design of the bearings in the final-drive reduction gears, which had been giving trouble. The design of a satisfactory internal starting handle was finally abandoned, and the exhaust pipe on the outside of the hull was re-positioned to prevent it overheating the petrol tank situated immediately behind.

In 1934, orders were placed for Mark IIC vehicles, 60 from the Royal Ordnance Factory and 25 from Vickers-Armstrong, of which eight were destined for the Defence Force of the Union of South Africa. On this model a single Solex downdraught carburettor replaced the twin Zeniths, a Vokes pattern panel air-cleaner replaced the AC type and an improved design of induction manifold was fitted as standard. The exhaust pipe was again repositioned and fitted with a ventilated guard and vacuum servo brakes were adopted. At first the change of carburettor failed to produce the anticipated improvement in performance until a minute difference was discovered in the internal diameter of the induction pipe. When this was rectified it resulted in a marked increase in power and performance along with a decrease in fuel consumption.

In 1935, the Mark IID was introduced. It was essentially the same as the IIC, except that two-piece hinged brake shoes were fitted, giving greater braking efficiency and ease of adjustment. To prevent overcooling and wear on the engine in cold weather, a thermostatic control was provided for the cooling system. One hundred vehicles of this Mark were ordered from the Royal Ordnance Factory and 57 from Vickers-Armstrong of which 12 are believed to have gone to India, the orders being placed between April and June 1935. This was the last variant of the Light Dragon Mark II series produced and, by 1937, there were 339 vehicles of

A Light Dragon Mark IIC serving in its later role as a tractor for the new 2pdr anti-tank gun.

A view that shows the seating arrangements in a Light Dragon; a Mark IID in this case. In all these later models the headlamps were built into the front of the hull where they were less vulnerable.

all marks in service use. Despite the introduction of the Mark III Light Dragon from 1936 onwards, and the increasing use of wheeled artillery tractors, the Marks I and II Light Dragon continued to be used by regular artillery batteries. It was the tractor used to tow the 3.7in howitzers when the brigades of the RHA mechanised in 1936.

Trials using Light Dragons Mark IIC were carried out at MWEE during 1938 to test their suitability as tractors for the newly designed 2pdr anti-tank gun. Mark II Dragons went to France with the British Expeditionary Force (BEF) in 1939 and were mainly used to tow the guns of the recently formed Anti-Tank Brigades.

The Light Dragon Mark III

Despite the satisfactory performance of the Mark I and II Light Dragons they were thought to be somewhat costly and, as the mechanisation of the Royal Artillery gained momentum after 1935, there was felt to be a need for a cheaper and simpler version. In December 1934, Vickers-Armstrong had demonstrated a new design of light tracked vehicle, which could be used either as a gun tractor or machine-gun carrier. In March 1935, a contract was placed for an artillery tractor having a mild steel plate body, seating for seven men including the driver, and provision for battery staff equipment and a Lewis gun.

The vehicle incorporated a number of novel features, although it was based largely on standard commercial components. The engine was a Ford V8 rated at 81 bhp and mounted centrally in the hull with a radiator at the front just behind the driver. Drive was taken through a standard Ford truck gearbox giving four forward and one reverse speeds to the driving axle, which was also a standard Ford commercial component, mounted at the rear. The suspension consisted of one-and-a-half pairs of Vickers light double-spring-type bogies on each side with a single return roller mounted above the front bogie. Track adjustment was carried out using the front idler wheels, and the tracks

The prototype vehicle for what became the Light Dragon Mark III. Powered by a Ford V8 engine, driving to a rear sprocket, this new Vickers design displayed another change in the suspension arrangement. Just visible at the front is the steering wheel that replaced the levers used on earlier models.

were the same malleable cast-iron type as fitted to the previous marks of carrier and light tank. Perhaps the most novel innovation was the method of steering where the initial movement of the steering wheel, which now replaced the conventional levers, caused the front cross-shaft to move laterally, carrying the main bogies with it. This permitted a small degree of steering, sufficient to correct small deviations from course, without having to apply the brakes. Further turning of the wheel brought brakes into play on the differential for tighter turns. Provision was also made on the vehicle for the fitting of a vacuum servo brake system to connect with a braked trailer or gun carriage whose design was also under consideration at this time.

The prototype was capable of average speeds of 18mph on roads and 16mph across country and could achieve a maximum of 30mph towing a gun and limber. It was considerably lighter than its predecessors, weighing only 3.4 tons fully laden against the 4.15 tons of the Mark IIs. There was room for one crewman alongside the driver, while the remainder sat on either side of the engine facing inwards.

It is recorded that this vehicle was sent to 30 Battery of the 10th Field Brigade in December 1935 for one month's trial and, in all, the prototype completed 2,625 miles before being dismantled for examination. Generally, there was very little that needed improvement, an exhaust manifold needed rerouting to improve oil cooling and there was a tendency for the rubber tyres to become detached from the rims of the bogie wheels. A requirement was also expressed for a sprung pattern of towing hook. The combined steering and braking system led to a tendency to slew when braking on a bend so a fully compensated linkage was designed for the brakes, independent of the steering system. An order was placed for 28

A production version of the Light Dragon Mark III with its canopy rigged. Notice the protected housings for the headlamps and the little 'aero' windscreens for the driver and front crew member.

vehicles, later increased to 69, with Vickers-Armstrong in April 1936 and a further order for 50 with the Royal Ordnance Factory.

During 1937, a further 48 vehicles were issued to units and all were fitted with Solex carburettors, resulting in improved economy and performance. In the same year, a Light Dragon Mark III was sent to Canada to undertake trials in the snow and mud. There it was found necessary to fit special angle-iron spuds to the tracks to improve traction and for a scraper to clear packed snow from the sprockets and brake drums. This was an interesting early introduction of the vehicle into Canada in view of the fact that Canadian industry became the largest volume producer, during the Second World War, of the Dragon's progeny, the Universal Carrier. One Light Dragon Mark III was also supplied to Australia.

During the year experiments were carried out raising the idler wheel by five inches. This was a modification that had already been carried out successfully on the machine-gun carrier and resulted in a much-improved cross-country performance. It was found that there was no appreciable difference in the

Dragon's performance when it was towing a gun, but when it was running alone there was a marked increase in speed and the risk of the front idlers striking the ground was reduced.

After 1938, no more Mark IIIs were ordered as the emphasis switched to the production of 6 x 4 and 4 x 4 wheeled artillery tractors and, apart from the production of some self-propelled guns and support vehicles during the war it ended the Artillery's involvement with tracked vehicles for the time being. The other development from the prototype Vickers tractor was the Universal Carrier, which proved to be one of the most versatile vehicles of the war. There was one specific variant, the Artillery Observation Post Carrier, which was produced without the normal weapon mounting but modified to carry observation-post personnel and equipment. These carriers operated as OP vehicles with armoured and mechanised infantry formations throughout the Second World War.

The 6 x 4 and 4 x 4 field artillery tractors

The final thread in the story of field artillery tractor development concerns the 6 x 4 and 4 x 4 tractors, which appeared in the late 1930s, and in the case of the 4 x 4 tractor, it was the most prolific type of tractor used during the Second World War. The development history of the wheeled tractors is particularly interesting because in many ways it mirrors both the changes and developments in commercial vehicle design during the period, and also the changes in government defence policy and the interaction between the two.

Of the two main contenders in the race to produce a satisfactory cross-country vehicle, it was the 4 x 4 tractor that was first off the starting blocks, and which eventually became the winner. However, for much of the race, the 6 x 4 tractor was the favourite and looked to be first to the winning post. As has already been described, four-wheel-drive vehicles were produced during the First World War, although these were strictly of American design and manufacture. Following the failure of the 1922 tractor trials to produce anything remotely suitable for Army use, a small group of RASC officers, working largely on their own initiative and with little outside encouragement, set to work to produce an effective four-wheel-drive tractor. The requirement seemed to be based, not so much on the specific need for an artillery tractor, but on a more general need to have a tractor capable of towing various items of specialised equipment such as water sterilisers, laboratories, workshops and the semi-mobile, anti-aircraft guns into forward areas off metalled roads. Such loads were likely to be in excess of five tons.

There was no problem designing a tractor with sufficient power to meet this requirement, and a new factor that had emerged since the end of the First World War was the large-section pneumatic tyre. The iron- or steel-spoked wheels with solid rubber or metal tyres, used hitherto, were not only heavy in themselves but also required strongly built chassis because of the lack of resilience in the wheels. The advent of the pneumatic tyre meant a lighter chassis, greater load carrying capacity, less fatigue for the crew and, most importantly, improved traction in rough going.

The Hathi 4 x 4 artillery tractor

In 1922, the RASC Experimental Department at Aldershot produced an experimental tractor made up from components of captured German tractors and vehicles stored in Aldershot. The resultant vehicle, known as the 'Hathi' (from the Hindustani for an elephant) was no beauty, but as a concept was far ahead of its time. The cross-country performance of this vehicle so far exceeded expectations that a specification was drawn up, in October 1923, for the production of a commercial version of the vehicle. The specification required a brake horsepower of not less than 80, a winch with a capacity of 5 tons, the ability to tow a trailed load of 5 tons up a 1-in-4 gradient, the ability to stop and start on a 1-in-5 gradient, and to be able to maintain an average speed of 22mph over 2 hours. A high ground clearance was required of at least 10in beneath the axles, and 20in beneath the remainder of the vehicle, yet the overall height of the vehicle had to be kept low to make it inconspicuous. The required turning circle of 55ft demanded a short wheelbase, yet the need to negotiate ditches and climb banks meant that the vehicle-frame overhang at the front had to be kept to a minimum. On top of all this, the total weight of the vehicle was not to exceed 5 tons. To meet all these conflicting requirements, and produce a satisfactory tractor would be most engineer's idea of a nightmare, and it is entirely to the credit of Thornycroft, who won the War Department contract, that they produced a remarkable vehicle. Twenty-four were delivered, and the first was demonstrated at trials in October 1924. The curious dumpy appearance of the vehicle was an inevitable result of the design requirements.

The engine was a Thornycroft GB6 6-cylinder unit, which developed 90bhp. The vehicle exhibited a number of novel features, extensive use being made of aluminium castings to save weight. The draw-bar arrangement was of a design that later became a standard fitting on most War Department vehicles, having a number of transverse laminated leaf springs with the draw hook bolted to the centre. The ends of the springs were attached to the main longitudinal chassis members, which took the majority of the pulling effort and the leaf springs had the effect of cushioning the jolts and jars from the trailed load. The Hathi had permanently engaged four-wheel-drive, which necessitated a design of front-axle final drive, capable of steering while remaining waterproof. This vehicle was the first to use wheel scotches, which were attached to the frame and used during winching operations to transmit the reactive force directly to the chassis rather than through the wheels, axles and suspension. The system was developed by the RASC Experimental Department, and later became a standard feature on most military winch vehicles.

A Thornycroft Hathi tractor during cross-country trials at Wool. It is numbered in the RASC series and fitted with twin sets of wheels all round, to take the overall chains that aid traction in the mud.

MOVING THE GUNS

The Hathis were trialled extensively in Britain as well as in South Africa, Australia and India. A photograph exists of one undergoing trials in Malta attempting to haul two 60pdr guns (combined weight of 248cwt) of 4th Medium Battery up Madelina Hill in Malta in 1927 – and not succeeding! Largely because of its high tractive power, the Hathi was used as a tractor for the AA Brigades, towing the 3pdr 20cwt AA on its travelling platform.

Despite its initial promise, the concept of a four-wheel-drive tractor did not progress at this stage, possibly because in 1927, responsibility for the development of mechanical vehicles passed from the Quarter Master General's Department, which supervised the RASC developments, to the Master General of the Ordnance Department, who were more concerned with developments emanating from ROF Woolwich, and MWEE at Farnborough. It may be that this resulted in a change of direction in favour of the current interest in half-track and full-track vehicles at the expense of the wheeled 4 x 4s.

However, there was one late development of the Hathi, which provides a convenient link with the parallel development of the 6 x 4 tractors. In an article in the *Automobile Engineer* in October 1928 on the Hathi tractor, it was mentioned that the RASC Experimental Department was working on a six-wheeled version, which necessitated a complete redesign of the chassis. However, the combination of six-wheel drive, together with the ability to fit overall tracks to the rear bogie, heralded a tractor of considerable promise. Such a vehicle was produced by P Company RASC, and it was sent for trials at MWEE in May 1928 with the trials number of 100. The vehicle was fitted with double wheels all round to enable the overall tracks to be fitted to the rear wheels and chains to the front wheels.

Unfortunately, the arrival of the 6 x 6 Hathi coincided with the successful development of the WD patented tandem rear bogie, which enabled 6 x 4 vehicles to be produced on commercial chassis at relatively low cost.

It was this development that led to the family of military 6 x 4 vehicles, variants of which were used both as artillery tractors and battery staff vehicles.

6 x 4 vehicle developments

The original development of this type of vehicle was a result once again of the pioneering efforts of the staff of the RASC Experimental Department at Aldershot. Initial interest was kindled by the French Renault 6 x 4 vehicle, which undertook a Trans-Sahara expedition

The six-wheel drive Hathi under test with the Royal Marines. It is also fitted with overall chains wrapped around twin wheels on each axle, which it probably needs to haul a piece of medium artillery in these conditions.

at much the same time as the Citroën-Kégresse crossings. The achievements of the wheeled vehicles attracted rather less publicity than the half-tracks, but were of more long-term interest from the military point of view. Owing to the small-scale production of vehicles necessary for military use, it was an inescapable fact that the only way of producing a vehicle suitable for military application was to ensure that there was also a civilian market for it. While the advocates of the half- and fully-tracked solutions pressed on in the hope that a market for such vehicles would develop in the colonies, the wheeled enthusiasts, perhaps more realistically, concluded that more civilian interest would be generated in the cheaper 6 x 4 vehicle.

The principle designers working on the 6 x 4 solution were Colonel Niblett and Captain C.H. Kuhne, both of the RASC. Working with a very limited budget and against a certain amount of official lack of interest, these enthusiasts took the original Renault design of a double rear axle and modified and improved it to produce what became the War Department patented tandem rear bogie. By 1925 the work of this small band of enthusiasts was being taken rather more seriously, and the Mechanical Transport Advisory Board decided that, for the bulk of the Army's transport, the 6 x 4 design was the answer. Consequently, provisional specifications were drawn up in 1925 for a light 6 x 4 vehicle in the 30cwt class and a medium vehicle in the 3-ton class. The specifications were drawn up with the active participation of a number of leading manufacturers, who no doubt saw the potential of a future military market. The final specifications were produced in 1927 and were drafted in the form of what would now be known as a performance specification. In other words, the specifications did not lay down how a particular performance was to be met, rather it defined the desired performance and left the manufacturer to design his own solution to the problem. Anxious to ensure that sufficient of these types of vehicle would be available in an emergency, the War Office firmly extended the existing and very effective subsidy scheme on 30cwt 4 x 2 vehicles to cover the new classes. Also, it made freely available various patented designs, notably the double rear-axle final drive.

There were a number of dissenting voices to this general policy, however. The major setback to the scheme, which became increasingly obvious as few commercial manufacturers took up the 6 x 4 option, was that the military vehicle requirement was out of line with that of the civilian operator. Firstly, few civilian operators required vehicles with the same degree of cross-country mobility as the Army. Secondly, the civilian vehicle taxation system operated against the type of vehicle the Army was attempting to promote. The Treasury Rating formula used to calculate the horsepower on which the tax was rated penalised larger engines, and although the tax did not directly apply to commercial vehicles, it certainly had an influence on the size of engines manufactured in this country, compared to the rest of Europe and the United States. In the main, commercial operators wanted vehicles that were light and therefore cheap to operate in relation to their payload. The second driven rear axle required by the military was at odds with this principle.

By 1927, there was a clear understanding by the Mechanical Transport Advisory Board of the need to harmonise with civilian requirements:

> 'The War Department realise to the full, its dependence on commercial resources, in respect both of the existing vehicles, and of the capacity to produce further large numbers in an emergency. The War Office has been guided by one main principle, namely,

MOVING THE GUNS

A Light Dragon Mark II of 30 Battery hauling one of the little four-wheeled Battery Staff trailers.

that vehicles must be of types which can be recommended for commercial use. The War Department may always indicate what it desires but insistence, in specifications for ordinary transport vehicles, on the adoption of new ideas, must always be tempered by a clear realisation of what is commercially practicable at the moment.'

As it became increasingly obvious that the military authorities could neither afford to develop small quantities of specialised vehicles nor to rely on civilian operators to provide the type of vehicle they wanted, they were forced to look for other sources of supply. Even loosening of the tight specifications for the subsidy vehicles in 1932 and the introduction of annual vehicle trials in North Wales did not encourage the production of the required 6 x 4 vehicles. So serious was the potential shortfall in vehicles of the required specification that the Government set up the Crosland Committee in 1934 to investigate to what extent civilian pattern 4 x 2 vehicles could replace 3-ton 6 x 4s. The main conclusion of the Crosland Committee was that over 50 per cent of the stated requirements for six-wheelers could be replaced by 4 x 2 vehicles obtained by impressment and hiring of vehicles on mobilisation. The findings of the Crosland Committee happened to coincide with a move away from the so-called Eastern Plan with its emphasis on the defence of Colonial interests in India and the Middle East to the Western Plan, which envisaged an Expeditionary Force being sent to mainland Europe.

The Crosland Committee did not discuss the necessity for specially designed vehicles for specific roles – which goes some way to explain the decision taken in 1936 to adopt a 6 x 4 Field Artillery tractor at the same time that the remainder of the Army was moving away from the 6 x 4 option towards the 4 x 2 and 4 x 4 vehicles. However, before moving on to consider the circumstances that led to the adoption of the 6 x 4 tractor, it is necessary to review briefly the various 6 x 4 vehicles used by the Artillery during its earlier period. They were employed in two roles – as gun tractors or as Battery Staff vehicles.

The Morris Commercial D type 6 x 4 gun tractor

Morris Commercial Motors were the principle suppliers of 6 x 4 vehicles in the 30cwt class using the WD patent rear bogie. Their D Type vehicle, introduced in 1928 and designed to meet the requirements of the 1928 subsidy scheme, was extensively trialled as a gun tractor. Before the advent of reliable low-pressure pneumatic tyres, the performance of the wheeled tractor was markedly inferior to the full-tracked and half-tracked tractors being evaluated at the same time. However, it was considerably cheaper than the specially designed vehicles and was eventually chosen as a suitable vehicle to be used as a gun tractor by the Territorial Army, both in its normal-control and forward-control versions.

The D Type eventually gave rise to the 'CD' Type chassis, which was used as the basis of the 6 x 4 Field Artillery

Tractor described later. D Types used in British service had standard pattern cargo bodies. The Indian Government, however, produced a number of D Type tractors fitted with special artillery tractor bodies with equipment storage and crew seating.

Battery Staff vehicles
The Gunners had a particular requirement for vehicles capable of carrying the Battery Staff personnel. These were the Command Post Officer and his staff of assistants and signallers, and the Observation Post staff consisting in the early years of the Battery Commander and his assistant, range finders and signallers. Between them, these personnel carried a considerable quantity of equipment and the problem was to find a suitable vehicle able to carry the necessary equipment and personnel across country, fast enough to arrive in advance of the rest of the battery, yet inconspicuous enough to be able to be used close to an observation post.

Various vehicles were tried, some of which have already been described.

One of the famous Morris Commercial D Type six-wheel staff cars carries King George V as he reviews a Dragon-hauled battery of 60pdrs.

The Citroën-Kégresse half-track Battery Staff car was rejected because it was too small and too slow, and the Crossley-Kégresse version disappeared when half-tracks went out of fashion in the early 1930s. Austin Seven and Ten, and Morris Eight 4 x 2 cars were tried and found to be lacking in space and cross-country performance.

In 1928, one vehicle each from Morris and Crossley was ordered for trials with a special Battery Staff body fitted to their standard commercial 30cwt 6 x 4 chassis. In 1930, seven Crossleys were purchased and used in service by

Based on a semi-forward control version of the Crossley BGV2 30cwt chassis, these big battery staff cars were also supplied to the Canadian Army.

MOVING THE GUNS

9th and 10th Field Brigades. A further batch of six was ordered in November 1930, fitted with a new gearbox and a different size of low-pressure tyre. A final total of 26 vehicles were in service in 1931.

A similar batch of Morris Commercial vehicles based on the D Type chassis was ordered in 1930, and a further batch in 1931 with a larger 17bhp engine. By 1930, however, it was felt that the vehicles might prove too bulky and conspicuous and that future developments were likely to be in the direction of a battery staff vehicle based on the Carden-Loyd (Vickers) 2-ton tractor. Of the two types of vehicle, the Morris was found to be more reliable and the Crossley staff car was eventually abandoned.

The D Type Morris Commercial Battery Staff Car was replaced in 1936 by a version based on the CD 30cwt chassis. This elegant looking vehicle with its canvas canopy was known as the 'prairie schooner' and a large number of these vehicles went to France with BEF in 1939.

The Morris Commercial 6 x 4 CDSW field artillery tractor

The requirement for a wheeled artillery tractor came about with the realisation in 1934 that, to meet the rapid expansion of the artillery likely to occur during an emergency, it would be necessary to supplement the existing tracked tractors with wheeled vehicles, which could be produced in a much shorter time and more cheaply than the Dragons. The recent development of the wide-section, low-pressure tyre, with a cross-country tread (a development, incidentally, for which the Army was almost entirely responsible) meant that wheeled tractors with a good power-to-weight ratio and tractive effort could produce a cross-country performance as good as a tracked vehicle in all but the most severe conditions. To cope with these conditions, it was proposed to retain a small number of Dragons in each battery.

During the autumn of 1934, trials were carried out on a variety of vehicles to test their suitability for this role. At the trials in November it is recorded that the following vehicles, some military and some civilian, took part:

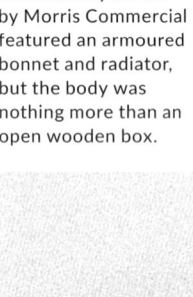

The prototype CDSW field artillery tractor by Morris Commercial featured an armoured bonnet and radiator, but the body was nothing more than an open wooden box.

106

- Leyland Terrier 3-ton 6 x 4
- Morris JB6 3-ton 4 x 2
- Morris CS 3-ton 4 x 2
- Thornycroft EE/SC6 3-ton 4 x 2
- Morris CD 30cwt 6 x 4, with winch
- Morris C 30cwt 4 x 2
- Leyland KG2 30cwt 4 x 2
- Morris CS8T 15cwt, with winch
- Morris CS8T 15cwt, without winch.

Each vehicle towed an 18pdr gun and limber, and carried various loads in the rear of the vehicle. At an early stage in the trial the performance of the lighter vehicles was so promising that the more conspicuous 3-ton vehicles were eliminated from further trials.

In December, the second trial was held at Farnborough and was watched by the CIGS and his staff. A cross-country course was devised with various obstacles whose difficulty was increased by torrential rainfall in the week preceding the trials. Results of the trials were quite promising. The Morris vehicles fitted with winches were able to extricate themselves from situations where the other vehicles floundered, but the low position of the radiator on the Morrises presented a problem and the cooling fan tended to throw water all over the engine.

The conclusions reached from the trials were that a gun tractor with a fair performance was possible from a commercial vehicle similar to those tested; the performance of the 6 x 4-type tractor was superior, especially when fitted with overall chains on the rear wheels; the inconspicuous Morris truck was particularly well suited to the role; a ground anchor and winch with fore and aft paying out leads was essential; it was desirable to dispense with the limber and carry the ammunition in the vehicle; and finally, the promise of pneumatic tyres on the gun carriages and brakes operated by the towing vehicle would greatly improve the cross-country performance of the vehicle and gun.

As a result of the trials, a design was produced for a six-wheeled tractor to be made by Morris Commercial using their CD 30cwt chassis. The prototype had an angular, lightly armoured front similar to that fitted to the Morris scout vehicle and a standard wooden cargo body. Twelve of these were produced and delivered in June 1935 for trials with 32nd Field Brigade stationed at Deepcut.

The vehicle was built, as far as possible, from standard Morris Commercial components. The engine used was a 3.49 litre six-cylinder engine, which developed 70.5bhp at 3,250rpm. It had a five-speed gearbox and drive was transmitted through the Morris Commercial patented worm-driven rear-axle assembly. The vehicle achieved a creditable power-to-weight ratio of 13.9bhp/ton and was capable of carrying a load of two tons, although the actual weight of crew and equipment was only one ton. This reduced the adhesion of the rear axle but nonetheless it was found unnecessary to carry additional ballast.

MOVING THE GUNS

A production version of the CDSW, serving with 8 Battery, 13th Field Brigade in 1937, shows the final design of artillery tractor body, and the unarmoured front end.

Comparative trials were held at MWEE against a Morris Commercial CS8T 15cwt truck and a standard Morris Commercial CD 30cwt 6 x 4 lorry, both fitted with winches, and the tractor was found to have a far superior performance. The field trials conducted by 32nd Field Brigade showed few problems though the low-slung radiator still gave ground clearance problems and was modified in the same manner as the CS8T truck. A demonstration was given at Farnborough in November in front of the CIGS when the tractor was pitted against a Light Dragon Mark IIC and a Light Dragon Mark III (Vickers).

The field trials were so satisfactory that a contract was placed in 1936 for a quantity of the new 'Tractor six-wheeled Field Artillery Mark 1/L (Morris Commercial)' as it was known officially, though later it came to become known as the 'Tractor Field Artillery 6 x 4 Morris Commercial CDSW'. The vehicle as finally produced had a specially designed body with the standard and characteristic Morris Commercial design of 'front end', and an open body with crew seating and lockers for the stowage of gun stores and equipment and the overall chains for the rear wheels. Despite recommendations to the contrary, there was no ammunition stowage on the vehicle and a limber was towed behind. The insistence on the retention of the limber was a peculiar British trait, which it is difficult to justify. The advantage was that the gun detachment had a considerable supply of 'ready' ammunition available on the gun position while the tractors could be parked safely elsewhere out of sight and danger. Also, the limber ensured that a larger total quantity of ammunition could be carried by each sub-section. Against this was the disadvantage of an increased trailed load, which affected the vehicle's performance. Also, the combination of gun and limber made manoeuvrability more difficult and reversing practically impossible unless the gun and limber were unhitched and manhandled. It may simply have been retained through conservatism because the use of the limber persisted almost exclusively in the British and Commonwealth armies until late into the Second World War when the Type 5 Bodied Morris Commercial Quad appeared, which was specially designed to carry ammunition on the tractor. The CDSW had an overall canvas hood supported by metal hoops. The cover was invariably left off the CDSW tractors supplied for use in India, earning them the nickname 'toast racks' from the shape of the supporting hoops.

The relatively large-scale production of CDSW tractors after 1936 (306 by the end of 1937) led to the production of the Mk IID Light Dragons being stopped in the same year and the final issue of Mark III Light Dragons in 1937. Thus, in the period up to the beginning of the Second World War, the Artillery was beginning to find itself with an increasing variety of gun tractors, wheeled and tracked, a situation compounded further by the advent of the 4 x 4 artillery tractors in 1938.

Before dealing with the 4 x 4 tractors, however, it is worth recording that there was one serious competitor to the Morris Commercial CDSW, which showed considerable promise but which did not, in the end, come to anything. In 1936, Fordsons produced a six-wheeled tractor from standard Ford components as a possible alternative to the Morris Commercial. The vehicle was fitted with a Unipower four-wheeled rear bogie produced by the Universal Power Drives Ltd. The 3.6-litre Ford V8 engine developed 81.2bhp at 3,750rpm and gave the vehicle a power-to-weight ratio of 18.4bhp/ton. The vehicle was tested against a Morris Commercial CD 30cwt lorry and a CDSW tractor and was found to be faster with a trailed load than either of the other vehicles. There were problems, however, with the cooling system and the types of tyres. In 1939, however, despite having carried out 10,000 miles of trials satisfactorily it was decided not to proceed with the vehicle. Presumably, the reason for this decision was that the Royal Artillery had decided by 1939 to cease production of 6 x 4 tractors in favour of the 4 x 4 Quads and that the Fordson was now obsolete. Another version of the Fordson tractor was fitted with a Sussex-pattern rear bogie and a driven front axle of the American Marmon-Herrington system. This tractor apparently had excellent cross-country performance, although its suspension was judged to be lively. It, too, was abandoned.

The 4 x 4 field artillery tractor

From about 1937 onwards, the military and commercial producers finally came to a conclusion that had been reached by many continental and American producers – and the British military in 1926 – that there was a role for a cross-country vehicle fitted with a forward-drive axle. To be fair, this acceptance did depend on a couple of technical developments – a reliable low-pressure pneumatic tyre with a good cross-country tread and a reliable front-axle final drive, capable of being steered. Nonetheless there appeared to be a marked reluctance on the part of the authorities to even consider this solution.

The impetus probably came from a number of continental designs trialled at MVEE, notably the 'Tempo' four-wheel-drive car from Germany, the Czechoslovakian 'Tatra' and the Alvis Straussler design of transmission originally developed in Austria. There was also the realisation that the 15cwt range of vehicles introduced in larger quantities after 1935 as the primary transport vehicle of the newly mechanised infantry divisions had a creditable cross-country performance even though they were 4 x 2. Finally, there was an acceptance that with the CDSW the British Army had fallen into the all-too-familiar trap of going for the best – a highly specialised vehicle, expensive and relatively difficult to produce.

MOVING THE GUNS

The Guy Quad Ant
4 x 4 field artillery tractor

In 1937 a specification was issued for a four-wheel-drive field-artillery tractor based on a short 4 x 4 chassis. Initially, there were three main contenders – from Commer, Guy and Morris Commercial.

Guy Motors had already produced a four-wheel-drive version of their standard 15cwt 4 x 2 Guy Ant, which was known as the Guy Quad Ant because of its four-wheeled or 'quadruple' drive. This was the general name by which the subsequent family of five types of artillery tractors, regardless of make, came to be known. The Guy Quad Ant was produced as a standard GS vehicle with a cargo body suitable for use as a 'platoon truck' or as a possible tractor for the 2pdr anti-tank gun. It was relatively easy for Guys to adapt this basic vehicle to meet the requirements of the field-artillery tractor specification. The prototype had a wooden body with crew seating in the rear and a projecting locker at the back. The vehicle had an overall canvas hood.

Two prototypes were produced, one with a conventional Meadows petrol engine and the other with a Gardner compression ignition engine. In addition, the compression ignition engine version had steering on all four wheels and was fitted with a winch. The compression ignition version was not pursued and the petrol engine version completed 10,000 miles of trials during 1938. The Mechanisation Board reported, 'General reliability was good, it has a good fording capability and petrol consumption and is the best field artillery tractor of any tested hitherto. The vehicle was also tested in Egypt where its performance was very satisfactory.'

A clue to the origin of the curious 'beetle' shape of the Guy, and other patterns of Quads, is contained in the Mechanisation Board report for 1939, which states, 'to permit of decontamination, an all metal body to the Chief Superintendent of Design's design was fitted, involving an increase in weight of 17cwts'. Thus, the characteristic shape of these vehicles was born of the need to be able to wash down the vehicles to rid them of chemical contamination, such as mustard gas – a very real fear in the pre-war years, which fortunately did not come to pass. It is interesting to note that the field-artillery tractors appear to have been the only vehicles to which a specially designed 'anti-gas' body work was fitted.

One of the prototype Guy Quad Ant field-artillery tractors. The ingenious front-end design allowed the driver's legs to fit alongside the engine, thus permitting the shortest possible wheelbase.

110

The design, which was finally approved featured an all-metal body that provided protection for the crew of six. The vehicle also carried the various gun stores and the sloping rear roof was equipped to carry the spare wheel and, later on, the traversing platform of the 25pdr gun. Thirty-two rounds of ammunition were carried in the new pattern No 27 Artillery Trailer, or limber, which was towed behind the vehicle. An order for 396 of these tractors was placed with Guy Motors and the majority were delivered in time to equip units of the BEF who went to France in 1939 and 1940. Practically all these vehicles were destroyed or abandoned in France and Guy Motors did not produce any further models after 1938 and 1939.

An early production model of the Guy Quad Ant on test by the makers. The characteristic shape of a Quad body – designed to make them easy to wash down after exposure to poison gas – is clearly shown.

The Commer Spider 4 x 4 tractor

The second of the three 4 x 4 tractors was an experimental vehicle produced by Commer in 1936. The engine was a 4.086-litre six-cylinder unit developing 80bhp at 3,100rpm and a power-to-weight ratio of 17.7bhp/ton. It was first tested at Farnborough in October 1936 and the Mechanization Board reported, 'The performance of this vehicle was very good, and was superior to the Morris Commercial six-wheeled field-artillery tractor. With Parson's type non-skid chains, its performance on the slopes of Miles Hill, in bog and wet grass slopes was excellent.' It also reported that braking, cooling and steering required modification to meet WD requirements. One criticism of the vehicle was that it was high and conspicuous as the engine was mounted over the front axle. By 1938, the Commer firm had been absorbed by Karriers and the Karrier 'Spider', as it was then known, was reported as having a performance comparable to the Guy Quad Ant. Karriers went on to produce a 3-ton GS Cargo truck based on this chassis as well as a version with a shorter wheelbase weighing 5 tons. During trials in 1939, the performance of this vehicle was reported to be very good and superior in many respects to that of the Guy Quad Ant. Although it was 'noted as suitable for WD use', the final version – known as the Karrier KT4 Field Artillery Tractor – was never used in British Army service, though a quantity were ordered for use by Indian Army Artillery units.

The Morris Commercial C8 field artillery tractor

The origins of this tractor lay also in a 15cwt 4 x 2 platoon truck, the CS8T, produced in 1934 to meet the requirements for a light truck made

MOVING THE GUNS

The original Morris Commercial Quad, based on an Austrian designed chassis, sports a body that was obviously inspired by the six wheeled CDSW.

as far as possible from commercial assemblies to mechanise the first line transport of infantry divisions. The vehicle was produced as a cheaper replacement for the Tractor Light GS – a fully tracked light utility tractor produced to a Carden-Loyd design. Although the performance during comparative trials was considered to be slightly inferior to the tractor, the initial cost was some 30 per cent less and its general reliability was so vastly superior that maintenance costs were also greatly reduced. It is interesting to note that as early as 1934 this vehicle was being considered as a possible field-artillery tractor.

However, the vehicle which Morris Commercial produced in 1937 as their contender for the new field-artillery tractor specification had totally different origins. It was developed as a result of links that the firm had recently made with the Austrian manufacturer Steyr-Daimler-Puch. Morris Commercial adapted the Daimler design of transmission, which consisted of a central tubular-backbone to the chassis, which carried a propshaft to a centrally mounted gearbox. Individual half-shafts connected to epicyclic final drives at the four wheel stations, each of which had independent suspension. Four-wheel steering was also provided together with an optional choice of four-wheel drive. Trials at MWEE were very satisfactory and the performance was rated better than the CDSW. This vehicle was called by the manufacturers the Morris Commercial Quad. However, as the development story unfolds it will be seen that although the vehicle began life as the potential Morris Commercial Field Artillery Tractor, it did not, in fact, fulfil this role, and the somewhat unconventional chassis became the basis of the prototype Morris Commercial Type Q Light Armoured Car, whereas the vehicle that became the Morris Commercial FAT and was to become known universally as the 'Quad' came from a different source.

Continuation trials in North Wales in 1938 showed that the performance of the original Quad was not as good as the Guy Quad Ant and that there were a number of problems with steering and the transmission. Its independent suspension was rated as excellent though there were problems of wheel adhesion when a wheel lifted to surmount an obstacle. For these reasons the Morris Commercial Quad was abandoned as an artillery tractor but was considered suitable as the basis of an armoured car.

The artillery tractor that was finally approved was built as a four-wheel drive version of the CS8 15cwt truck. At the 1938 trials in North Wales, the vehicle was tested towing an 18pdr gun and limber against both a Morris Commercial Quad and a Guy Quad Ant and its performance was found to be better than both. The cooling system was not satisfactory and had to be modified as did the design of the front suspension. The prototype of this vehicle had a conventional wooden GS body fitted. The design of the bodywork went through many changes, and it is not at all clear from the surviving photographs of the trials vehicles which were Morris Quads and which were Morris Commercial Type CS8/FWD. An early version had crew seating and lockers with an overall canvas hood, rather similar to a shorter version of the CDSW; later ones had all-steel, but partly open, bodywork while the pattern finally approved was all-steel with crew accommodation for six men including the driver, stowage lockers for gun equipment, camouflage nets and a limited quantity of ammunition. The vehicle had the familiar humpback shape similar to the Guy Quad Ant, designed also with decontamination in mind.

The original tractor was fitted with the Morris Commercial six-cylinder 3.49-litre engine, which was replaced in 1939 by their newly developed EF four-cylinder engine. At this point the designation of the vehicle changed to Morris Commercial Type C8/FWD Field Artillery Tractor. Modifications were made during 1939 to the steering to correct an excessive wobble, to the winch drive and to the final drives to reduce the gear ratios. The Quad was finally recommended for WD use in mid-1939 just before the outbreak of war. Morris Commercial were heavily committed to the production of 15cwt trucks as they were designated the primary producers of this type in 1938 and it is not known whether any Morris Commercial field-artillery tractors were produced in time to join the BEF in France.

Although it is beyond the scope of this book, it is worth recording that the Morris Commercial C8 tractors were the most numerous of the British-built Quads and went through three

The first design of FAT body fitted to the four-wheel drive version of the Morris Commercial CS8T, 15cwt chassis.

MOVING THE GUNS

In its penultimate form the Morris Quad body featured a solid curved roof, suitable for washing down, but still retained the open sides with nothing more than canvas screens to keep out the weather.

marks and a complete redesign of the bodywork during the course of the Second World War.

It was never an ideal vehicle – being slow and somewhat underpowered compared to the various later Canadian-built versions. It was not armoured in any way and was prone to catch fire if hit by splinters or small arms fire. Its manoeuvrability was severely hampered by the insistence on retaining the limber. Yet it was a vehicle that, more than any other, earned the affection both of the crews who used it and also of the remainder of the Army who received support from the guns it towed.

Other experimental 4 x 4 tractors

Reports of the Mechanization Board after 1937 indicate a general feeling of urgency about mechanisation. There is an indication that a large variety of vehicles were tested by MWEE at Farnborough and at the annual War Office vehicle trials in North Wales during this later period with a view to providing the Army with a pool of vehicles, suitable for use in an emergency. The policy was adopted after 1935 of contracting a small number of specialist vehicles from manufacturers but relying mainly on impressed lorries for the bulk of the Army's needs. Manufacturers were therefore encouraged to send suitable vehicles to MWEE for testing, and the North Wales trials became the regular testing time for civilian cross-country vehicles.

Quite a number of vehicles are reported as being tested as possible field-artillery tractors during this period. Some were rejected out of hand and others voted as suitable for WD use, but are heard of no more. Some that emerged in 1938/39 reappeared later when full-scale production of military vehicles began in Canada in 1940.

A four-wheel-drive field artillery tractor by Chevrolet was tested in 1939. It had selective four-wheel drive with an auxiliary low-ratio gearing. It was reported as having a good performance but suffered from so many defects that it was noted as unsuitable for WD use. Similarly, a GMC four-wheel-drive tractor was tested at MWEE in 1938 where its performance was said to be similar to the Morris Quad and Guy Quad Ant. Further trials were due to be carried out in 1939, and it reappeared in the trials of that year as a medium tractor when it was noted as 'showing promise'.

Latil tractors of French manufacture had first attracted the attention of MWEE in 1928 when a four-wheel-drive-and-steer vehicle had been tested with an 18pdr in tow. One fitted with low-pressure tyres in place of the Latil-

5 FIELD ARTILLERY – CONSOLIDATION, 1930-39

patented spuds was purchased in 1929 but was found to be too slow, and to have insufficient traction. This particular vehicle ended its days as a breakdown vehicle with the RAOC in Aldershot. However, in 1937 it was reported that Latil tractors, assembled under licence in England, where they were used commercially in forestry work and heavy haulage, were being considered as field-artillery tractors for the Indian Army. Trials were carried out at MWEE on behalf of the Indian Government towing an 18pdr and limber. The performance was said to be good, but they suffered from a lack of adhesion because of inadequate tyres. A more powerful Mark II version was produced which, with a larger body, was considered to be suitable for use as a Medium Artillery Tractor, though its performance was not considered to be as good as the Scammell.

Fordsons at Dagenham produced a four-wheel-drive Field Artillery Tractor in 1939 made of standard Fordson components and the Marmon Herrington front-wheel-drive assembly. They produced forward-control and normal versions, of which the former was noted as being suitable for WD use provided various defects were rectified.

In 1939, Garner Mobile Equipment Ltd had submitted a 3-ton vehicle for test by MWEE as a field-artillery tractor. Its power-to-weight ratio was nearly double that of the Guy Quad Ant. Despite a number of defects, it was also noted as suitable for WD use.

Finally, there were two conversions of standard four-wheeled vehicles into 6 x 4 versions, which were tested as possible Field Artillery Tractors. A Bedford 30cwt and a Dennis 30cwt were each fitted with a Scammell four-wheel-drive rear bogie, and tested using a 18pdr gun. The performance of both vehicles, however, did not match that of the Morris Commercial CDSW and no further development took place.

Morris Commercial CB Field Artillery Tractor on the road to Damascus. Note the circular traversing platform for the 25pdr gun/howitzer being carried on the limber.

MOVING THE GUNS

6 MEDIUM AND HEAVY ARTILLERY, 1919-39

Shire and Clydesdale horses were favoured by medium batteries and made magnificent spectacles at reviews and parades, but Gunners with experience of the First World War knew how impractical it was to look after and feed such animals under war conditions. The 1920s saw the gradual replacement of horses by tractors and by 1938 all medium and heavy batteries were fully mechanised.

6 MEDIUM AND HEAVY ARTILLERY, 1919–39

The Medium and Heavy Batteries of the RGA discovered early on the necessity to mechanise. They were the only branches, other than the anti-aircraft sections, who used mechanical transport during the First World War, when extensive use was made of Ruston and Holt tractors to haul the bewildering variety of medium and heavy guns and howitzers used.

After the war, the RGA rationalised the stocks of artillery remaining and decided to retain the 60pdr gun and the 6in 26cwt howitzer as the standard medium-artillery pieces, and to place the remaining heavy and siege guns on a care and maintenance basis to be held in reserve as mobilisation stores. The Medium Brigades of the RGA consisted, after the war, of a mixture of tractor- and horse-drawn batteries, depending to some degree on where they were stationed. Thus, in 1925, for instance, 1st Medium Brigade, stationed at Shoeburyness, had two tractor-drawn 6in howitzer batteries and two horse-drawn 60pdr gun batteries; 2nd Medium Brigade stationed at Ambala in India had three tractor-drawn 6in howitzer batteries and one horse-drawn 60pdr gun battery; 3rd Medium Brigade in Malta had all four batteries tractor-drawn; 4th Medium Brigade at Roorkee in India had one horse-drawn 6in howitzer battery, while the remaining two 6in howitzer batteries and the 60pdr gun battery were all tractor-drawn; and 5th Medium Brigade stationed at Larkhill had two tractor-drawn 6in howitzer batteries and one each horse-drawn 6in howitzer and 60pdr gun batteries.

However, in common with the field artillery, there was a realisation that mechanisation was inevitable. Heavy draught horses of the type required by the medium batteries were even more difficult to obtain than the light draught horses of the field batteries. While the Shires and the Clydesdales favoured by the medium batteries were a magnificent spectacle at reviews and parades, those Gunners with experience of the conditions of the First World War knew of the impracticalities of looking after and feeding such animals under war conditions. The 1920s, therefore, saw the gradual replacement of horses by tractors. By August 1927, there were only three horse-drawn batteries in India and one in England; by early 1929, only two remained in India and by November 1930, all medium batteries were fully mechanised.

The types of vehicle varied considerably throughout the period. Initially, stocks of existing wartime vehicles were used; Holt and Ruston tractors and FWD lorries. At the 1926 Demonstration,

A Dragon, Medium Mark III viewed from the same angle as the Mark II*, but with the nearside ammunition lockers open.

The FWD/Roadless tractor B4E1, shown at MWEE towing a 60pdr gun. By the time this picture was taken the vehicle had been fitted with hub reduction gears on the track drive sprocket and front-driven wheels. However, it was never adopted for service.

two vehicles were shown as medium artillery tractors; one was a FWD chassis fitted with a Roadless half-track rear bogie and the other was the Medium Dragon Mark III.

The FWD Roadless medium artillery tractor

Four Wheel Drive Motors Ltd of Slough was an independent company with no commercial connection with the original American parent company. In September 1926, they produced two vehicles for trials by the Army as medium artillery tractors, known as B4E1 and B4E2. The chassis of these vehicles were fitted with Roadless Traction half-tracked bogies and the front axle was also driven. The 42bhp engine was mounted high in the frame of the vehicle and offset to one side to allow room for the driver who sat in a semi-forward-control position.

One of the two prototypes was returned to the makers in 1929 to be fitted with hub reduction gears in the front axle and in the drive sprockets of the rear bogie. The front axle reduction gear was covered by a domed axle cap, which was a distinctive feature of FWD and, later, AEC vehicles. The hub reduction gears were fitted with a view to the vehicle being used to tow Territorial Army medium artillery.

B4E1 was trialled by MWEE against a standard FWD six-wheeled tractor and was reported as being 'not ... suitable for adoption in the Service as an artillery tractor in its present form'. The other one was fitted with a new type of track with rubber joints, known as the E4 Type, but fractures of the track shoes prevented further trials. Both vehicles remained at MWEE until 1933 when they were disposed of after it was decided that the test results were unsatisfactory and the vehicles so heavy and cumbersome that they were damaging their own suspension.

The Medium Dragon Mark III

This vehicle was a development of the Dragon series of vehicles originally produced for field-artillery haulage. In 1924, a modified version of the Dragon Mark II was produced for towing medium artillery. The Dragon, Medium Mark III had ammunition lockers designed to take 60pdr and 6in howitzer rounds. It was also fitted with reduced gearing on the final drives to enable it to haul the heavier medium-artillery pieces. In 1927, it was decided to discontinue the use of the Mark II Dragons for field-artillery haulage and the 28 vehicles then in service were modified for use by medium-artillery batteries by the provision of appropriate ammunition stowage, improved transmission and steering clutches. These vehicles were then known as Dragons, Medium Mark II*.

B4E2 used a standard Roadless Traction bogie fitted to the old wartime FWD Model B chassis. There is no evidence available to show if the one tested by the British Army ever had a body fitted, but it seems unlikely. Some were, however, sold to the Portuguese armed forces.

6 MEDIUM AND HEAVY ARTILLERY, 1919-39

When the Dragons Mark II were modified to serve as Medium Artillery Tractors the work not only involved a change of gear ratios in the final drive, but enlarged ammunition lockers on the sides to accept the larger rounds. In this form they were classified Dragons, Medium Mark II*.

The Dragon, Medium Mark III underwent various design modifications throughout its life. Ten Mark IIIAs were produced by Armstrong Whitworth in 1926. In this model, the engine compartment was enclosed and ventilation louvres fitted to the top plates and the sides. The suspension system was also modified. Ten Mark IIIBs produced in 1928 reverted to an open engine compartment. In 1930, the Mechanical Warfare Board reported an absence of mechanical problems and attributed it to careful maintenance by personnel who, by then, had become accustomed to mechanised equipment.

One further version was produced with the order of five Mark IIICs in March 1931 from the Royal Ordnance Factory. They were generally similar to the Mark IIIBs with further improvements to the cooling and ventilation of the driver's compartment. The problem was never satisfactorily resolved and 3rd Medium Battery, in a move from Portsmouth to Larkhill that took from 6.30am to 11.30pm, reported that, 'the drivers had to go sick with their feet – owing to the heat'. It was necessary to change drivers frequently on long journeys for this reason alone. Mechanically-driven fans

This front view of a Dragon, Medium Mark IIIA shows the cover over the engine compartment, restyled headlamps and open ammunition lockers unstowed.

MOVING THE GUNS

A Dragon, Medium Mark IIIB of 44 Medium Battery on the road towing a 60pdr gun. The heat shields around the open engine compartment indicate that it was one of the machines rebuilt to Mark IIID standard.

were fitted to the driver's compartment of all marks in an effort to solve the problem. Another characteristic of the earlier Dragons was the overheating of the steering brakes on the rear final-drives. This particular problem was solved by placing two gunners at the rear of the Dragon, armed with Pyrene extinguishers, which they squirted onto the brake-drums from time to time – a particularly hazardous operation as the combustible by-products of the fluid were highly toxic.

No further Mark III Dragons were produced after 1934. They were a costly vehicle to produce, particularly as the 90hp Armstrong Siddeley engine was non-commercial and difficult and expensive to maintain. From October 1934, the Army began to look for a cheaper replacement for the Mark III Dragon and found it in a 6-ton tractor being developed by Vickers.

The Vickers 6-ton tractor and the Medium Dragon Mark IV

In 1928, Vickers Armstrong produced a medium tank and an experimental 6-ton tractor based on the same chassis. In 1930, both this tractor and others produced by Rushton and Blackstone were trialled as potential medium-artillery tractors. The possibility of using such a tractor commercially or in the Colonies was of interest to the manufacturers and the military. It is interesting to note that the Vickers tractor was trialled by the Royal National Lifeboat Institution (RNLI) to assess its potential for hauling lifeboats over sandy foreshores, a role for which it was found not to be suitable without extensive modification and waterproofing. The United Africa Company also looked at the Vickers 6-ton tractor in June 1930 as they had a requirement for tractors to haul logs in West Africa.

The first trials of the vehicle were held in May 1930 at MWEE and in July at Vickers' works at Chertsey, hauling a 60pdr gun and carrying a 2-ton load on the vehicle. As a result of these trials, an order was placed for two vehicles with Vickers Armstrong in January 1931 for delivery in March. The two vehicles, known as B12E1 (T905) and B12E2 (T906), were fitted with an 80hp Armstrong Siddeley air-cooled, horizontally aligned, four-cylinder petrol engine. The track was of a new design, made of manganese steel.

The engine was placed centrally at the rear of the vehicle and the drive was taken forward through a gearbox giving four forward gears, an emergency low gear and one low reverse speed. Steering was by way of steering brakes and clutches on the driving sprockets. The suspension consisted of two transverse tubular members evenly spaced between the front and the rear of the hull. At each end of these tubes, there were two pairs of small bogie wheels connected to the cross members by leaf springs, giving eight small bogie wheels on each side of the hull. The drive sprockets were mounted at the front and were considerably higher than the idlers at the rear, giving a characteristic 'wedge-shape' to the suspension and running gear.

Trials were conducted at MWEE, in North Wales and at Bovington in July 1931, towing 6in howitzers and 60pdr guns and limbers to ascertain the advantages of the new tractors over the Medium Dragon Mark III. The general conclusion was that the vehicles had little to offer over the existing Dragons in terms of performance, though it was thought that the Vickers tractor allowed greater control over the towed load. The vehicle generally was found to be unreliable with a number of defects developing in the engine, transmission, gearbox, final drive, suspension and hull. The Mechanical Warfare Board reported in 1931, 'there can be no doubt from the experience so far gained that the durability of these vehicles leaves much to be desired. In this respect they have proved very much inferior to the Armstrong Siddeley design of Dragon.' Trials continued through 1932 and further engine defects were reported. Finally, in 1933, it was reported that no further vehicles of this type were being ordered.

By 1934, however, there appeared to be a change of mind, as it was reported that, although the Medium Dragons in service had been most satisfactory and had proved themselves to be 'robust and reliable vehicles under arduous conditions', they were costly and the non-commercial Armstrong Siddeley air-cooled engine was expensive to maintain. In October 1934, therefore, the Army began to look for a cheaper replacement. Vickers-Armstrong, in the meantime, had continued the development of their 6-ton tractor, despite the Army's earlier rejection of it, and had just produced a trial vehicle for the India Office. This machine was trialled at MWEE at the end of October before it was sent out to India where

trials staff were most impressed with its performance.

The vehicle was essentially the same as the earlier model but with a commercial AEC compression ignition engine which developed 130hp. It had a performance equal to that of the Mark III Dragon but had a much-improved suspension, smoother running and a quieter engine. Its cross-country performance was much enhanced and was capable of 19mph across country without the towed load. In addition, its weight at 8½ tons was considerably lighter than the Mark III Dragon. The design of the tractor was similar in other respects to the earlier 6-ton tractor. The trials were so promising that two vehicles were ordered from the manufacturers in December 1934, the first being delivered to MWEE in September 1935. The vehicle was extensively trialled towing a 60pdr gun with a total weight of 6½ tons. With this equipment in tow it was capable of a maximum speed of 16mph and a cross-country speed of 13mph. The most desirable feature was

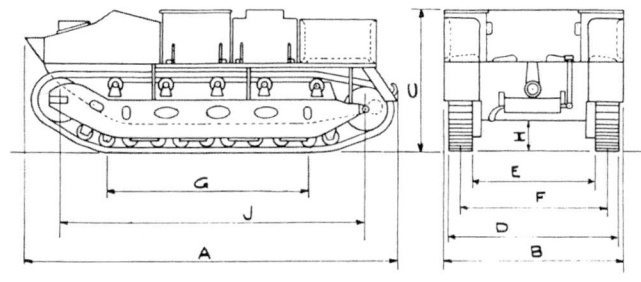

Data sheet for Dragons in the Medium Mark II* and III series.

MOVING THE GUNS

An interior view of a production Dragon, Medium Mark IV. Notice how the big AEC diesel engine dominates the interior and how the seating is arranged round it.

for field trials. It is recorded that a further 18 were ordered in November 1937 for use in India, though neither documentary nor photographic evidence is known to exist of the use of these vehicles in India. It is thought that Medium Dragons Mark IV were used by the BEF in 1939 and 1940, and presumably were destroyed or abandoned in France during the retreat to Dunkirk.

The Scammell Pioneer

In 1934, the Mechanisation Experimental Establishment organised a trial run from Shoeburyness to Plymouth. It involved three six-wheel drive tractors; an AEC/FWD, a Leyland and a Scammell, towing a 6in, 45-calibre gun and carriage. The gun was split into two loads, each weighing about 9½ tons, and the tractors took turns to pull each item. At an average speed of 10mph, the 278-mile journey was accomplished without any trouble worth speaking of; but, what is more important, on no occasion did any of the vehicles concerned ever engage their front axle drive or use their lowest gears. The evidence was there for all to see and, coupled with the success of the Morris Commercial CDSW Field Artillery Tractors, led the Royal Artillery to consider the advantages

its relative quietness compared to the Armstrong Siddeley air-cooled-engine Dragons and the Vickers Medium Tanks. The second prototype was delivered in December 1935 and differed from the first in that it had welded bogie frames and semi-elliptical springs in place of the leaf springs of the earlier model. The manganese steel track was particularly noted for its ease of steering. In June 1936, a production run of ten vehicles was ordered from Vickers-Armstrong

This sharp side view of a Dragon, Medium Mark IIID reveals the final form of headlamp design and the sprung return rollers, mounted in pairs, which were features of this version.

The first of the Vickers-Armstrong Tractors, B12E1, showing the unusual suspension system.

of developing larger 6 x 4 tractors to handle medium and heavy guns as well. Such vehicles would be less complicated than the six-wheel-drive types which, in all but a few cases, did not live up to expectations, and a good deal cheaper than the big Dragons. Also, of course, they would be that much faster on the road if not as effective across country. In 1935 contracts were issued with Albion Motors, for an artillery tractor version of their current 6 x 4 subsidy three-tonner, and Scammell Lorries Ltd, for a similar type based on their Pioneer chassis – which was already enjoying considerable success on the overseas commercial market. Both vehicles were to be powered by the Gardner LW six-cylinder diesel engine.

The Albion soon faded from the scene. During trials at Farnborough in 1936, the Scammell contender not only beat it convincingly, it also proved superior to an AEC/FWD 6 x 6 and an imported Tatra. The Gardner engine developed 98.6bhp and, driving through a six-speed gearbox with worm-drive rear axle and final spur gear reductions produced a torque ratio, in the lowest gear, of 111 to 1. In practical terms this meant that the tractor could manage a towed load of 36 tons, on a level road, at walking pace, or at least 15 tons on a steep gradient. Further, the Scammell patent rear bogie combined with an undriven, semi-pivotal front axle almost eliminated the problem of wheelspin by keeping all wheels in good contact with the ground surface, even on very rough going.

A Dragon, Medium Mark IV prototype with 60pdr gun attached. The suspension arrangements, it will be noted, derived directly from B12E1 although in every other respect it is a much bigger vehicle.

123

One of the most famous artillery tractors of all time, the 6 x 4 Scammell Pioneer first entered service in 1937. This early example features spoked front wheels, an anti-aircraft mounting above the rear crew compartment and, on this occasion, overall chains fitted to the rear bogie.

Hardy Motors of Slough, through their connection with AEC, produced the Hardy 4/4 service lorry with four-wheel-drive. It was not adopted when first offered in 1931 but, in a later form, entered service as the AEC Matador.

Scammell Pioneer was associated to its everlasting credit with the 7.2in and 8in howitzers of the Heavy Regiments RA.

The AEC Matador
Another classic lorry and gun combination of the Second World War was the 5.5in Medium Gun and AEC Matador four-wheel-drive tractor; but the origins of this famous vehicle can be traced back to an experimental prototype, which appeared in 1931 for an entirely different purpose. When AEC joined forces with the British FWD concern in 1929 this included another firm, Hardy Motors Ltd, which had been producing rail-equipped FWDs for some years. In 1931, to avoid confusion with the American company, all FWD products were built under the Hardy Motors banner at the AEC factory, and this included diesel railcars as well as all-wheel-drive trucks. Thus, it was that in 1931 they approached the War Office with a design for a four wheel-drive version of the AEC Monarch, a commercial 4 x 2 rated at 4 tons. As the Hardy 4/4 two were tested, not as artillery tractors but for their suitability as replacements for the 6 x 4 load carriers then in service. Initial trials were successful enough to encourage the War Office to order an improved model in 1932. It was a forward control type, powered by an AEC 65bhp four-cylinder engine with a four-speed gearbox and auxiliary reduction. Using the primary box, it ran as a 4 x 2 but engagement of the auxiliary box also brought the front axle into operation. Trials with MWEE in North Wales and, in 1933, with the RASC, proved that the new lorry was in most respects as suitable for general service purposes as the 6 x 4, but at this stage no attempt was made to order any. Instead, the War Office agreed to classify it as suitable for impressment once sufficient commercial examples were in service. But here was the rub. As with the 6 x 4 itself there was very little interest among commercial operators for such a vehicle and few, if any, were sold.

By the end of the year, 60 chassis were on order and plans were drawn up to use them as tractors for medium, heavy and anti-aircraft artillery as well as recovery vehicles for the Royal Army Ordnance Corps (RAOC). In 1937, a horizontal winch was designed that took up less space while Dunlop and Goodyear produced new types of 13.50-20 tyres, with flexible walls, that improved cross-country performance. By 1938, the new tractor was in service with batteries equipped with 60pdr guns but, during the Second World War, the

6 MEDIUM AND HEAVY ARTILLERY, 1919–39

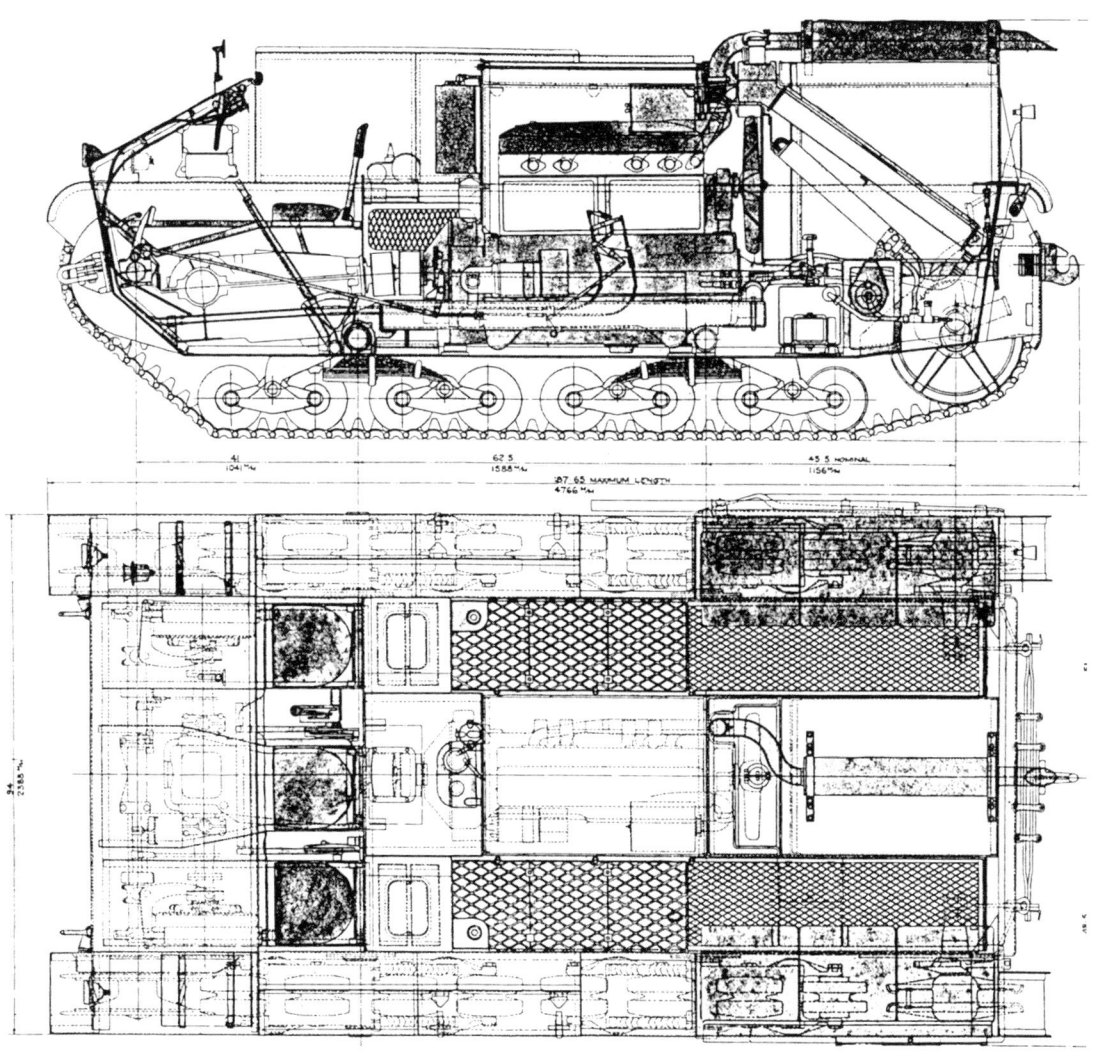

Sectioned plan and side elevation of a Mark IV Dragon.

The extra maintenance, not to mention the very high loading platform inevitable on such a big four-wheel-drive lorry made it too expensive and specialised for the average haulier.

There things rested until 1938, when a similar vehicle, albeit with a fully enclosed cab and capable of taking either a petrol or diesel engine, was tested as a Medium Artillery Tractor or 3-ton load carrier, which could also accept special, technical bodies like workshops or stores. Tests conducted in 1939 revealed that it was a better proposition as a gun tractor than any of its rivals, being faster than the Guy Lizard, Karrier Spider or Albion. Reliability trials were still going on when war broke out, but it was already clear that the Matador, as this vehicle came to be known, was going to prove highly satisfactory. In passing it should be noted that another AEC Matador, a 4 x 2 load carrier in the 5-ton class, had been examined by MWEE in the 1930s but, apart from the name, there is nothing in a military sense to connect the two.

MOVING THE GUNS

7 ANTI-AIRCRAFT ARTILLERY

There were two fundamental roles for anti-aircraft artillery, each of which demanded a different means of transporting the gun – defence of the Field Army in France, and the home defence of Britain. With the interwar rolling policy of 'no war for ten years' it meant there was little money to spare for replacing the Hathi tractor or the wartime Peerless lorries.

7 ANTI-AIRCRAFT ARTILLERY

Anti-aircraft gunnery was a science, which had developed from something that few people had paid scant attention to at the beginning of the First World War, into a highly developed and complex discipline by the time of the Armistice.

In September 1914, the threat from enemy aircraft during the Retreat to the Marne led to the hasty provision of anti-aircraft guns to the BEF in France. These were 1pdr 'pom-poms' supplied by the Royal Navy and mounted on lorries. By Christmas 1914, the 13pdr 6cwt guns used by the RHA had been modified and placed on an improvised mount to produce a form of anti-aircraft gun which, because of its evolution, had severe limitations in terms of laying, fusing and loading. Other weapons were becoming available around this time; 3in guns from the Admiralty, small quantities of French 75mm auto-cannons and 3pdrs produced by Vickers.

There were two fundamental roles for anti-aircraft artillery, each of which demanded a different means of transporting the gun. Firstly, there was the defence of the Field Army in France. Initially, anti-aircraft cover was required for the protection of the various HQs and installations on the lines of communication stretching back to the coast. The standard 13pdr field gun was bored out and re-lined to produce an anti-aircraft gun known as the 13pdr 9cwt, which had a maximum ceiling of 19,000ft. For Field Army use, the gun was mounted on the back of a lorry. The most common type of lorry used was the Thornycroft J Type, of which some 5,000 saw service during the First World War in this and other roles.

Just before the war, work had started on the development of a gun designed specifically for anti-aircraft use. By 1916, quantities of this gun, known as the 3in 20cwt, began to arrive in France. It was originally designed to be fitted to a fixed mounting for static defence but was also used in France as a lorry mounted gun. The weight of the gun and mounting was such that the American Peerless TC 5-ton truck was used to carry it, and this combination performed satisfactorily throughout the war. Indeed, Peerless anti-aircraft guns remained in service after 1918 and some of these – by then vintage – chain-driven vehicles, with their wooden spoked wheels, were trundled out of reserve in 1938 during the Munich Crisis, much to the amusement of the citizens of London.

The number of anti-aircraft sections multiplied during the war as the air threat increased and, by the end of the conflict, the anti-aircraft system involved the coordination and control of guns manned by the Royal Artillery, machine-guns provided by the infantry, searchlights of the Royal Engineers (RE) and fighter aircraft of the RAF. In 1918, a scheme even evolved to link the reporting of aircraft movements in France with a similar system in Britain to give early warning of raids on the homeland.

Air defence was given, nonetheless, low priority both in terms of quality of personnel and of equipment. In June 1918, a committee reported that anti-aircraft batteries should be reorganised with six guns and that there was a need for a lighter, more mobile piece of equipment. Sadly, with the coming of peace, these lessons were largely forgotten.

The other main role for the anti-aircraft branch was that of the home defence of Britain. This was the responsibility of the Admiralty until 1916 when the Army took over. As the home air-defence system evolved, mainly to defend London, the 3in 20cwt gun was used either on a fixed mounting, which it was originally designed for, or on a semi-mobile platform. The so-called travelling platform was mounted on

A 3in 20cwt anti-aircraft gun mounted on a 5-ton Peerless truck. Although they saw active service in the First World War this one was photographed in the 1920s and some of these venerable vehicles were still in service in 1938.

127

MOVING THE GUNS

A Thornycroft J Type anti-aircraft lorry in action on the Western Front during the First World War. Notice how the body has to be stabilised during firing and how the sides fold down to increase the available working space for the gun detachment.

axles with small solid wheels and was invariably towed by a Holt tractor. To come into action, four radial arms swung out from the corners of the platform, which was then raised by levelling jacks. The combination would have probably achieved, at best, a road speed of 5mph and it took at least half-an-hour to get the gun into action – hardly the most mobile piece of equipment!

An experimental 3.6in gun was produced in prototype form in 1918 and underwent firing trials in 1919. It fell victim, however, to post-war economies and was never pursued. It was an interesting development in that its travelling platform was tracked and designed to be towed behind a Holt tractor. It was an attempt to solve the problem of improved cross-country performance, which unfortunately never came to anything. By all accounts, it was a far better gun than either the existing 3in 20cwt or the rather futile attempts some ten years later to misuse the Birch Gun as an anti-aircraft weapon.

Post-war developments

Although there appeared to be little progress in terms of equipment during the war, the Anti-Aircraft Branch of the RGA had evolved a well-tried system of air defence and it might be thought that this experience would be retained and built on in the years following 1918. This was not to be and the entire organisation – with the exception of one regular Anti-Aircraft Brigade of the RGA and its associated Royal Engineer Searchlight Battalion – was disbanded. The coalition government of Lloyd George, with its rolling policy of 'no war for ten years', could not shoulder the burden of a large and expensive air-defence system.

For some six years, the Anti-Aircraft Branch of the RGA practically stagnated. From the large variety of weapons left over at the end of the war, the 3in 20cwt was retained as the primary weapon although it was mounted on a more mobile four-wheeled trailer with sprung axles and pneumatic tyres. The platform was steadied in action with outriggers and levelling jacks and there was room on the platform for the crew to travel in relative comfort. Some of the old 13pdr 9cwt guns mounted on Peerless trucks were retained as a reserve. The 3in 20cwt gun was towed initially by the Hathi tractor, and then by the FWD 6 x 4.

The post-war organisation consisted of the regular Anti-Aircraft Brigade of three six-gun batteries stationed at Blackdown and one much under-strength Territorial Brigade stationed in London. The Territorial Army Anti-Aircraft Brigade was equipped with a few static mountings for training purposes only.

The return of the Conservative Government in 1923 under Baldwin resulted in the re-formation of the Committee on Imperial Defence with a brief to examine the state of the nation's defence. The subcommittee that looked at air defence matters, the Steele Bartholomew Committee, recommended a vast expansion of the air defences of the country. However, the return of a Labour Government in 1924 led to the re-introduction of the 'no war for ten years' philosophy – but not before there had been a modest increase in the anti-aircraft cover with the formation of five new Territorial Army Anti-Aircraft Brigades.

Baldwin's Conservatives returned in 1925 but there was little money to spare for enhancing the armed forces and little progress was made. The TA brigades either manned fixed defences or used the wartime travelling platforms towed, when the need arose, by hired lorries. Practice camp was accomplished by borrowing equipment from the Regular brigade, itself still equipped with the Hathi tractor or the wartime Peerless lorries. In 1927, the formation took place of the second Regular brigade of three batteries stationed at Portsmouth and equipped primarily for the defence of the naval port.

After 1931, international and national events brought about a gradual change in attitude towards the armed services in general and anti-aircraft defences in particular. A disastrous air-defence exercise in that year highlighted the deficiencies. The National Coalition Government abandoned the pacifist policies of its predecessor and gradually began to allocate more resources towards re-equipping the forces.

The search had begun in 1928 to find a replacement for the then ageing Hathi tractors. Experiments were carried out at MWEE on a six-wheeled version of the Hathi and the eight-wheeled Armstrong Siddeley version of the Pavesi. The experiments showed that great improvements in cross-country performance could be obtained from vehicles with a driven front axle and

The experimental 3.6in anti-aircraft gun on its special tracked trailer mounting. It was intended to be towed into action by a Holt tractor, although progress would have been slow. Notice the extreme difficulty in loading the gun at maximum elevation.

MOVING THE GUNS

experiments concentrated on suitable six-wheeled drive vehicles. Guy Motors and Leyland were already in the process of producing vehicles of this type as were Scammells. Orders were placed for samples from Leyland and Scammell and it was agreed to test an existing vehicle produced by Guy for the Indian Government. A vehicle was already ordered from the FWD Company who had considerable expertise with front-driven axles.

The general specification for these vehicles dictated a draw-bar effort of between 12,000 and 15,000lb, some 50 per cent greater than the Hathi. Each was fitted with a different design of transmission and final drive, which enabled comparisons to be made between the different types. The front axle assembly of the Guy had the advantage of being able to be fitted to any of Guy Motors' six-wheeled vehicles including their armoured car and ammunition truck, both in service with the Indian Army. The four contenders were tested by MWEE between 1929 and 1931 to examine their ability to tow the 3in 20cwt AA gun on its four-wheeled trailer.

The Guy 6 x 6 and 8 x 8 tractors

The Guy 6 x 6 vehicle was only on loan for testing prior to being sent out to India and arrived at MWEE in March 1931 for a demonstration to compare its performance against that of an experimental 8 x 8 Guy vehicle delivered the previous year. The 8 x 8 vehicle was itself a development of the standard Guy 6 x 4 chassis used for the Indian Army armoured car and ammunition lorry. The Guy 8 x 8 vehicle was intended to be used as a salvage or heavy haulage vehicle with greater tractive effort and better cross-country performance, without any appreciable increase in size and without departing too much from standard design. The vehicle was fitted with a 95hp six-cylinder engine and a supplementary gearbox to provide power to the two front axles and the winch. Comparative trials with the 6 x 6 vehicle were held in February 1931 at MWEE and in

The magnificent eight-wheel-drive Guy at MWEE. Looking below the spare wheel one can make out the bevel gearbox and layshaft running forwards to drive the two front axles. Because of its great length the chassis had to be very flexible.

7 ANTI-AIRCRAFT ARTILLERY

Leyland Motors' abortive design for a six-wheel-drive tractor based on their forward control Terrier 3-ton chassis.

North Wales. The general conclusions reached were that the added expense and technical complications of the 8 x 8 were not justified by any great gain in performance except in exceptional circumstances. The bevel gear pinions of the front-wheel-drive gave constant problems throughout the trials and experiments were finally brought to a halt in 1933. The conclusion at the end of the trials was that the 8 x 8 vehicle achieved an overall gain in tractive effort in the order of 10 per cent but at the expense of increased fuel consumption, greater weight, increased cost and difficulty in maintaining the complicated transmission system.

Just before the Guy 6 x 6 was shipped out to India in March 1931, a demonstration was held to compare its performance against the 8 x 8 hauling the 3in 20cwt AA gun. At the trial it was generally considered that the performance of the 8 x 8 was better, despite the fact that it was some 2 tons heavier. The Guy 6 x 6 was never adopted for AA gun haulage in the British Army. In India, it took part in comparative trials against the 6 x 4 Guy and Thornycroft vehicles and the Holt 5-ton tractor as a medium artillery tractor, but was not adopted in that role.

The Leyland 6 x 6 tractor
A six-wheel-drive vehicle produced by Leyland was the second of the four vehicles tested by MWEE. Its planned delivery in 1929 was delayed by production difficulties and it was finally delivered to MWEE in October 1930 in time for a demonstration to delegates of the Imperial Conference. A six-cylinder engine was fitted in place of the normal four-cylinder Leyland Terrier. The vehicle underwent the usual trials in North Wales and took part in comparative trials against the other contenders.

The Leyland was not particularly satisfactory and had a history of mechanical problems culminating in a serious transmission failure in 1933. It was judged not to be suitable as an anti-aircraft tractor and ended its days as a heavy breakdown truck.

The Scammell 6 x 6 tractor
The Scammell was delivered in 1929 and from the outset its performance was inferior to the FWD. It appeared to be used mainly as a breakdown vehicle at demonstrations and on manoeuvres although it was supplied as a contender for the AA gun tractor. It appeared to be prone to transmission brake-drum failures resulting in several catastrophic

131

MOVING THE GUNS

An AEC/FWD R6T tractor of 15 Anti-Aircraft Battery pulling a 3in 20cwt AA gun on its wheeled carriage. A pillar-mounted Lewis gun is provided for close-in protection and the picture shows the curious little seat alongside the engine, designed to give the passenger a stiff neck.

burstings of the drum casing. In 1931, MWEE reported that the 'machine had given general satisfaction principally because of the simplicity of design. Its chief drawback from a military aspect is its bulk and conspicuousness.'

It is surprising that this vehicle did not gain widespread support in view of the success of the later models of Scammells during the war and beyond. The experimental vehicle was still in service in 1938 when, fitted with 13.50-20 Trakgrip cross-country tyres in place of the originals, it was used to test the relative advantages of 6 x 4 over 6 x 6 drive. In the latter mode, a 30 per cent increase in tractive effort was observed.

The FWD 6 x 6 tractor

The vehicle that was ultimately to be selected as the AA gun tractor was a version of the FWD tractor delivered for trials in April 1929. Initial trials against the Hathi were so satisfactory in terms of ease of manoeuvre, towing, winching and maintenance that a contract was placed at the end of 1929 for a further nine vehicles fitted with the AEC 6,126cc six-cylinder engine in place of the Dorman IC engine fitted to the prototype. This was a move that foreshadowed the takeover of the FWD Company by AEC in 1929. A specially designed metal body was fitted with additional seating placed longitudinally alongside the engine at the front of the vehicle.

Of the nine vehicles, six were issued to the 1st Anti-Aircraft Brigade at Blackdown for extended trials. Two of the six were fitted with 'mock-up' armoured bodies for trials as armoured AA tractors in support of an armoured force. One was fitted out as a RAOC heavy breakdown vehicle. A further two vehicles were ordered, one of which was fitted with the AEC diesel engine.

The FWD Company designed and fitted the special all-metal body for AA use.

Constructed of 1/8in mild steel plate, it had lockers at the forward end for the stowage of stores and equipment. The winch rope passed in a channel beneath the floor, which also carried non-skid chains, spades and other equipment. Folding doors were fitted at the rear in place of a tailgate and seating was provided along the sides of the body for the gun detachment. A folding hood similar to the type fitted to touring cars of this period, was provided at the front end of the lorry body and when it was erected it extended along the length of the body. A similar, smaller hood extended forward over the driver. A curious and distinctive feature of the vehicle was the forward bench seat for two crew members fitted lengthwise alongside the engine.

It was recorded in 1930 that its performance over difficult country towing the 3in 20cwt gun was inferior to the Dragon, but that it was both faster and cheaper to run over roads and moderate terrain. Originally, the vehicle was fitted with 10.50-20 low-pressure tyres with a standard commercial tread. Subsequently smaller 9.00-22 tyres with bar treads able to take overall chains were fitted on the rear bogies and non-skid chains on the front wheels. The result was a dramatic increase in ground adhesion.

The two additional vehicles remained at MWEE, one fitted with the AEC six-cylinder petrol engine while the other was fitted with an AEC diesel engine. The petrol engine tried initially was the standard AEC 95hp engine used commercially in buses and lorries. The larger cylinders and pistons of the 110hp engine were fitted experimentally, which increased the capacity from 6,590cc to 7,983cc. A further batch of six vehicles was then ordered, which were modified to take the larger engine.

The first compression ignition engine was the standard AEC Acro type but problems were experienced with cooling. FWD offered to exchange the Acro engine with a new version designed by Ricardo, which featured a spherical pre-combustion chamber. The six-cylinder engine developed 130hp at 2,400rpm and was described as a 'neat and compact unit'. Trials were carried out in North Wales and the engine was reported to be generally satisfactory, although there was difficulty in starting in cold weather.

The petrol engine version was the one chosen for service use and the War Department made a few small purchases each year. After the initial order for nine in 1928, a further six were ordered in 1931 – one of which was a RAOC breakdown truck – further unspecified quantities in 1932 and 1933, and six in 1934. In October 1939, a review was started to find a replacement vehicle, which could be used for anti-aircraft and medium artillery haulage and also for recovery work. The FWD was considered to be expensive because of its non-commercial design, its transmission was too costly and, in war, it would be difficult to increase production. This did not prevent the placing of a further order for 11 vehicles in September 1935. These were fitted with a modified design of rear axle and other improvements.

The expansion of anti-aircraft artillery
From 1934 onwards, the search began for a replacement for the FWD for anti-aircraft haulage. The stated design criteria for this vehicle, which would also be used for medium-artillery haulage, were: simplicity, rapid production and availability, and a weight restricted to the capacity of the military medium girder bridge. It was decided that the chosen vehicle would have to be made from standard commercial components available from within the trade. To achieve this might mean sacrificing front-wheel-drive and accepting lower cross-country performance. The vehicles tested for this role were primarily to be used in the medium-artillery role and are described more fully in Chapter 6.

The need to replace the ageing FWD/AEC tractors coincided with other important developments. The failure of the 1932 Disarmament Conference and the gradual build-up of the hitherto banned German Air Force, and also of the Italian Air Force in North Africa, led to a general realisation that disarmament was never going to be achieved through the League of Nations. The government, tacitly if not officially, abandoned the 'no war for ten years' policy and began allocating more resources towards the re-equipping of the armed services. A further three TA anti-aircraft brigades were authorised in 1932 and a third regular brigade in 1935, though this was primarily allocated to the defence of port installations abroad.

A regular Anti-Aircraft Brigade at this time consisted of three batteries each of three sections. Two of the sections comprised the basic fire unit of two anti-aircraft guns commanded by a subaltern. By now all the 3in 20cwt guns of the regular batteries were mounted on the four-wheeled trailer towed by the AEC/FWD tractor. The third section of each battery had Lewis Light AA guns carried in Morris 30cwt 6 x 4 trucks. Each heavy AA section had, in addition, two 3-ton vehicles pulling trailers carrying the Vickers predictors and the height-finding equipment and a further three 3- or 5-ton ammunition vehicles. The officers travelled in Morris or Austin light cars and there were two motorcycles to each section. This was the published establishment. However, in practice, most batteries were seriously deficient in equipment and relied on the hiring of vehicles from contractors to go on annual practice camp.

In 1934, the Crosland Committee was tasked to study the extent to which the Army's fleet of 3-ton 6 x 4 vehicles could be replaced or augmented by civilian-pattern 4 x 2 types. The 6 x 4 had never won widespread support in the civilian market and, as a result, military vehicles of this type were invariably specially designed and therefore expensive. In addition, there was insufficient industrial capacity to enable large quantities of this type to be produced in a hurry. In general terms, the Committee recommended that 50 per cent of the 6 x 4 vehicles required by the Army could be replaced by 4 x 2 vehicles. The Committee did qualify its recommendations by suggesting the types of use to which the lower mobility four-wheelers could be put.

As far as the Anti-Aircraft Branch was concerned, the Crosland Committee recommendations had two effects. For the air defence of the Field Army where cross-country mobility was a prime consideration, six-wheeled vehicles were

7 ANTI-AIRCRAFT ARTILLERY

considered essential and the search continued for a replacement for the AEC/FWD. For the home-defence units, mobility was a lesser concern and reliance was placed on the provision of four-wheeler vehicles. The general policy was that the majority of such vehicles would be obtained in an emergency by hiring or impressment.

In 1934, a committee was set up under General Thompson to review the anti-aircraft defence requirements of the Territorial Army. It recommended the formation of an Anti-Aircraft Division in the south of England. While the implications of this recommendation were being considered, international events added an unexpected impetus. In October 1935, Italian troops invaded Abyssinia and the potential threat to Egypt and the Suez Canal was considered serious enough to warrant the dispatch of the regular 1st Anti-Aircraft Brigade from England to Alexandria. Although the brigade was not tested in action, the crisis provided a timely warning that the Regular Army had insufficient resources to cover overseas commitments, let alone the defence of an expeditionary force or the home defence of the United Kingdom. A further expansion of up to six Regular brigades was authorised and, for the first time, Light Anti-Aircraft Batteries were included in the organisation, although there was as yet no suitable weapon other than the existing, inadequate Lewis gun.

The Thompson Committee recommended an organisation of 58 Territorial Army anti-aircraft gun batteries supported by 24 searchlight battalions of the RE. As far as equipment was concerned, a new anti-aircraft gun, the 3.7in, was at firing trials stage by 1935 and was intended to be the mobile gun for the Regular brigades. On the LAA side, Lewis guns continued to be

Part light anti-aircraft gun tractor, part furniture van, the prototype Morris Commercial CDSW Bofors tractor had a fully enclosed crew compartment behind an equally well protected cab.

MOVING THE GUNS

the main weapon until the arrival of the Swedish 40mm Bofors gun, which completed firing trials in 1937.

As for the new TA batteries, it was obvious that neither existing equipment nor the production of the 3.7in gun would meet the demand for guns to equip the new units. There were two solutions: firstly, in 1937, production of the new weapon was switched to provide it with an immobile mounting so that the gun could be used in the static role of the Air Defence of Great Britain by the TA batteries, while the regular batteries continued with the existing 3in 20cwt gun on its mobile trailer. This was a fortuitous decision, as it turned out, for it meant that it was the older, obsolete equipment that was destroyed or left behind in France in 1940 while the more modern guns remained relatively unscathed in England, able to take their part in the Battle of Britain later in the year. Secondly, the Admiralty offered a number of 4.5in guns which, mounted on specially adapted mountings, became static AA guns manned by TA units as part of the Air Defence of Great Britain.

The transport implications of this rapid expansion of the Air Defence branch were considerable. Because of their largely static role, the TA units were to rely on the use of impressed and hired vehicles. These were to be used to get personnel to the gun sites, which were in most cases within the locality anyway, and to move stores and ammunition from magazines to the guns. Events in September 1938 put the system to the test, when, during the Munich Crisis, the

As provided for service use, the CDSW anti-aircraft gun tractor was a much more spartan affair, with canvas replacing the coach-built bodywork of the prototype.

international situation deteriorated to such an extent that TA anti-aircraft units were mobilised and deployed to their wartime locations. The organisation for call-out worked well but the resources were inadequate. There was an acute shortage of transport and all sorts of means were used from buses and coaches to Thames barges.

The Munich Crisis passed, and the authorities were given a brief respite in which to make improvements. However, by then, priority was being given to the production of aircraft and guns for the Air Defence of Great Britain and the Anti-Aircraft Brigades of the Regular Army received no further significant improvements in their vehicle requirements. The BEF that went to France in September 1939 had to rely for its anti-aircraft protection on a gun that dated back to the last war, hauled by a variety of vehicles, some of them hastily impressed civilian lorries. The conflicting demands for limited supplies of transport by all branches of the Services meant that even by 1940, AA brigades in France were still short of 15 tractors out of a reduced scale of 106, and much borrowing of transport went on simply to put guns and equipment into anticipated deployment positions. In practice, of course, most of this equipment was lost or destroyed in France, forcing the authorities to tackle the problem of re-equipping the anti-aircraft units afresh.

The Morris Commercial CDSW 6 x 4 LAA Tractor

After scouring the armaments factories of Europe for a suitable light anti-aircraft gun, the Director of the Royal Artillery decided to accept the Swedish 40mm Bofors gun and issues began in 1938. It was also necessary to find a suitable tractor to tow it. Whereas previously the Lewis gun sections of the Light Anti-Aircraft Batteries could easily be transported in standard GS 6 x 4 lorries, the new gun required something more specialised. The gun itself was mounted on a four-wheeled trailer weighing about 3 tons. The new gun had a rate of fire of 120rpm, which meant that there was a considerable ammunition carrying problem. In addition, the high rate of fire meant that it was necessary to change barrels fairly frequently, so each gun had to carry a spare. The solution was to adapt the Morris Commercial CDSW chassis for this role. By 1938, the CDSW was a well-proven vehicle used throughout the Army in a variety of roles. The LAA requirement demanded crew seating for six, locker stowage for gun stores and a limited amount of 'ready' ammunition, stowage for a spare wheel for the gun trailer and for the spare gun barrel.

The prototype was fitted with rigid coachwork, which clearly owed its origins to commercial vehicle body designs of the time. It had a pantechnicon-style of body of the 'Luton' type with stowage space that projected above the driver's seat. A less military-looking vehicle is hard to imagine. The production model, however, was more business-like with a canvas hood for the drivers and crew compartments, and stowage and ammunition lockers that were accessible from the outside of the vehicle. The spare gun barrel was carried in a trough that ran the length of the rear body. It was also fitted with the standard CDSW 4-ton winch, which could pay out to front or rear.

The Morris was well suited to its role, and those that were not lost in France served right through the war in all theatres; supplemented by similar versions mounted on Bedford L, Chevrolet and Ford chassis.

MOVING THE GUNS

8 THE MECHANISATION OF THE TERRITORIAL ARMY ARTILLERY

In 1930, the decision was taken to mechanise the Territorial Field Artillery with a forward-control, light six-wheeler – the subsidy type Morris Commercial D Type 30cwt 6 x 4 lorry. Luckily, by 1939 it was decided to produce 4 x 4 tractors as the standard regular Field Artillery tractor, releasing the Morris Commercial CDSW 6 x 4 tractors for the expanding Territorial Artillery.

It seems curious that the artillery units of the Territorial Army should have become mechanised before most of the Regular Army, but on examination it is obvious why. Once demobilisation was completed after the end of the First World War, the policy first introduced in 1908 was re-established of having a small permanent Regular Army whose prime role was 'Imperial policing', backed up by a larger army of reservists and 'territorial' volunteers. These would be mobilised in an emergency and rapidly expand the size of the national army. In the Royal Artillery in 1924, for instance, there were 69 TA Artillery brigades of all types against the Regular Artillery total of 92 brigades, not including depots, ammunition columns and reserve brigades.

8 THE MECHANISATION OF THE TERRITORIAL ARMY ARTILLERY

Bedford MW 15cwt trucks were issued to anti-tank brigades of the TA shortly before the Second World War. This wartime picture shows such a vehicle serving as a portée for the unpopular little 25mm Hotchkiss anti-tank gun; a type imported from France when supplies of the excellent 2pdr ran short.

The Territorial Artillery units were no strangers to mechanisation. Indeed, some of the earliest experiments into the use of mechanical traction, particularly of field artillery, were carried out either officially, or unofficially, by Territorial Artillery units. The requisitioning of the Aveling and Porter traction engines during the volunteer review at Dover Castle in 1869, already mentioned, is typical of the improvisation for which the Territorial Army was, and is, well known. Similarly, the experiment with the battery of Ehrhardt guns towed behind Sheffield Simplex cars in July 1914, also described before, might have had more impact on artillery mechanisation were it not for the fact that war broke out only a couple of weeks later. The Regular Artillery adjutant of the battery recorded after the war, 'I am convinced that had this experiment been tried earlier, great alterations in traction for guns of all kinds would have been made both before and during the early part of the War . . . I was making out a description of the experiment with drawings and photographs when the superhuman efforts required from a Territorial Force Adjutant on mobilisation put a stopper on it.'

Horsed units of the Territorial Army had a problem never really experienced by their Regular Army counterparts. Although most units held their regular weekly 'drill nights', the main training for the year was carried out at 'Annual Camp', usually held during the summer months. It was obviously impractical for a Territorial unit to keep and maintain its full complement of horses throughout the year only to use them for two weeks in the summer. They relied, therefore, on civilian contractors to provide quantities of horses of the right size for the use of units during their annual camp. Commanding officers received an allowance from which they paid for the hire of the horses.

The problem that this system generated is graphically illustrated in an article in the *Royal Artillery Journal* by Lieutenant Colonel Heindryk, who commanded the 59th (4th West Lancs) Medium Brigade after the First World War:

> 'A Brigade of Artillery arrives at Amesbury or Trawsfynydd complete with personnel, guns and harness. After a short delay, a train load of horses, which none of the officers or men have ever seen before, comes in. The horses are detrained, allotted to batteries and the unfortunate Battery Commander proceeds, to the best of his ability, to sort them into teams. After harnessing, the batteries march to camp. Scenes of incredible confusion take place, resulting in kicks, galls, and what is more serious, accidents to men. (I know of one case in 1907, in which eleven men, from one battery alone, went to hospital on the first day.) This sort

The detachment for this 60pdr form up behind their gun, which is about to set off behind a Fordson Model N farm tractor, while the officer looks down from his charger. They are members of 59th Medium Brigade RA, Territorial Army, at Okehampton, North Devon in 1923.

139

MOVING THE GUNS

The original Peerless portée, which was demonstrated at Camberley in 1926. The limber straddles the trail of the 18pdr, the muzzle of which pokes through a hole in the back of the cab. With the tailgate down one can see the loading ramps stowed on the floor.

of thing is a severe task, even for the experienced and fully trained regular driver, and it is one which no partially trained driver should ever be asked to undertake. Furthermore, it frequently happens that on arrival in camp, the Board casts a number of horses and the one or two day's delay in waiting for these to be replaced causes a loss of time for training when every minute of it is of value.'

Additionally, by the early 1930s, there was the problem of being able to hire sufficient numbers of suitable horses, not only for the artillery units, but for all the other horsed units as well. The problem of being able to find sufficient horses for the Army on mobilisation became a practical reality for Territorial units at Practice Camp each year. As the use of the 'light van' draught horse (the nearest civilian equivalent of the artillery draught horse) declined in commercial usage in favour of the internal combustion engine, so it became increasingly more difficult to provide horses for the Territorial units.

With their usual resourcefulness, some Territorial units found ways of overcoming the problem and many interesting experiments, some more official than others, took place in the 1920s. In 1923, for instance, the 59th (4th West Lancs) Medium Brigade went to Annual Camp at Okehampton with two batteries horsed, and the other two batteries using commercial Fordson agricultural tractors specially hired for the occasion. There was much interest in the possible use of agricultural tractors at this time, largely because considerable quantities would be readily available on mobilisation. The 1923 trial showed that the standard Fordson tractor needed modifying, particularly in respect of the wheels and tyres, before it would be entirely suitable. Further trials were carried out in 1925 at Okehampton, again using Fordson tractors. The principle advantages were seen to be: equal mobility compared to a horsed team, particularly on roads; economy in personnel; better use of training time and financial economies.

In the following year, *Motor Transport* magazine reported the movement through London of 65th (8th London) Field Brigade, their guns being hauled by Fordson tractors supplied by Willets of Colchester, the local Fordson dealers. The Fordsons used patent twin rubber-tyred wheels with steel strakes, which could be withdrawn when running on metalled roads. Apparently, it was estimated that there were 15,000 Fordson tractors available in the country at the time, which would have produced a very useful pool of artillery tractors in the event of war, together with a large number of trained drivers.

Yet all these experiments seem to have been, at best, semi-official. In most cases they seem to have been carried out at the whim of a particular commanding officer using, or some might say mis-using, his horse allowance to experiment with mechanical traction. At the official level, some work was being done, and it would seem from the commentary that accompanied the Dominion Premiers demonstration at Camberley in November 1926, that the Morris-Roadless shown there was designed with the Territorial Artillery in mind. Six of these vehicles were purchased for trials but it is not known whether any were actually trialled by a Territorial unit. The experimental use of a First World War-vintage Peerless lorry to portée an 18pdr gun and limber, shown at the same demonstration, was also carried out for the Territorial Artillery.

However, in 1930, the decision was made to mechanise the Territorial Field Artillery with a forward-control, light six-wheeler. This was the subsidy type Morris Commercial D Type 30cwt 6 x 4 lorry. These were to be held in pools under the administration of the Quarter Master General. 'Battery staff cars in sufficient numbers will be hired for Annual Camp as heretofore.' This was presumably a reference to the facilities of the Artillery Transport Company of York, a civilian firm set up after the war by two demobilised Gunner officers. The firm had a number of cross-country vehicles, which were hired out to Territorial Army regiments for exercises. At one time the Company owned 6 Citroën-Kégresse staff vehicles, 12 Citroën-Kégresse tractors, 6 Crossley-Kégresse tractors as well as a number of Morris Commercial D Type 6 x 4 lorries. When the vehicles were not being used by the military, they were available for hire by forestry and

Morris Commercial D Type six-wheelers, running with overall tracks on the rear bogie while moving the guns of a TA Battery during annual camp at Redesdale.

141

MOVING THE GUNS

A column of 2dpr anti-tank guns being towed by Bedford MW 4 x 2 15cwt tractors in 1939.

agricultural concerns or were available for general contract work. Despite the massive increase in mechanisation after the Munich Crisis in 1938 and the doubling of the Territorial Army in 1939, vehicles were still being hired from the Artillery Transport Company for Annual Camp as late as August 1939. At the same time, medium artillery brigades of the Territorial Army were to be provided with a pool of medium six-wheelers, which would have been any of the subsidy type 3-ton 6 x 4 lorries. The Mechanical Warfare Board accepted that these may not give the best possible cross-country performance, but for reasons of economy it was not possible to re-equip the Territorial medium artillery with the standard medium-artillery tractor of this period, the FWD/AEC R6T/850.

So the authorities, for reasons that were largely beyond their control, pinned their colours firmly to the mast of the 6 x 4 tractors so far as the Territorial Artillery was concerned. Unfortunately, the Army's faith in this type of vehicle was not shared by civilian operators who preferred a lorry with a higher payload-to-weight ratio. As a result, the anticipated pool of civilian-owned vehicles, which could be impressed in an emergency, failed to materialise. Luckily, by the time war broke out, the decision had been taken to produce 4 x 4 tractors as the standard field-artillery tractor and sufficient numbers of these were being produced to equip the Regular batteries, thus releasing the Morris Commercial CDSW 6 x 4 tractors for the use of the expanding Territorial Artillery.

In 1939, it was decided to form ten Anti-Tank Brigades from existing Field Brigades of the Territorial Army Artillery. The 2pdr anti-tank gun was considerably lighter than the 18/25pdr or the 4.5in howitzer and did not therefore require as large a tractor as the current 6 x 4 vehicles. Various 15cwt 4 x 2 vehicles, which had been widely adopted in the rest of the Army, were trialled as anti-tank gun tractors. The Morris Commercial CS8, Bedford and Guy 15cwt trucks were all used as anti-tank gun tractors and were the vehicles used, and abandoned, in France in 1940.

As a postscript, this account is given by **Richard Peacock**, who served as a Gunner in 121st Field Regiment Royal Artillery (Territorial Army), which captures the atmosphere of Territorial gunnery in the period immediately before the outbreak of war in September 1939.

When war was declared in September 1939, my TA unit was at Annual Camp at Bridlington on the Yorkshire coast. We were the 121st Field Regiment, Royal Artillery (Territorial Army) being the 'second line' Regiment of the 69th Field Regiment, based in Leeds. We existed as a result of the Minister of Defence, Mr Hore Belisha, ordering that all TA should duplicate themselves as part of the preparations for war in 1939. I had enlisted earlier that year and, because I could drive, I was a Driver IC (Internal Combustion).

At Camp, we had very little equipment with which to train. There were about six guns. As I remember they were wooden wheeled 4.5-inch howitzers which had come by rail from Leeds. To tow the guns at Camp and for driving instruction we had very ancient six-wheeled Morris Commercial D Type tractors. These had been hired, as was the TA custom, from the Artillery Transport Company of York. This firm was run by an ex-Regular Army officer who knew of the TA transport requirements each summer. In addition, he carried out general transport work, mainly using ex-WD vehicles. We had as well a few up-to-date army vehicles, for example, Morris Commercial 8cwt PU 4 x 2 wireless trucks and Morris and Commer 15cwt GS 4 x 2 trucks. These were on loan from our 'first line' and from other units who were not on Camp at the same time as us.

The South Notts Hussars, 'first line' TA Field Regiment, had lent us three Morris Commercial CDSW 6 x 4 tractors. These vehicles were the latest field artillery gun tractor and I was very lucky to have one 'on charge', much to the envy of my friends.

The day after war was declared, our unit had to return to Leeds to be billeted in schools for the second week of camp as 'aid to the civil power' to prevent looting and so-on in the event of air raids. At the same time, the three CDSW's had to be returned to the South Notts Hussars at Nottingham.

We left Bridlington about 3pm in the charge of a Sergeant and headed for Nottingham. Leeds, our home town, was not quite on the direct route but nonetheless that was our first stop. The Sergeant had decided that a break for liquid refreshment was in order and the pubs were open. I did not drink at that time so I went home by tram for a meal having arranged to meet the others at closing time. We set off down the A1, the others being well oiled by this time. Towards midnight, one of the other tractors ran off the road and down an embankment due, I'm sure, to the alcoholic intake of the driver. After several attempts to reverse out, it was decided to use the vehicle's cross-country performance and drive it through a hedge, right across the field and back on to the A1. A very clear track mark was left right across the field, which was on the inside of a long bend on the A1.

Eventually we arrived in Nottingham in the early hours of the morning to be 'greeted' by the RSM. This was my first experience of a really irate RSM who wanted to know why it had taken 12 hours to drive a distance of 130 miles. He was also far from impressed at the considerable amount of damage done to the front and rear of his vehicle. Fortunately, it was not up to me, a mere Driver IC, to offer an explanation but it's a journey I shall never forget!'

APPENDIX A
NOTES ON THE ORGANISATION AND EQUIPMENT OF THE ROYAL ARTILLERY

The purpose of this appendix is to explain, in general terms, the basic organisation of units in the Royal Artillery, the types of equipment they used, and how they were used. The section is included to be of help to the layman who may not be familiar with the many technical and organisational terms that are second nature to a Gunner. The organisations and equipment described refer mainly to the interwar period, the period with which this book is primarily concerned. For organisations and details about earlier periods, the reader is referred to the various standard histories of the Royal Artillery for those periods.

Organisation

The basic weapon of the Royal Artillery is the gun. (Some would argue that the shell or round is the weapon, the gun the means of delivering it.) A single gun is served by a detachment and is usually commanded by a sergeant, sometimes known as the 'number one'. Two single guns, each known as Sub-Sections, form a Section, usually commanded by a Subaltern Section Commander. A complete Section would consist of the two guns, the means of towing them (either horses or tractors), detachments for the guns, drivers for the vehicles or teams of horses, and a first-line supply of ammunition carried in wagons or limbers.

A number of Sections form a Battery, with the number of Sections depending on the equipment and the role of the Battery. The war establishment of a Horse or Field Artillery Battery was three Sections, but the peacetime 'Lower Establishment' would have only two Sections, the guns, harness and equipment of the centre section being held in mobilisation stores. Medium, Heavy, Light and Mountain Batteries had two Sections with a total of four guns in the Battery. A typical Field Battery of six guns was commanded by a Battery Commander (BC) in the rank of major. In addition to the gun sections, there were a number of specialist tradesmen who formed the Battery Staff. These were the Observation Post (OP) Party and the Gun Position Officers (GPO) Party, whose functions are explained more fully later on. For administrative convenience, the Battery might be organised into two Troops, each commanded by a Captain Troop Commander. A Field Battery would consist of about 80 officers and men at the 'Lower Establishment'.

Until 1938, a Battery of the Royal Artillery was a self-contained unit, largely responsible for its own administration. This was the responsibility of the Battery Captain (BK) and the Battery Quartermaster Sergeant (BQMS) who, assisted by a small staff, looked after the ration account for the men, the forage account for the horses, for the ammunition supply in time of war and for all the technical equipment and stores. They were assisted by a number of specialist tradesmen, such as farriers, saddlers, wheelwrights, carpenters, clerks, cooks and fitters for the guns and vehicles.

It was because the Battery was the smallest independent unit, that the traditions of the Royal Artillery and the loyalties of the Gunners tended to be concentrated at Battery level, unlike most other units in the British Army.

APPENDIX A

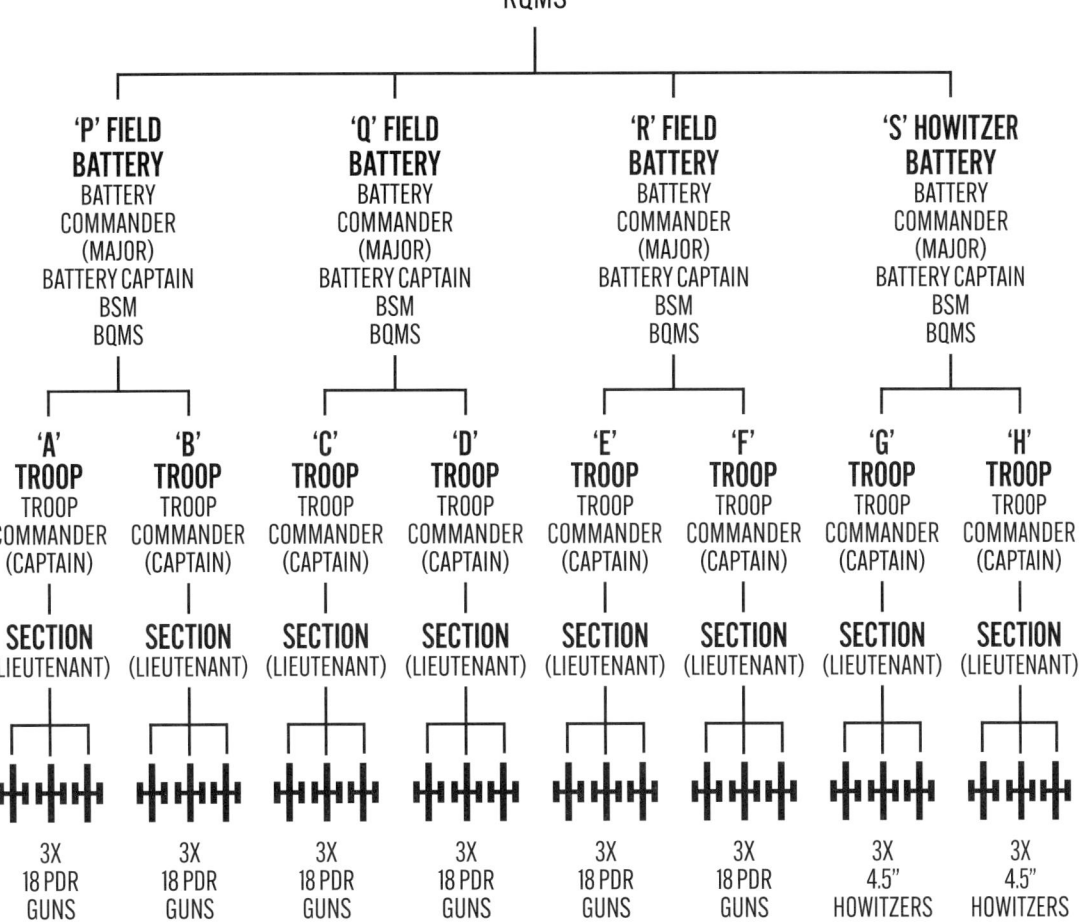

After 1938, many of the administrative functions of the Battery were taken over by the Royal Artillery Brigade and individual Batteries lost some of their autonomy.

A number of Batteries (depending on equipment and role) formed what was known, until 1938, as a Royal Artillery Brigade. Confusingly, an Artillery Brigade, commanded by a lieutenant colonel, did not relate in size, function or level of command to an Infantry or Cavalry Brigade commanded by a brigadier. It was more equivalent in terms of personnel and number of sub-units to an Infantry Battalion or Cavalry Regiment. Indeed, in 1938, Artillery Brigades were renamed Artillery Regiments to avoid this confusion. In the 1920s and 1930s, Artillery Batteries were brigaded together as a matter of administrative convenience but the Brigade had little function in peace or war. Indeed, many Batteries, particularly of the RHA or those in India, were posted at single Battery stations and were not brigaded at all.

Where Field Batteries were brigaded, they were in the proportion of three gun Batteries to one howitzer Battery. Horse Artillery Brigades were of three Batteries only. Medium Brigades usually consisted of three howitzer Batteries to one gun Battery.

Three Brigades of Field Artillery formed the Divisional Artillery, commanded by the Commander Royal Artillery (CRA) in the rank of brigadier. Some Brigades were known as Army Field Brigades and were used as a reserve or to supplement the Divisional Artillery as necessary. They were commanded by the Brigadier General Royal Artillery (BGRA). The single Heavy Brigade of the interwar period came under the command of the Corps Commander and was the responsibility of the Counter Bombardment Officer (CBO) at Corps. This unit existed more on paper than in reality, its guns and equipment being placed in 'care and maintenance'.

The Royal Regiment of Artillery was itself split into three branches: the Royal Horse Artillery (RHA), the Royal Field Artillery (RFA) and the Royal Garrison Artillery (RGA). The traditional role of the RHA was the close support of the Cavalry using a Battery of four or six guns in support of a Cavalry Regiment. One RHA Brigade was stationed at Aldershot in support of 1st Cavalry Brigade and another was in Egypt in support of 3rd Cavalry Brigade. Remaining Batteries were in various

single Battery stations at home and abroad. Horse Artillery Batteries used a lighter version of the standard field gun, which was designed to be towed behind a team of six horses at the gallop. The RHA tended to use 'direct fire' methods (see later notes).

The RFA provided the artillery support for the bulk of the field army on the basis of a Battery of four or six guns in support of an infantry battalion. The gun used by the RFA did not need to be quite so mobile as the RHA weapon and the detachments tended to travel in accompanying wagons or march beside the guns, unlike the Gunners of the RHA who were all mounted.

There had always been a degree of mobility of officers and NCOs between the RHA and the RFA, with the RHA being regarded as a corps d'élite for selected officers and men. Until 1924, the RGA had always been a separate branch with very little cross-posting into the other two branches. To some extent this was a result of the variety and specialised nature of the branch's armament. As its name suggests, it was originally responsible for the fixed defences of the port installations of this country and abroad, and coast defence was the main preoccupation. From the time of the Boer War onwards, when there was seen to be a need for mobile Medium, Heavy and Siege Artillery in the field, the RGA took on a more mobile role and adopted field-artillery methods of fire control. During the First World War, the RGA manned the greatest number of artillery pieces deployed in the field.

The RGA also looked after the specialised discipline of anti-aircraft artillery after the Army took this job over from the Admiralty in 1915. By the end of the First World War, the RGA was the biggest branch and probably the most advanced technically in terms of the variety and complexity of equipment. It was not, however, the most popular branch to serve in, lacking the glamour of the other two branches. In 1923, it was decided to unify the three branches of the Royal Artillery and the RFA and RGA titles disappeared, although the RHA was retained as a corps d'élite. After that date, officers of all three branches were able to move freely between them and the regiment undoubtedly benefited from the exchange of ideas and experiences. Thereafter, Batteries were designated as 'Field Batteries' or 'Medium Batteries' of the Royal Artillery.

Equipment

From 1913 until the 1930s, the RHA was armed with the 13pdr QF gun. This was a lighter version of the standard 18pdr QF gun and was designed to be towed behind a team of six horses at the gallop. It had a range of 6,500yds and, at the beginning of the First World War, could only fire shrapnel. This was detonated as an airburst using a powder-burning fuse. The correct elevation of the gun and the setting of the fuse depended as much on the experience of the Number One as on the application of mathematical settings from range tables. A Quick Firing (QF) gun was characterised by the use of 'fixed ammunition', where the projectile and propellant were fixed together and could thus be loaded quickly. It was also designed with a buffer and recuperator system to absorb the recoil of the gun in the top carriage, allowing it to be reloaded and re-laid more quickly.

In the late 1930s, the RHA was armed with the 3.7in Howitzer. This was originally designed as a light mountain howitzer and was chosen as a stop-gap weapon during the experiments to find a suitable close-support weapon for the mechanised formations in the 1930s. A howitzer has the ability to fire a heavier shell at a lower velocity – usually over a shorter range. Its main characteristic is its ability to fire in the 'higher register', i.e., above 45 degrees. It also has a 'separate round' where the shell and charge are loaded separately and, by varying the propellant charge, it is possible to achieve a great variety of ranges and trajectories. Thus, the howitzer was eminently suitable for bringing down 'plunging fire' deep into enemy trenches, from behind cover. It was this characteristic and the fact that its ammunition was high explosive (HE) detonated by a direct-action fuse and, later, smoke, that made it attractive as a close-support weapon for armoured formations before the advent of the 25pdr gun-howitzer.

The RFA did not need to be so mobile and its Batteries were armed with the 18pdr QF gun, which could fire an 18lb shrapnel shell to a range of 6,500yds or to a maximum of 7,800yds if the gun trail was dug in. By the end of the First World War, one battery out of the four in a Field Brigade was armed with the 4.5in howitzer. This weapon could fire a 35lb HE shell 6,600yds, although a small proportion of shrapnel was also held by the howitzer battery.

The carriage design of the 18pdr QF gun underwent many changes after the war. The Mark V carriage had split trail legs to increase maximum elevation and range. This meant that it could also achieve greater angles of traverse without moving the carriage. The two Mark V guns in each Battery tended to be placed on the flanks of a Battery position where their improved angle of traverse was useful for anti-tank protection.

Towards the end of the interwar period, the search had begun for a replacement for the 13pdr, the 18pdr and the 4.5in howitzer. The gun that emerged, the 25pdr gun-howitzer, combined the characteristics of both gun and howitzer. It was capable of firing in the high and low register, it had separate rounds but the propellant was contained in a number of separately packed charge bags. Thus, the number of charges could be varied to alter the muzzle velocity required and the gun could be used in virtually any role from low-velocity howitzer through to a very high-velocity anti-tank gun.

In 1938, the Royal Artillery took on the specialist anti-tank role using the newly issued 2pdr anti-tank gun. Five Regular Field Regiments were converted into four-battery anti-tank regiments and allotted one to each divisional artillery. An anti-tank gun needed to be able to fire a small calibre shot at very high velocity over a relatively short range. It also needed to be small and inconspicuous and able to be traversed rapidly. The 2pdr gun met all these requirements and was capable of penetrating any known German armour at the time it was introduced.

At the end of the First World War, the RGA of the field army had a bewildering variety of Medium, Heavy and Siege guns and howitzers, from which it selected the 60pdr gun and the 6in 26cwt howitzer as the standard weapons of the medium artillery batteries. Both these guns saw little change, except in carriage design, during the interwar period, though replacements in the form of the 4.5in gun and the 5.5in gun-howitzer were at trials stage at the outbreak of war in 1939.

Employment of Artillery

Until the Boer War, artillery tactics were relatively simple. A Battery of guns supporting an infantry or cavalry attack would gallop forward in full view of the enemy, unlimber and come into action and engage the enemy with 'direct fire', that is, by firing at a target that could be seen from the gun position. The Boers, however, were unsporting enough to actually fire at the gun detachments with rifles. Moreover, they used the newly invented smokeless propellant, which meant that the Gunners, even if they were able to retaliate (rifles and carbines were not carried by gun detachments at this stage), were unable to identify where the rifle fire was coming from. The Gunners found that their aim was being spoilt by these 'uncivilised' tactics and, as losses mounted, they took to placing the guns behind cover where the detachments were relatively safe from small arms fire. They also, incidentally, took to providing shields on the guns, a move which was roundly condemned by *The Times* as 'encouraging cowardly behaviour' on the part of the detachments.

This move presented a technical problem – that of directing the fire of the guns onto a target that could not be seen from the gun position, this being known as indirect fire. The solution was to have an observer forward who could see the target, who was in communication with the Battery and who could adjust the fire of the battery on to the target. In the early days, this was the job of the Battery Commander and, because the means of communicating were fairly rudimentary (voice, semaphore or telephone), the observer was never deployed very far from the Battery.

The guns were directed onto the target by a process known as ranging. On arrival at a gun position, the individual guns were laid parallel to each other with the use of a compass. A section of two guns would commence the ranging process under the direction of the Observation Post Officer (OPO). Any changes in bearing of the guns would be recorded in relation to a fixed aiming point, such as a prominent tree or church tower visible to all the guns in the Battery. The changes in bearing would then be applied to all the guns in the Battery so that they remained parallel with each other. When the OPO was satisfied that the ranging guns were on target, the remaining guns of

Howitzers with wooden-spoked artillery wheels before their conversion to pneumatic tyres are towed by Morris Commercial D Type 6 x 4 tractors.

the battery would open fire and fire would be brought down around the target. The method became rather more sophisticated with the adoption of dial sights on the guns and directors in each battery.

The problem with indirect fire was that the process of ranging inevitably gave away the fact that a target was about to be engaged, thus presenting the enemy with the opportunity of moving the target or of taking retaliatory action. To overcome this problem, predicted fire was used. The bearing and distance of the target in relation to the guns was worked out trigonometrically and fire could be brought down without the need for any preliminary ranging. Its success, however, depended on the accurate location of the guns and the target on the same type of map projection. Predicted fire rose to a high degree of sophistication during the firing of timed barrages during the First World War and was dependent on the development of accurate survey methods and an understanding of all the other variables which affect the accuracy of a shell – meteorological conditions, the muzzle velocity of individual guns, the effect of wear on barrels, small differences in the weights of shells and differences in the characteristics of different batches of propellant. It was not until well into the First World War that all these variables were understood well enough for the Gunners to be able to guarantee supporting fire with an acceptable level of safety for our own troops.

Apart from the dramatic effects of improvements in wireless communications, by and large, the artillery tactics developed during the First World War were those continued throughout the interwar period and which the Gunners went to war with in 1939.

149

MOVING THE GUNS

APPENDIX B
THE MECHANISATION OF THE ROYAL HORSE ARTILLERY

In April 1934, the War Office announced that the Royal Horse Artillery (RHA) was to become mechanised. Traditionally, the role of the RHA was the close support of the cavalry using, since 1913, the 13pr QF gun as its principal weapon. This gun was a lighter version of the 18pdr field gun and its weight was dictated by the need to be able to tow it, at a gallop, behind a team of six horses. As the Cavalry Brigades began to mechanise in the early 1930s, it became increasingly difficult to justify the retention of horse-drawn batteries equipped with an obsolete gun. Indeed, in many instances in the First World War when mobility became a low priority, RHA batteries re-equipped with the heavier 18pdr gun.

Mechanisation had been a fairly traumatic experience for the field batteries but was even more so for the RHA which, since its formation in 1793, had relied solely on its horses for the close support of the cavalry. The more pessimistic officers saw it as the beginning of the end. How on earth was the traditional 'dash' and 'élan' of the RHA to survive the process of mechanisation?

In 1934, the 13 regular batteries of horse artillery were serving in various stations at home and abroad. A Battery 'The Chestnut Troop', B Battery, and O Battery 'The Rocket Troop' were brigaded together in 1st Brigade RHA and were stationed in Egypt in support of 3 Cavalry Brigade. Their main

Mahout, a Light Dragon Mark IIB of M Battery, Royal Horse Artillery, beautifully turned out, as one would expect from the RHA, with a pair of wooden-wheeled limbers in tow.

function was the protection of various British interests in the Middle East, notably the Suez Canal. D Battery, J Battery and M Battery were brigaded together in 3rd Brigade RHA and were stationed in Aldershot in support of 1 Cavalry Brigade. C Battery, K Battery and L Battery were loosely brigaded in 2nd Brigade RHA, with C and K Batteries at Newport and L Battery at Trowbridge. F Battery was an independent battery stationed at St Johns Wood, London, and performed the ceremonial functions now carried out by the King's Troop. The remaining batteries formed independent units in India: E Battery in Meerut, G Battery at Sialkot, J Battery at Risapur and N Battery at Trimulgherry.

In England, M Battery was the first to mechanise, being warned in late 1933. By the end of the following January, the Battery had bade a sad farewell to the first batch of horses, which were sent back to the Remount Centre at Arborfield. The officers' chargers and a

Dragons of M Battery RHA, preceded by their battery staff vehicles, await the signal to enter the portals of Windsor Castle for the Royal Inspection by King George V in June 1934.

number of troop horses were retained and the equestrian life of the Battery seems to have continued unabated with notable successes at the Aldershot Point-to-Point in March. Indeed, it seems that one particular horse should perhaps have been included in the batch of horses returned to the Remount Depot for it is recorded that Lieutenant

MOVING THE GUNS

Colchester was thrown from his charger 'Simple James' during the Grand Military at Sandown on 16 March and broke his collar bone. Not three weeks later, the same horse threw Mr Shorland during the Royal Artillery Steeplechase, also at Sandown, where he suffered the same fate. Whether both officers were pleased to receive replacements in the form of Austin Sevens is not recorded.

By April 1934, six of the guns chosen to replace the 13pdrs, the pneumatically-tyred 3.7in howitzers and their limbers, had arrived. On 19 April, King George V and Queen Mary inspected a Dragon-drawn section of two guns at the Royal Pavilion at Aldershot, the Dragons being borrowed from 10th Field Brigade for the occasion. By 4 May, the Battery was complete with its 12 Dragons and was inspected for the first time as a mechanised Battery by the GOC Aldershot Command on 9 May. By the middle of May, the vehicle establishment was:

- 4 Morris Eight two-seaters with wireless
- 3 Austin Seven two-seat cars
- 4 motor cycles
- 12 Light Dragons Mark II
- 2 Morris 30cwt 6 x 4 lorries.

The Battery retained 10 officers' chargers and 20 troop horses, so perhaps life was not so bad after all.

On 18 June, the King inspected M Battery in the Quadrangle at Windsor Castle. The Battery paraded in front of an impressive inspection party including, in addition to the King and Queen, the Princess Royal, Princess Julianna of the Netherlands, Princess Alice and the Earl of Athlone, the Earl of Harewood and the Commander-in-Chief Aldershot Command. The King apparently took a great deal of interest in the vehicles and equipment and examined everything in the minutest detail. Each Dragon in the Battery was given a name beginning with the Battery letter 'M', as had been the custom with the horses. Queen Mary, however, was not impressed

152

APPENDIX B

Another Mark IIB of M Battery RHA, *Mars*, is shown with the pneumatic-tyred version of the 3.7in howitzer and its attendant limber. This rear view of the Dragon shows the expanded metal cover fitted round the silencer.

with the name *Moscow* on one of the Dragons, a name that was rapidly changed after the inspection!

The other two batteries of 3rd Brigade, D and J, mechanised during 1935. The Royal Tournament of that year was an emotional event as, on the last night, it was announced that it would be the final occasion on which a horsed battery of the RHA would be performing the famous Musical Drive. The audience apparently rose to their feet and removed their hats in salute as the teams rode out to the strains of 'Auld Lang Syne'. In practice, of course, a horsed battery remained at St Johns Wood until the outbreak of the Second World War and the Riding House Troop, now the King's Troop, was re-formed after the war to carry out ceremonial duties.

J Battery held its last full-mounted parade in October 1935 and all its horses, except 15, were dispersed among the Royal Artillery Mounted Band – for which the Brigade now assumed responsibility – and the Remount Depot. Two instructional vehicles were received about this time, which were described as being 'rather ancient and indifferent'. Despite the fact that no vehicles had by then been received, a 'tactics week' was held in February 1936 during which the problems of horse artillery support of mechanised cavalry were discussed. By March 1936, the Battery was having to borrow vehicles and guns from M Battery in order to get on with driving and maintenance training and in April the Battery Commander reported that driver training was seriously handicapped by the lack of vehicles.

By April 1936, the first vehicles began to arrive. Four Austin 7s and two 30cwt lorries arrived on 29 April, four 3.7in howitzers on 15 May and the first two Dragons were issued on 15 June together with three Austin Sevens fitted with wireless. By the end of June, the shortage of vehicles throughout the Brigade was such that, on one day of each week, each battery was allowed a full complement of vehicles in order

153

MOVING THE GUNS

Light Dragons of 1st Brigade RHA in Egypt during a trial run into the Western Desert in 1934. Canopies have been rigged in this case to keep the sun off.

to be able to carry out one full day's training each week. However, with the arrival of four Dragons on 22 June, the Battery was able to take part in the 1st Cavalry Brigade exercises in August and September although it was still short of six Dragons and two guns more than nine months after the mechanisation process began.

The experience of J Battery was very typical of many units at this time, with insufficient men and equipment to enable them to maintain a fully operational state. In September 1935, 1st Division was sent to Palestine to deal with an Arab uprising. Had a similar emergency arisen a few months earlier requiring the Cavalry Brigade, the RHA would have been hard pressed to have provided proper mechanised artillery support.

Both D and J Batteries took part in the Cavalry Brigade exercises in 1936 and learnt at first hand many of the lessons already learnt by the other mechanised batteries of the field artillery. Protection of the battery on the move, concealment of the battery from the air, the importance of good vehicle maintenance and, not least, the ability to read a map accurately from a fast-moving vehicle were all lessons that had to be learnt by the former masters of the horse.

Finally, just to prove that the 'old and bold' were adaptable, it is recorded that the newly posted-in Battery Sergeant Major of J Battery arrived in February from the Depot Royal Artillery, having learnt to ride a motorcycle and drive a motor vehicle in a fortnight, having never done either before. This was no bad achievement (for a man who presumably had grown up with horses since he was a youngster) and was a typical example of the enthusiasm and determination in the former horsed batteries at this time.

In Egypt, A Battery (the Chestnut Troop) was the first battery of 1st Brigade, RHA to mechanise, being warned on 7 April 1934. By the end of July, horses had been returned to the Remount Depot and the battery had received 12 Light Dragons — 6 for the guns, 3 for ammunition wagons and 3 for Battery Staff. In addition, there were seven two-seater cars and four motorcycles. Six 3.7in howitzers were issued with experimental pneumatic carriages (possibly the 'Egypt' carriages mentioned earlier) and three ammunition wagons.

Driving and maintenance training continued throughout 1934 and, by December, the Battery was able to complete its first Drill Order as a mechanised battery. The Battery received reports from England of M Battery's experiences during the year and applied them to its own training. However, the first exercise in the desert brought many equipment defects to light. The little Austin Sevens were quite incapable of tackling desert sand, while the existing vehicle establishment

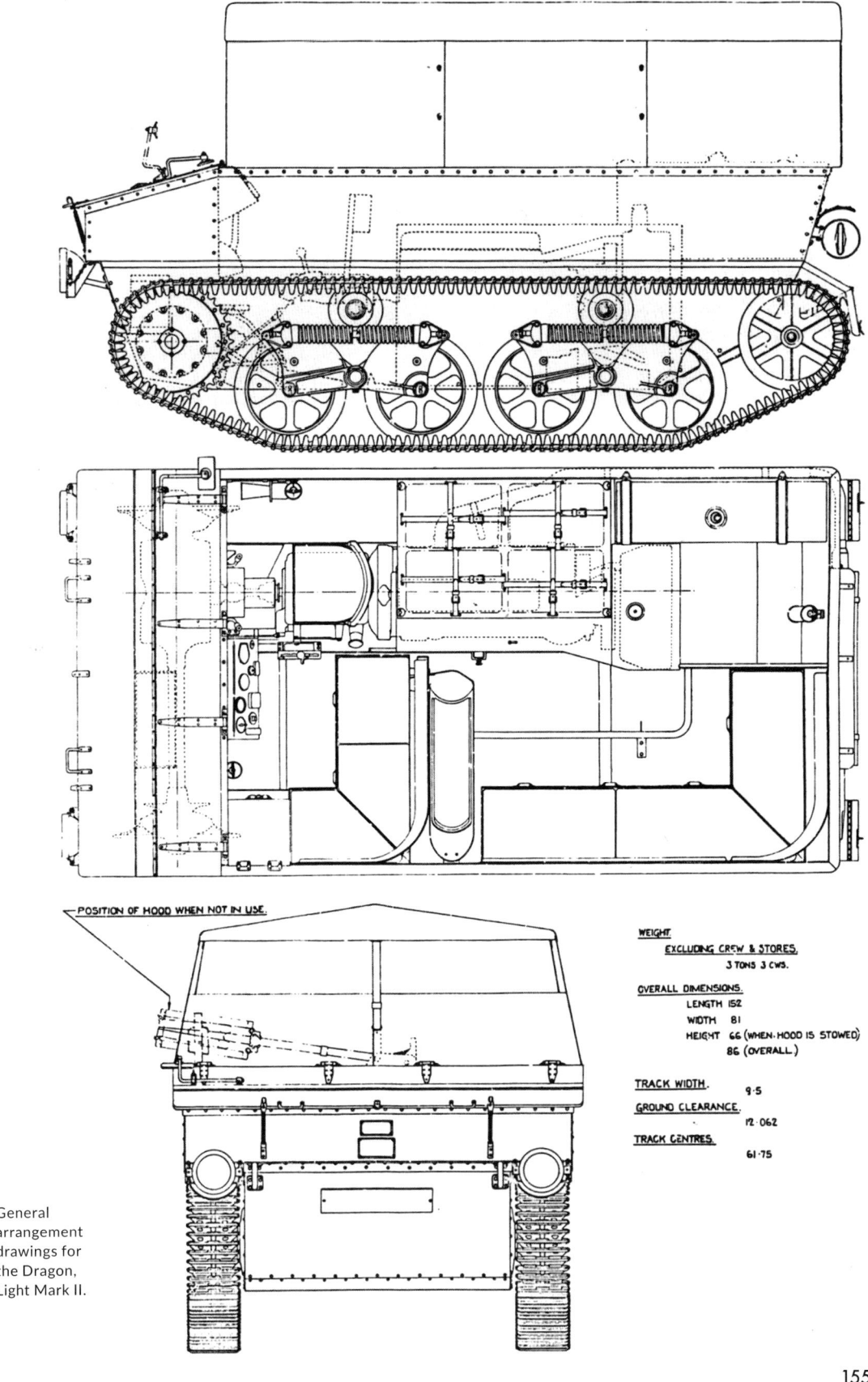

General arrangement drawings for the Dragon, Light Mark II.

MOVING THE GUNS

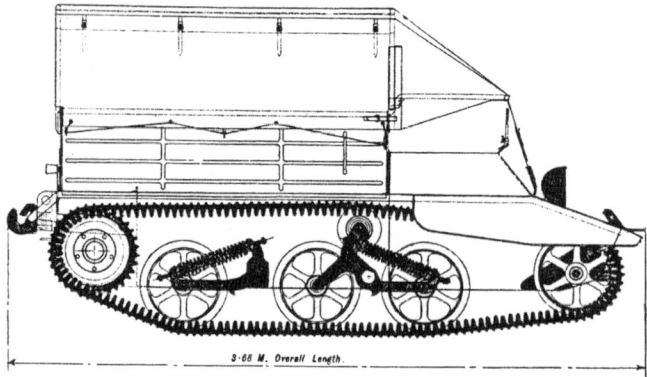

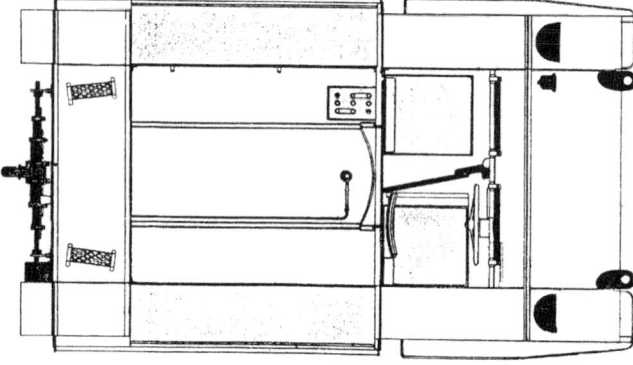

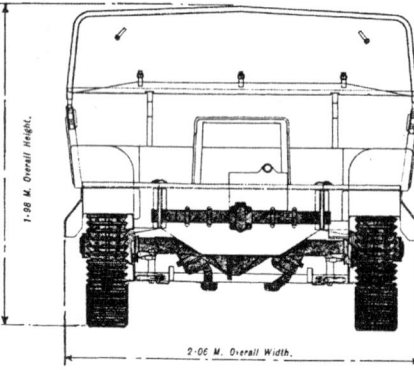

A manufacturer's drawing, from a sales brochure, showing the layout of the Light Dragon Mark III.

was insufficient to allow for any vehicle casualties. A note of exasperation is detected in a report that, 'a regrettable tendency was noticed amongst Staff Officers to utilise our Dragons in pulling Staff-cars through difficult places – this will have to be suppressed'!

However, by February 1935, the Chestnut Troop took part in the Cavalry Brigade exercises and, despite the fact that the drivers had converted from horses to tractors only some seven months before, there were few vehicle casualties apart from the Austin Sevens.

In the autumn of 1935, Italy invaded Abyssinia and for a time British interests in Egypt and the Canal Zone seemed to be threatened. The garrison towns on Egypt's western frontier, with names that were to become famous less than a decade later, such as Mersah Matruh, Sidi Barrani and Sollum, were fully manned and the Chestnut Troop formed part of an armoured mobile force ready to move at 24 hours' notice. The threat receded during the year, however, and the force was eventually stood down in August 1936.

B Battery began its mechanisation process after its return from the Western Desert in April 1936. The horse establishment was reduced to 15 troop horses and the officers' chargers. The Battery was issued with the latest, brand-new Light Dragons Mark IID and 3.7in howitzers. Driving and maintenance training began in earnest despite the fact that the Battery had to provide detachments to man guns mounted on Ford rail 'trollies' in Palestine during the disturbances there in 1935 and 1936. In June 1936, it is recorded that, on the death of the battery Commander from bronchial pneumonia, a horse team was provided for the last time for the funeral carriage, the horses being borrowed from O Battery.

The third battery in Egypt, O Battery (the Rocket Troop), began the mechanisation process in October 1935 with the arrival of four Austin Sevens, followed by two 30cwt lorries in December. Three Austin Tens filled with wirelesses were issued for trials as possible replacements for the Austin Sevens. No 45 Battery of 20th Field Brigade, stationed nearby at Helmiah, which was already mechanised, helped train the Horse Artillery drivers in the techniques of driving in the desert. Twelve Light Dragons were drawn from Ordnance during April and the 3.7in howitzers were issued in May and June. It is interesting to note that it was decided not to issue the four-wheeled staff trailers to carry the wireless sets pending the issue of Austin Tens. By 16 April, the Battery was fully mechanised and on 29 April was able to provide a fully mechanised gun section for the mobile column, which was still on standby for the Abyssinian crisis.

During 1936, 1st and 3rd Brigades swapped stations, with 1st Brigade returning to England and 3rd Brigade replacing them in Egypt. Both Brigades were now fully mechanised and had picked up a lot of practical experience.

The remaining horse artillery batteries in England and in India generally did not mechanise until 1937 or 1938 when the general mechanisation was fully under way. Some batteries in India were not mechanised at the outbreak of war as was the case with K Battery at St Johns Wood.

As the threat of war loomed, the conflicting demands for new equipment within the Army and between the Services had its effect on the progress of mechanisation and there were considerable delays in the provision of new equipment. F Battery, for instance, stationed at Risalpur, was expecting to be completely mechanised by October 1937 and the first two Light Dragons Mark IIC were issued in April 1937. However, by November it was apparent that mechanisation would not be achieved before Christmas at the earliest and the Battery took part in Brigade training in November half-mechanised and half horse-drawn. As late as March 1938, although the Battery had disposed of all its horses, it had only received eight 15cwt trucks and was still short of six lorries and eight Light Dragons. Similarly, neither G Battery at Meerut nor C Battery at Trimulgherry were mechanised by 1939.

Back in England, the remaining Batteries mechanised slightly earlier. I Battery at Newport performed the last horsed musical drive at the Southern Command Tattoo at Tidworth in July 1937 and was fully mechanised by January 1938. L Battery at Trowbridge received its first Morris 15cwts in December 1937 and the first Light Dragons Mark II arrived in January 1938. N Battery, who returned from Trimulgherry to Newport in 1936, were fully mechanised by January 1938 when their vehicle establishment was:

- 6 Light Dragons
- 2 15cwt trucks
- 2 30cwt lorries
- 6 8cwt lorries
- 6 Norton motorcycles

An indication of the urgency of the situation is reflected in the report in the Battery diary that, once the vehicles were received, driver training 'was carried out morning, noon and night'. Of course, the Munich crisis passed and the country was given a brief respite in which to continue to rearm.

K Battery, the battery stationed at St Johns Wood, apparently mobilised in 1939 as a horse-drawn battery. Its horse 'reinforcements' were drawn from what remained of the civilian draught horses left in London. Rather than split up teams that had worked together for years, they were allocated to sections as teams. The gunners irreverently nicknamed the gun sub-sections so formed with the names of the firms who had supplied the horses. Thus, the 'Whitbread sub-section' and the 'United Dairies sub-section' entered the Army List unofficially for a short time. The story that the 'United Dairies sub' would not move – and then only at a sedate pace — until it heard the clank of empty milk bottles behind, is, no doubt apocryphal.

MOVING THE GUNS

APPENDIX C
VEHICLE DEVELOPMENTS IN INDIA

Despite the fact that the Army in India had taken delivery of a Burrell-Boydell traction engine in the 1860s, this did not mark the start of a continuing interest in mechanisation. The real change did not begin until the First World War and, even then, it did not appear to have affected the Royal Artillery. Things were slightly different overseas and the Mesopotamia Expeditionary Force, which was administered from India, had some motorised anti-aircraft batteries in service along with Caterpillar (Holt) Companies of the ASC operating with medium-artillery batteries.

After the war things began to improve but the first event worthy of note was the arrival, in 1923, of the prototype Dragon No 1. However, the purpose of its visit was only loosely connected with the artillery. It had been dispatched for trials to evaluate the possibilities of employing tracked vehicles on the North West Frontier with a view, perhaps in the future, of sending tanks out there. In 1925 the first positive steps were taken with the purchase of a number of 5-ton Holt tractors to work with the medium batteries. These were full-tracked vehicles, powered by a 56hp engine and not fitted with the small forward-steering roller that was a feature of the wartime model. Although somewhat underpowered and too slow for long trips, they easily coped with the worst sandy conditions that India could offer and remained in service well into the 1930s. They could be coupled direct to the 6in howitzer but when towing the 60pdr gun a limber was necessary. They also towed a large-tracked trailer, which carried ammunition and on which the detachment sat in elevated, but vulnerable, isolation. Holt tractors accompanied 16 Medium Battery to China in 1927.

Naturally the Army in India was influenced by developments in Great Britain and, as a consequence, purchased various sample vehicles for evaluation. As has been seen, many of these vehicles were also trialled by MWEE in Great Britain before being sent out to India. Among the types tested were a four-wheel-drive Hathi, similar to the British version apart from a larger radiator, and a 30cwt Crossley-Kégresse half-track. It is not altogether clear if this vehicle was chosen specifically for artillery haulage, although this must have been one potential use.

Reports suggest that a far higher degree of interaction existed between the various arms of service in India than was the case at home, no doubt stimulated by the distance factor. This cooperation manifested itself in the establishment of the Mechanical Transport Advisory Committee (India), which first met in 1924. Its members represented all the user branches of the Army as well as the RAF. Any new vehicle arriving in India

One of the big Holt 5-ton caterpillar tractors, towing a 60pdr gun and one of the clumsy-looking trailers. These were large, box-bodied contraptions on Holt-style running gear, presumably to carry ammunition. The precarious arrangements for carrying the detachment were probably an afterthought; it would doubtless have been quicker and a lot more comfortable to march.

158

The original Woolwich-built tractor AT 1, masquerading as His Majesty's Tank *Dragonind*, one of the first military tracked vehicles to be tested on the sub-continent.

seemed to have been examined by all and sundry, regardless of its intended use.

In 1926, an Armstrong Siddeley Pavesi was supplied to India but it probably made no better impression there than it did in Britain and no more appeared. Indeed, it seems that little progress was being made towards mechanisation among the Gunners, but this could be explained by the lack of suitable vehicles.

In 1929, the Royal Artillery in India took delivery of a batch of Guy 3-ton 6 x 4 lorries specially designed for hauling medium artillery in tropical conditions. The chassis was a Model CAX6 but the body appears to have been supplied by Vickers Ltd, with whom the contract was signed. Called 'ammunition lorries' in some official documents, they were referred to by the Mechanisation Board in Britain as 'tractor lorries'. This was the name given to vehicles with a shorter load-carrying body than usual in order to enhance their performance as gun towers. The six-cylinder engine was housed in a longer bonnet than usual, which also contained a radial-pattern Still-type radiator, presumably intended to give improved cooling in hot climates.

At least nine were supplied and, in comparative trials with a Holt tractor, the Guy was generally favoured for greater speed and comfort. Nonetheless, it was not as effective in soft sand as the Holt, and showed a tendency to dig in its undriven front wheels on soft going. It was also criticised on account of its long bonnet, which limited the driver's visibility across country and for the complicated controls required for the supplementary gearbox. The towing hooks also proved troublesome and, judging from the many reports on the subject in the Military Transport Advisory Committee Minutes, was one

159

MOVING THE GUNS

The experimental six-wheel-drive version of the Guy, along with other military and civilian vehicles, bogged down at a river crossing. Even the old bus seems to have got further than the Guy, and the event has attracted a good audience.

A column of trucks led by two of the Guy CAX6 ammunition lorries on an Indian road. The front-mounted tow bar could be used to help emplace a gun although one source has claimed that it was done to enable the trucks to double-head a gun if the situation required it.

that was never satisfactorily resolved. The Guys were only ever considered to be an interim solution to the gun tractor problem and some experts advocated a forward-control version of the 3-ton Thornycroft instead, provided it could be fitted with a six-cylinder engine.

The two underlying problems of mechanisation in India could be summed up as distance from source of supply and finance. The latter factor, for instance, ruled out the use of tracked Dragons, which many Royal Artillery officers in India would have preferred to either Holts or lorries. Not only were they expensive machines to purchase in the first place, but they also required a lot of specialist maintenance and a large stock of spare parts. The distance from Britain also inhibited the speedy adoption of new models. The normal practice was to purchase for trials two examples of any new model that appeared suitable and then to follow this with a small order for more extensive tests. If these proved satisfactory, a larger order was placed and the vehicles entered service. Due to the lengthy delivery time, however, this process took about 12 months longer than it did in Britain. The problem was not helped by the lack of a really effective testing organisation in India. A small trials establishment existed at Chaklala and, by 1929, it was hoped that a more extensive unit could be set up in conjunction with MWEE at

APPENDIX C

The great earthquake that devastated Quetta in 1935 gave the two Morris-Roadless half-tracks a chance to show what they could do pulling down buildings. Although based on the FAT Mark II used by the Royal Artillery in Britain, these vehicles carried a much simpler style of body.

Farnborough, which was also planning to open a branch in India, mainly to subject British Army vehicles to hot weather trials.

Following trials of the Guy, consideration was given to the idea of obtaining some six-wheel-drive tractors for India and, in 1929, two prototypes were purchased. One was an impressive looking Scammell and the other was a modification of the Guy. Oddly, it was the latter, which had a complicated (some would say highly vulnerable) form of layshaft drive to the front axle, which was found to be the better of the two. No more were ordered, however, and one suspects that expense was the determining factor.

The mechanisation of field-artillery batteries in India began in 1929 with the appearance of two Morris-Roadless half-tracks, based on the Mark II Field Artillery Tractor being used at home. There is no evidence to suggest that

MOVING THE GUNS

This Morris CDSW 'toast rack', with its 18pdr and limber, has been prepared for a military funeral. The gun itself will be the funeral carriage while the tractor has shrouded headlamps. Once again, the unit is 98 Field Battery, 1st Field Brigade, and the location is Nowshera.

An 18pdr on a special two-wheeled portée trailer, being towed by a Morris Commercial CD Type 6 x 4 tractor, also of 98 Field Battery. The leading vehicle is another Morris design, the 8cwt PU light truck.

they were ever adopted as service vehicles and the two trials vehicles remained on strength for some years. There are photographs of them being used in salvage work following the earthquake in Quetta in 1935. The vehicle finally chosen was the Morris Commercial D Type 30cwt 6 x 4, a batch of which arrived in 1930 to equip 1st Field Brigade, Royal Artillery. Although the type was widely used by the Army in Britain in a variety of roles, it was never adopted as a gun tractor except for the use by the Territorial Army Artillery units. They were supplied as a basic chassis and cab to India and were fitted with a special artillery body at the Gun Carriage Factory at Jubbulpore. They were widely criticised for being underpowered and were followed by the more substantial CD Model in the mid-1930s. There is a photograph of one of this model towing an 18pdr gun on a special portée trailer. The Morris Commercial CDSW Field Artillery Tractor was also adopted for use in India after 1938, a move designed, in part, to rationalise vehicles and equipment at home and in India in the event of a British Expeditionary Force needing to be reinforced by an Imperial Service unit of the Indian Army.

Although the Royal Artillery was originally denied the use of modern Dragons in India, the matter was eventually reconsidered. This was prompted initially by the RTC wishing to replace its rather ageing fleet of armoured cars in India with Light Tanks. The change began with the arrival, in 1929, of a pair of Carden-Loyd Mark VI carriers. One of these, bearing the name *Cachy*, was photographed towing a small-tracked limber and a rather ancient and unidentified field gun. Since the two-man machine-gun carrier had been constantly criticised by the RTC for being underpowered, its use as a gun tractor seemed doomed from the start, and so it proved. In 1932, however, there appeared from Vickers-Armstrong a pair of their new 2-ton tractors of the type that was to become the Light Dragon Mark I in British service. Although they appear to have performed well, the argument in favour of wheeled tractors, that they were more versatile and could be used for other purposes, seemed to have settled the matter in favour of the Morris Commercial tractors.

In 1934, a 50hp Caterpillar tractor, powered by a diesel engine, was tested as a medium artillery tractor at Ambala. Unfortunately, its cross-country performance was at the expense of a very slow road speed, and it was rejected. This tractor incidentally, was a commercial model destined for a customer in Afghanistan and the trials report revealed that it left for Kabul driving on its own tracks. Not only must this have been an epic journey in its own right, but it also seems highly likely that the vehicle would have been virtually worn out by the time its new owner took delivery of it in Kabul!

The trial appears to have rekindled interest yet again in the idea of Dragons for medium-artillery haulage and the subsequent discussion produced some interesting comments. On the one hand, the Gunners appreciated the advantages of diesel engines for this type of haulage but, on the other hand, they felt that, as a matter of principle and for sound military reasons, they should adopt the type of vehicle being used at home. Against this, others felt that any vehicle with an all-metal body, such as the Dragon, would be a liability in India, presumably on the grounds of heat retention. This comment was endorsed by Captain R.M. Jerram, who represented RTC interests on the Advisory Committee. Since the RTC had operated all-metal armoured cars in India since 1922, and was now using Light Tanks in large numbers, they would be more aware of this problem than most, but Jerram is not known to have advocated the use of wooden tanks.

Two Carden-Loyd Mark VI carriers were supplied to India for tests with the Royal Tank Corps. Both came complete with special sun roofs and modified cooling arrangements. Cachy was also tested briefly as a gun tractor, using this rather ancient field piece, but the Model T Ford engine would probably have been defeated by anything less level than this basketball court.

A War Office summary published in 1937 mentions, amongst other things, that 18 Mark IV Medium Dragons were on order for India at this time. This was the last pattern of Medium Dragon to be supplied to the British Army and was fitted with an AEC diesel engine. This order may, therefore, have resulted from the 1934 deliberations. In the event, there is no evidence to suggest that they were ever delivered to India or, indeed, that they were ever built.

Examples of the Vickers 2-ton tractor also went to India for trials. Although at first glance similar to the Light Dragon Mark I, notice the earlier style of leaf-spring suspension and absence of a front stowage locker.

APPENDIX D
THE PROGRESS OF MECHANISATION FIELD BATTERIES

Date See Note 1	Brigade See Note 2	Formation See Note 3	Batteries See Note 4			
1923 Apr	9	Army	19	20	28	76(H)
1924 Apr	1	Army	11	52	80	98(H)
1928 Feb	10	Army	30(H)	46	51	54
1931 Feb	21	Army	P	O	Y	Z
1932 May	20		41	45(H)	67	99
1935 Feb	4		4	7	14	66(H)
Aug	14	Army	38(H)	61(H)	68	88
Aug	32	Army	115(H)	120(H)	121	
Nov	33		101	113(H)	114(MH)	
1936 May	30		111(H)	112(H)	117	
May	31		116(H)	118(H)	119	
Nov		1RHA	A	B	O	
Nov		3RHA	D	J	M	
1937 Feb	2	1 Division	35(H)	42	53	87
Feb	13	2 Division	2		8 44	82(H)
Feb	16	2 Division	27	34	72	86(H)
Feb	18	2 Division	59	93	94	95(H)
1937 Feb	19	1 Division	29(H)	39	96	97
Feb	24	1 Division	22	50	56(H)	70
1938 May	13		2	8	44	82(H)
	14		38	61	68	83
	21		P	Q	X	Y
	26		15	48	71	40
	29					

1939 see Note 6

APPENDIX D

Location See Note 5	Destination, etc
Deepcut	to Bulford 1925 Oct
Bulford	to Deepcut 1925 May to China 1927 May then India
Deepcut	
Catterick	
Catterick	to Egypt 1936 Nov
Nowshera, India	
Colchester	
Deepcut	to Brighton ex 4 Light Bde
Bulford	ex 5 Light Bde
Norwich	ex 1 & 2 Light Bdes
Helmich, Egypt	ex 3 Light Bde
Abassia, Egypt	
Aldershot	
Bordon	
Aldershot	
Ewshott	
Deepcut	
Bordon	
Aldershot	
	All Batteries convert to Anti-Tank Batteries

Source: Philip Ventham, 1989

Notes

1 Date
The date listed is the date when the Brigade is first shown in the Royal Artillery Distribution Lists (the Blue Lists) as being mechanised. Individual Batteries may well have mechanised sometime earlier.

2 Brigade
This is the number of the Field Brigade, Royal Artillery, or Brigade of Royal Horse Artillery as appropriate. Brigades of Artillery (equating to Battalions of Infantry or Regiments of Cavalry), became known as Regiments in 1938.

3 Formation
This is the higher tactical formation, which the Artillery Brigade supported at the date in question. In general terms, a Brigade (or Regiment) of Artillery supported a Brigade of Infantry or Cavalry but were allocated to Divisions or Armies. The RHA Brigades supported Cavalry Brigades.

4 Batteries
These are the numbers or letters of the Batteries in the Artillery Brigade in question. Generally, there were four Batteries to a Brigade; some Brigades, depending on role, had three. (H) indicates a Battery armed with the 4.5in howitzer. In the case of 1st and 3rd Brigades RHA, all Batteries were armed with the 3.7in howitzer on mechanisation.

5 Location
The location of the Brigade at the date in question. Individual Batteries may have been detached elsewhere.

6 1939
After mid-1938, the Distribution Lists were no longer published 'for reasons of National Security'. However, the remaining 15 Field Brigades all mechanised in the period up to September 1939.

INDEX

A
Abyssinian Invasion 1935 135, 153, 154
Ackroyd safety oil engine 17
AEC 130hp compression ignition engine 121
　FWD R6T/850 6 x 6 Artillery Tractor 122, 123, 132
　Matador 4 x 4 Medium Artillery Tractor 124-5
Air Defence of Great Britain (ADGB) 136, 137
Air Defence School, Watchet 48
Air Defence Wing, Shoeburyness 47
Albion 6 x 4 Artillery Tractor 123, 125
Albion Motors 123
Alvis Straussler 109
Anti-aircraft Artillery 36, 79, 100, 127 et seq
Armitage, Lt Col 39, 44
Armstrong Siddeley Ltd 44, 67, 72, 73, 75,
Armstrong Siddeley
　8 x 8 Artillery Tractor 129
　80hp air-cooled engine 120
　82hp engine 46
　90hp engine 120
Armstrong Siddeley Pavesi, in India 159
Armstrong Whitworth, Sir William & Co Ltd 18, 46, 119
Army Service Corps (see Royal Army Service Corps)
Artillery Observation Post (AOP) carrier 100
Artillery Transport Company of York 141, 143
Artillery Transporters (ATI & AT2) 41, 43
Artillery Units (see Royal Artillery)
Ashanti War, 1873 11, 12
Austin Motor Co Ltd 71
Austin,
　Seven 4 x 2 car 91, 105, 152, 154, 156
　Ten 4 x 2 car 156
Automobile Engineer 102
Aveling and Porter Steam Sapper 11, 12, 13
　traction engine 10, 139

B
Baldwin 129
Battery Staff trailer
　2-wheeled 91
　4-wheeled 104
Battery Staff vehicles 105 et seq
Bedford 30cwt 6 x 4 tractor 115
　MW 15cwt 4 x 2 AT 139
Benz tractor 69
Bethell, Maj RFA 16, 17
Birch, Gen Sir Noel 46
Birch Gun 34, 46 et seq, 81, 85, 91
Blackstone tractor 120
Boer War 15, 146, 148
Boydell, James 7
Bray, William 8
British Expeditionary Force (BEF), 1939 98, 104
Broom and Wade tractor 19
Burford, H.G. & Co Ltd 55
Burford-Kégresse 41, 44, 55 et seq
　30cwt tractor 42, 44, 55, 56, 65
　3-ton tractor 56, 68
Burrell, Charles & Son Ltd, Thetford 8
Burrell traction engine 9
Burrell-Boydell engine 7, 8, 15

C
Carden-Loyd Carrier Mk VI 42, 66
　Tractor Light GS, 112
　trailer 66
Caterpillar, Holt, tractor 23, 25, 26, 158
Chaklala, Trials Establishment 160
Cheshire Regiment, 2nd Bn 85
Churchill, Winston 81, 84
Citroën, André 51
Citroën undercarriage 64
Citroën-Kégresse 51 et seq
Cletrac tractor 61, 64, 71, 72
Cleveland Tractor Co 60, 72
Commer Spider 4 x 4 artillery tractor 111
Crimean War 7
Crompton R.E.B Lt 10, 11, 14, 15
Crosland Committee, 1934 104, 134
Crossley-Kégresse 41, 44, 45, 53 et seq, 57, 65, 82
　15cwt artillery tractor 52, 53
　30cwt artillery tractor 53, 57
　30cwt Battery staff 53
　3-ton B3E1 artillery tractor 54
Crossley Motor Co 53

D
Daily Telegraph 34, 84
Dennis 30cwt 6 x 4 tractor 115
Department of Tank Design and Experiment, Charlton Park 39,
Diplock, Bramah J. 14, 17
Disarmament Conference, 1932 134
Dominion Premiers Demonstration, 1926 46, 54, 56, 60, 61, 141
Dragons,
　experimental, B1E1, B1E2, B1E3 72, 73
　Mk I 89
　Mk II 93 et seq
　Light Mk IA (2-ton tractor) 93
　Light Mk II 93
　Mk III 98, 99, 108
　Medium Mk II* 121
　Mk III 118, 119, 121, 122
　Mk IV 120
　'protected track' (PT) or Woolwich 74

INDEX

Duncan Prize Essay, 1921 35-6

E
Egypt undercarriage 64
Empire Marketing Board 77
emplacement destroyers 30
Experimental Armoured Force (EAF) 34 et seq
Experimental Bridging Establishment, Christchurch 44
Experimental Mechanised Force (EMF) 81 et seq

F
Fisher, Capt D.R.D. RFA 36, 37
First World War 23 et seq
Fuller, J.C. Maj Gen 34, 81, 82
Foden Steam Waggon 16
Fordson 71, 50
Fordson Agricultural Tractor 139, 140, 141
Fordson 4 x 4 artillery tractor 109, 115
Foster Daimler 60hp, 90hp, 105hp tractors 26, 27, 28, 68, 69
Foster, William & Co 26
Fowler, John & Co, Leeds 12
Fowler traction engine 12, 13
Fowler-Hay Siege Engine 12, 13
FWD Motor Co, Slough 78
  FWD 4 x 2 3-ton lorry 26, 69, 86
  FWD 6 x 6 artillery tractor 123, 132-3
  FWD Roadless artillery tractor B4E1, B4E2 117, 118

G
Gardner LW 6-cylinder CI engine 123
Garner Mobile Equipment 115
Garrett, Richard & Sons, Leiston 7
Glasgow tractor 68, 69, 71
GMC 4 x 4 tractor 114

Gun Carriers 28-33
  Mk I 60pdr, 6in how 28-9
  Gun Carrier Mk II, 1917 30, 31
  Gun Carriage Factory, Jubbulpore 162
Guy Motors Ltd, Wolverhampton 77, 79, 110, 111, 130
Guy,
  4 x 2 tractor 62
  6 x 4 tractor 62, 130
  6 x 6, 8 x 8 tractor 130-1
  15cwt 4 x 2 AT 142
  3-ton 6 x 4 CAX6 in India 159
  Ant 4 x 2 110
  Quad Ant 4 x 4 109-114
  Lizard 3-ton 4 x 4 125

H
Half-track tractors 40, 51, 73
Hardy Motors Ltd 124
Hathi tractors 70, 71, 75, 101, 129, 130
  4 x 4 tractor 100, 158
  6 x 4 tractor 100
  6 x 6 tractor 102
Hathi-Roadless tractor 79
Heavy Motor Car Order, 1903 17
Hedjaz Battery 32
Hinstin 51
Hobart, Col Percy 86
Holt Caterpillar tractors
  45hp, 75hp, 120hp 23, 25, 26, 37, 117, 128
Holt 5-ton tractor in India 131, 158, 159
Hornsby, Richard & Sons, Grantham 17
Hornsby Roberts chain-track tractor 18, 19
Hornsby Little Caterpillar 21
Horstmann suspension 91

I
Ingoldsby Transporter 74, 75
India, vehicle developments in, App C 158

J
Johnson, Lt Col Philip 39, 42, 51, 57, 58, 72

K
Karrier,
  KT4 FAT 111
  Spider 111, 125
Kégresse, Adolphe 51, 75
Kégresse trailer 66
Kuhne, Capt C.H. RASC 103

L
Landships Committee 27, 30
Lanz Tractor 69
Latil Model TL 77, 78
Latil artillery tractor 69, 70, 114, 115
League of Nations 33, 134
Leyland Motors Ltd, Lancs 131
Leyland,
  6 x 6 tractor 79, 131
  8 x 8 tractor 76
  60hp water-cooled engine 43, 44
  Terrier 3-ton 6 x 4 106, 131
  KG2 30cwt 4 x 2 107
Liddell Hart, Capt 34, 81, 82, 84
Light Artillery Transporter 46, 47
Lindsay, Col 86
Lloyd George 33, 128
Lorry Trials, 1901 16

M
Mallett mortar 7
Martel, Maj RE 84
Martel tankettes 57, 89
McCormick Deering tractor 71
Meadows 30hp engine 90
Meadows EPT 6-cylinder engine 93
Mechanisation Board 92, 110, 159
Mechanised and Armoured Formations, 1929 49, 86
Mechanical Experimental Establishment (MEE) 39, 48

167

Mechanical Transport Advisory Board 103
Mechanical Transport Advisory Committee (India) 158
Mechanical Transport Committee (MTC) 15, 21, 23
Mechanical Warfare Board 45, 63, 67, 68, 91, 97, 119, 121, 142
Mechanical Warfare Experimental Establishment (MWEE) 42, 53, 54, 55, 56, 58, 60, 63, 65,72, 73, 75, 77, 78, 90, 92, 93, 94, 98, 102, 107, 112, 114, 115, 117, 118, 120, 121, 124, 125, 129, 130, 131 132, 133, 158, 160
Mechanical Warfare Supply Department, Cricklewood 31
Mercedes Daimler tractor 69
Mesopotamia 25, 33
Mesopotamia Expeditionary Force 158
Military College of Science, Woolwich 54
Milne, Gen Sir George CIGS 81
Mobile Naval Base Defence Organisation (MNBDO) 78
Modern Formations, 1931 86
Morris Commercial Motors Ltd 57, 104
Morris,
  Eight 4 x 2 car 105, 152
  4 x 4 C8 artillery tractor 4, 111-3
  4 x 2 CS8 15cwt A/T 107, 108, 111-3
  6 x 4 D-type 30cwt 63, 104, 141, 142, 143,
  6 x 4 D-type artillery tractor, India 162
  6 x 4 CD-type battery staff vehicle 109
  6 x 4 D-type battery staff vehicle 106, 109
  6 x 4 CDSW Artillery tractor 106, 108, 109
  6 x 4 CDSW LAA tractor 106
  Quad artillery tractor 109
  Type Q armoured car 112
Morris Roadless artillery tractor 41, 57-9, 141
Morris Roadless artillery tractor, India 160-1
Munich Crisis 127, 137, 142, 157

N
Niblett, Col, RASC 103

P
Palestine 25, 154, 156
Paul & Bray traction engine 9
Pavesi 4 x 4 artillery tractor 67-9, 75, 89, 129, 159
Payne, Capt 94
Peacock, Richard 143
Pedrails, Roberts 17
Peerless, British Quad 26
Peerless 3-ton 4 x 4 60
Peerless TC 5-ton 4 x 2 AA lorry 127
Portholme tractor 30-1
'Purple Primer' 86

Q
Quetta earthquake, 1935 161, 162

R
Ransomes, Simms and Head, Ipswich 11
Renault 6 x 4 truck 102, 103
Roadless Traction Ltd Hounslow 51
Road Traffic Act 1930 37
Robey and Sons, Lincoln 10
Robey's Advance 10
Robert's Patent Chain Track 17
Rolls-Royce Armoured Cars 27
Royal Army Service Corps, Caterpillar (Holt) Coys 70-1

Experimental Department RASC 100-2
P Company RASC 102
Royal Artillery,
  employment, App A 144
  equipment, App A 144
  organisation, App A 144
Royal Artillery Institute 35, 44
Royal Artillery Institute, Proceedings of, 16, 35
Royal Artillery Journal 35, 36, 139
Royal Engineer Searchlight Battalion 128, 135
Royal Horse Artillery, mechanisation of, App B 150
Royal Marine Artillery 26, 59, 71, 78
Royal National Lifeboat Institution 120
Royal Naval Air Service (RNAS) 27, 28, 30
Royal Navy 26, 127
Royal Ordnance Factory (ROF) Woolwich 39, 41, 42, 43, 55, 74, 93, 97, 99
Royal Tank Corps 23, 77, 163
Ruston tractors 117
Rustons, Lincoln 25

S
Salonika 25
Scammell
  6 x 4 tractor 124
  6 x 6 tractor 79, 123, 131
School of Anti-Aircraft Defence, Biggin Hill 50
Seabrook lorry 28, 31
Self-propelled guns 34, 44 et seq
Shanghai Defence Force 40, 41, 47, 53, 55
Sheffield Simplex cars 25, 139
Somerset Light Infantry, 2nd Bn 81
South Notts Hussars 143

168

INDEX

Steam Gunners Nos 1 and 2 10
Steam Sapper 11-3
Steele-Bartholomew Committee 129
Stepney rims 64
Steyr-Daimler-Puch 112
Subsidy scheme 23, 103, 104

T
Talbot tender 32
Tank Board 44
Tank Corps, Gun Carrier Companies 29
Tank Corps Centre, Bovington 58
Tasker, William & Sons, Andover 14
Tasker Little Giant 17
Tatra,
   4 x 4 vehicle 109
   6 x 6 vehicle 123
Tempo 4 x 4 car 109
Territorial Army Artillery 58, 60, 130 et seq
Thompson Committee (on air defence) 135
Thomson Road Steamers 10
Thomson, R.W. 10
Thornycroft J.
   Type 3-ton 4 x 2 AA 127, 128
   Hathi 4 x 4 100
   oil engine tractor, 1909 17, 19
   steam waggon 16
   XB 6 x 4 portee 61, 63
Trackson 71
Trans-Sahara Expedition 102
Treasury Rating for horsepower 103
Trials,
   Lorry 1909 19
   North Wales 1938 112
   Subsidy 1911 23
   tractor 1901 16
   tractor 1903 17
   US Army 1912 26
   War Office Mechanisation 1930 58
   Wool 1925 75
   Wool 1927 58
   Wool 1930 58
Tritton, William 30

U
United Africa Company 120

V
Vickers Armstrong Ltd 91 et seq
Vickers Artillery Observers Vehicle 89, 90, 92
Vickers Carden-Loyd tractor truck 92
Vickers Light Tank 93
Vickers Ltd 34, 39, 42, 48, 55, 89
   Peerless half-track 73
   predictor (AA) 48, 50, 134
   transporter 41, 42
   Tropical Tank B6E1 41, 42
   Universal Carrier 99, 100
   2-ton tractor 106, 163
   3-ton tractor B3E3 92
   6-ton tractor B6E1l 120
Vulcan Holverta 4 x 4 75

W
Wentworth Woodhouse 25
Wilson epicyclic transmission 67, 93
Wilson, Walter 18, 30

Woolwich Arsenal 7, 8, 54
Woolwich, Royal Ordnance Factory (ROF) 39, 43, 55

Y
Ypres, Third Battle of, 1917 29, 32

MOVING THE GUNS

THANKS TO

The Tank Museum wishes to thank and acknowledge the following, whose kind support enabled *Moving the Guns* to be republished in late 2022.

Alan Atkinson
Benjamin Hutchins
Matthew Tyler
Ben Leah
Rob Shipman
Deborah Parkes
Iain Reid
Steven Harker
Jerzy Hevelke
Andy Dinh
Cameron Moeller
Duncan Stevens
Victoria Taylor
David Gorton
Robert Rewcastle
Samantha Field
Ildefonso Gómez Yáñez
Paul Lowther
Mick Graham
Jeff Freeman
John Walker
Robert Bull
David Pyle
Chih-Yung Chang
Donald James
Thor Greve
Peter Bailey
Ross Hillman
Mike McGurgan
Nigel Wilton
Colin Avern
Andy Rhoades
Derek Maunder
John Bagley
John Elgie
Todd Schavee
Peter Noble
Jordan Graham
Matthew Hudson
Adrian Hampton
Michael Mills

Steve Foster
Stephen Stuck
Kye Woods
Greg Jewell
William T Wright
Ken Macdonald
Chris MacKay
Michael Rhodes
Robert David Parkin
Michael Williams
Stephen Bettany
James Grover
Tom Morris
Nicholas Slater
Ian Stanworth
Julie Cox
Anthony Hillier
Peter Faulkner
Oscar Levy
Nigel Fairhurst
Stephen Harvey
Richard Stephen Purvis
Skyler Wake
John Shill
Ian Merriman
Stuart Carter
Janis Sorenson
Edward Adkins
Ian McKinnon
Neil Boston
Patrick Woodford
Geoff Titterton
Neil Atkinson
Gerald Pierson
Julian Davies
Michael Catt
Meredith Russell
Andrew Witherspoon
Andrew Bird
Dave Hickman
Kevin Hann

Ian Clarke
Alan Smith
Glynn Beresford
Warren Mason
Harry Johnson
Robert Hector
Richard Evans
Tom Williams
Ethan Beal
Gavin Kratz
James Mcinnes
P.D. Jarman
Geoffrey Boby
Douglas Nicholson
Jack Rimmer
Hugh O'Donnell
Chris Naden
Robert Mundell
Mike Whitcombe
Graeme Thomas
Wayne Birks
Michael Orris
Mike Warren
David Powell
Tim Yow
David Garoz Esteban
George Exon
Alan Atkinson
Graeme Carruthers
Stephen Belton
Paul Trevett
Ryan Brewis
Robert Peach
Peter Savill
David Hulme
Andrew Grayman
Anita Jennison
Samantha Green
Philip Livingstone
Wirton Philippe
Terence Young

THANKS TO

John Blackmore
Kevin Hudson
Graham Hough
Nigel Savage
Luke Webb
Steven Browning
Glenn Harrison
Robin Braysher
John Edwards
Michael John Bishop
Anna Bartoszewicz
Colin Webb
Matthew Kaye
Thomas Platt
Nicola Lillywhite
Martin Roberts
David O'Farrell
David Magee
Ian John Whitear
Colin Needham
James Hall
Lynn Norcliffe
Clare Wilkinson
Susan Anchor
Mark Ansell
Owen Adamson
Anthony Brown
David Rowland
Tom Badger
Maximilian Broden-Barbareau
Ian Roberts
Matthew Hynett
Kevin McAlinden
Graham Crymble
Alberto Corradine
Malcolm Ivison
Euan Smith
Martha Wells
David Morris
Bryan Donald Surridge
James Scrivener
David Allen
Melvin Avery
Wayne Weddle
Lindsey Haycock
Piers Wilson
Robert Mountford

Derek Gard
Charles Stevens
Edward Sealey
John Zahra
Thomas Breitenbacher
Neil Holden
John King
Axel Macdonald
Joshua Garston
Charles Canova
Tomasz Blaut
Darren Rolfe
Tim Lowe
Graham Hurst
Chris Ryan
David Farrell
Peter Morrison
John Doran
Roger Houston
Nigel Sait
John Gibbons
Simon Quinn
Austin Hindley
Simon Cannon
Peter Smith
John Hill
Peter Martin
Björn Unell
Tom van der Vlist
Ian Costar
Radu Dumitrean
Scott Parkinson
Rodney S. Arneil
Kathleen Moots
Paul Thomson
William Gunter
Bryn Stevenson-Davies
David Wade
Philip Dale
Roberts Daniel
Chris Simpson
Nicholas Noppinger
Alan Neocleous
Paul V. Scourfield
Nick Godwin
Alexander Burnett
Simon Burrough

Christopher Worsley
Marion Bahnerth
Alyssa Ryder
Mark Demmen
Mark Campbell
George McLean
Ron Owen
Robert Ingham
Rachel Bowen
Mike Burgess
David Richardson
Stuart Gumm
Alex Phillipson
Rick Williams
Brenton White
Hamish Davidson
Joseph Blackett
Ceri Thomas
David Johnston
Keith Bispham Miller
Paul Colebrooke
Joseph Checkley
Martin Gregory
Len Newman
Alan Northcote
Gordon Matthews
Neil Burt
Robert Scott
John Fearn
Gary Matfin
Graham Wilby
Tancred Cassar
Michael Rhodes
Jason Spicer
Tim Cook
Paul Tamony
Geoff Ayres
Robert Bond
Douglas McMillan
Keith Terry
Markku Hyttinen
Ross Kennedy
Trevor Corrin
Michael Monroe
Alan Ross
Tyler Steele
Gene Smith

MOVING THE GUNS

THANKS TO

Justin Grootenboer
Martin Jones
Terry Rowsell
Steve Bastable
Simon King
M.J. Roche
James Christopher Cutts
Peter Sutton
Mark McCuller
John King
Richard Payne
Richard Dallimore
John Robertsom
Terry Cotter
Stephen Lord
Steve Smith
Stephen Cairns
Alan Long
David Gray
Jan Cees Grinwis
Robert Metcalfe
Teresa Smith
Norm Day
Rebecca Addicoat
Samuel Greenhill
Neil Inglis
George Corrie
Daniel Boggild
Trevor Rawlinson
Richard Davies
Neil Mason
Jason Ward
Chris Bill
Andrew Perkins
John Melrose
Guenter Kortebein
Robert Swaine
Jason Field
Christopher Tubb
Johnny Doyle
Peter Vernon-Lawes
Andrew Wilkinson
Chris Binnie
Thomas Rye
Martin Mickleburgh
Paul Malmassari
Jedd Connolly

James Webb
Craig Cowie
Gavin Taylor
Sue Jenkins
John Zrimc
David Hewson
John Green
Ben Hughes
Anthony Cairns
Alexander Losert
Ryan Cook
Mark Yearsley
Maria Vazquez Lopez
Adrian Ferguson
Paul Lipscombe
Martin Clouder
Amanda Butler
P. Hennessy
Derryck Madden
Gary Norris
Jean Lewis
Malcolm McEwan
M.J. Hill
Ian Mcnally
Paul Hutchings
Dot Tracy
Amber Stahl
Michael Freeman
John Twigge
Stuart Bestford
Richard Bradley
Gary Hewings
David Mason
Jan Meyer-Kamping
Chris Stevens
Uwe Springhorn
Anthony Bird
Alan Johnson
Edward Shoop
Simon House
John Ingleby
Johan Van der Bruggen
Marc Lecuit
Phil Bargery
Kathleen Gulson
Philip Kaye
David Pepper

Keith Stafford
Peter Dicks
Gareth Sewell
Henry Boulton
Anbe Hironobu
Liam Cooney
William Walter Hill
William Gunning
Jeremy Bond
Annie and Michael Bradley
Mark Paines
Bennett Horner
Charles Taylor
Neil Cowell
Christopher Dunmill
Ian Price
Ian Hambelton
Nigel Barrett
Karolina Phelps
Richard Gibbon
Lee Smith
Colin MacNee
Peter Tipping
Philip Jobson
Brian Sanders
Alex Blair
Antony Vickers
David Foster
Richard Cooper
John Hutchinson
Mike Matthews
Steve Percy
David Fraser
James Andrew
William Pointing
Steven Bannister
Nick Vaughan
Gabriel Necsuleu
Richard Bishop
David Bottomley
Eugene Lefeuvre
Rob Carson
Brian McGinley
Robert Dickinson
Eero Juhola
William A. Siddons
Stephen Wall

THANKS TO

John Cavanagh
Nicholas Piper
Adam Burton
Sam Anderson
David Mansfield
Graham Rhodes
Martyn Keen
Philip McCarty
Paul Perry
Gwynne Fright
Matthew Lambert
Hamish Davidson
Piers Jackson
Cobweb Williams-Manton
Paul Bussard
Andrew Downs
Dwight Luetscher
Matthew Finck
Wayne Mills
Anthony Witham
Justin Rollinson
Thomas Paine
James Carty
Tony Price
Jared Lee
Scott Harwood
Brian Douglas
Javier Tapia
Campbell Harris
Edward Paul Anderson
Eddie M. Redfearn
Charles Hoagland
Lowell Wong
John Rauscher
Larry Geno
Glen Cooper
David Krigbaum
William Neilus
Adrian Symonds
William Mckibben
Chris Bridgman
Ka Ki Leung
Rejean Paquette
David Batho
Øystein Mork
Benjamin L. Apt
Larry Deornellas Jr

Geoffrey Mawson
Andy White
Kieran Hall
Merle Steeves
Steven Dyer
Rob Lee
Paul Demato
Nicholas Brodar
Tim Prestia-Cook
Oliver Pearcey
Patrick Bailey
Joseph Jolley
Andrew Noble
Franz Biedermann
Stuart Purvis
Robert Frisch
Alan Batten
John MacFarlane
Phil Eyden
John Simpson
Callum White
Alexander Estermann
Richard Cammack
Tim Wrate
Dave Howling
Josh W. Salazar
Jeffrey Ware
Eric Maple
Graeme Campsie
Mark Niblett
Murray Kennedy
Mark Mills
John Beck
George G Hill
Mark Ploszay
Friedrich Klett
David Woodside
Terry Hall
Richard Briscoe
Patrick Crelly
Keith Walker
J. Tweddle
Alan Mincher
Sidney Road
Lachlan Harris
Colin Bracher
Sean Smart

Andrew Hunter
Barry Canning
Daniel Moore
Paul Nuttall
Simon King
James Cridland
Matthew Zembo
Bob Baal
Aiden Terris
Craig Abrahams
Anthony Sampson
Fiona Jakielaszek
Simon Snodin
Charlotte Dillon
Philip Moor
Alan Titcombe
Martin Littlecott
Staley Snook
Oliver Austin
Filip Björklund
John Tapsell
Thomas Lucas
Robert Obermeier-Hartmann
Connor Coolbaugh
Alan Knuth
Ryan Maclam
John Buckle
Michael Guerin
Jack Shearer
Stuart Woods
Iain Mellors
Adrian Johnson
Michael Hall
Zebulon Swinney
Stuart Hanley
Duncan Curd
Nigel Chappell
John Parr
Jan Andersson
Bradley Mitchell
Trevor Povey
Alexei McDonald
Mark Bentley
Alvin Chan
Nicholas Sadler
Steve Merrett
Paul Button

THANKS TO

Doug Parry
Christian Bastow
Stephen Turner
Matt Davies
Neil Kindlysides
Gareth Williams
Ben Dummer
Gary Dhillon
Mark Fowler
Paul M. Wilde
Scott Gill
Julie Bettinelli
Frederick Brown
David Bullen
Geoffrey Giles
Andrew Pritchatt
Jacob Tierney
Nick Jones
Stuart Hudson
Matthew Smith
Michael Rorer
Richard Box
John Convery
Ray Peterson
Roman Smith
Colin Baddeley
Chris Pilags
Russell Barnes
Andrew David
Sean Smart
Pierre Pellerin
Nicholas Biddle
Paul Grainger
Robbie Macauley
Joshua Hiscock
Ian Rainford
Roger Peachey
David Paul Williams
Antony Kirmond
Eric Hollis
Justin de Lavison
Richard J. Tugwell
Stephen Gregory
Rodney Anderson
Hugh Dennis
Isaac Dennis
Martin Killick

Matt Klotz
Steven Barnes
Mark Hollowell
Ian Collins
Bryan Perrington
Alan Anstruther Black
K. Simpson
David Chapman
Tizian Dähler
Kirsty Meredith
Alexander Gibson
Steven Parkes
John Meadows
Lawrence Rhyce
Chris Burberry
Paul Cocks
Donald Holmes
Jason Hofer
Robert Coach
Alex Malcom
Philippa Bowden
Alexander Ridler
Gordon Chrisp
Paul Condren
Nigel Rumble
Chris Saulpaugh
David Mapley
Jim Evans
Ray Young
Grant Kenny
Mark Ambridge
Charles Jones
Ian Duffin
James Knight
Edward Hervey
Anthony Grindle
Kenneth Lilley
Colin Poulter
Marici Reid
Jacob Wright
Jordan Taylor-Jeal
Robert Feast
Nigel Colverson
Deborah Schouten
Jonathan Barnes
Mike Woolnough
Heather Brown

Larry Stone
Alfie Green
Phil Loder
Michael Woong
James Nicholls
Michael Brothwell
Nick Wynn
Neil Illingworth
Chris Wright
Michael Pytel
Nigel Titchen
Noah Bly
Phil Burrows
Tony Gaynor
Robin Elliott
Eric Dellaquila
Keith Matthews
Albert Lecuyer
Sarah Burt
Jaroslaw Chojnacki
Jean Grieten
Tim Ellerby
Thomas Hignell
Jonathan Frere
Rocco Plath
Nicholas Davis
Pat Coughlin
Gayle Bailey
Pierre Hedström
Steven Grace
Scott Kerr
Jonny Nilsson
Leonard Thomson
Sean Cuddy
Stuart Harrison
Brian Smith
W. Lindsay
Vivian Symonds
Ian Willy
Alan Lodge
Thomas Stromberg
Susan Logan
Kevin Dyke
Andrew Wood
Gary Burns
Bradley Kirk
Sean Holder

THANKS TO

Simon Barnes
Fraser Durie
Helen Rogers
Colin Little
Erik Miller
Neville Mullings
Dennis Krag
Paul Jones
Keith Allan Langton
Geert Arends
Keith Major
Bill Allan
Mark Bevis
Michael Patey
Ian Bullion
Stewart Garnett
Andrew Woodward
Jamie Todd
Ben Hughes
Nicholas M. Maris
Naomi Ecob
Arran Hartley
Oliver Beddoe
Mattias Sjösvärd
Colin Gibson
Samuel Tuck
Thomas Brooks
Paul Walsh
Tony Hearn
Alex Wrotek
Simon Norburn
John Andrews
Jason Singleton
Mark Barnett
Matthew Faiers
George Gillett
David Sedano
Sarah Gray
Daren England
Paul Liddiard
Terry Light
Brian Nelson
Charles Knapp
Ian Bryer
Kenneth Zichal
Chris Brook
Phil Puddefoot

Matthew Hurley
Jeremy Lawson
Cammie Lamont
Simon Smith
Thomas Sitch
John Hill
Aidan Lloyd
Kjartan Bergsson
M. Reynolds
Danny Hin
Paul James
Hongrui Zhang
Marcel Tromp
Tim Barr
Paul Nuttall
David Chapman
Carson Thomas
Allan Sinclair
Trevor Hayman
Kevin Page
James Carter
Andrew Osborne
Aaron Supinger
Glenn Bainbridge
Andrew Temple
Steven Blackburn
Tina Rydberg
Matthew Spreadbury
Lukas Milancius
Ben Couldwell
Thomas Williams
Børge Arild
Eisa Alkalbani
Alastair Powers-Jones
Liam Riordan
Stephen McGuire
Peter Feeney
Taylor Jay
Patrick J. McNamara
Kristine Janusas
Kjell Arne Randen
Anthony Stewart
Wes Lunney
Louis Devirgilio
Paul Taylor
Clive Thomas
Willem Marinus Stoutjesdijk

Leslie Stephenson
Kelvin Bampfield
Ethan Candy
Salvador Cadengo
Steven Adams
Cameran McKie-Jones
Daisy Ticehurst
Nikolas Eibich
Mario Saliba
Daniel Nye
Karen Lee Zachry
Panzerwrecks Ltd
Paul Hutchinson
John Wright
Michael Townsend
Ian Featherstone
Andrew A.
Matt Magee
Bryan Davis
Andy Kirk
Tom Williams
Scott Mccrindle
David Butterfield
David Hindmarsh
Simon Ashcroft
Liam Adams
Katie Jones
Jonathan Bordell
Graham Cooper
Martin Jones
Mark Hiles
Mark Gregory
Robin McEwen
Ewan Spence
Douglas Swanson
Alan Hall and Shade Kelly.